CANDLES BEHIND THE WALL

Candles behind the Wall

Heroes of the Peaceful Revolution
That Shattered Communism

Barbara von der Heydt

WILLIAM B. EERDMANS PUBLISHING COMPANY
GRAND RAPIDS, MICHIGAN

Library of Congress Cataloging-in-Publication Data

Heydt, Barbara von der.
Candles behind the wall : heroes of the peaceful revolution
that shattered communism / Barbara von der Heydt.
p.   cm.
Includes index.
ISBN 0-8028-3722-0
1. Dissidents—Europe, Eastern—Biography.
2. Christians—Europe, Eastern—Biography.
3. Europe, Eastern—Politics and government—1945-1989.
4. Europe, Eastern—Biography.   I. Title.
DJK31.H49   1993
947'.0099—dc20   93-35445
                                                        CIP

Quotations from *No, I'm Not Afraid* by Irina Ratushinskaya (Bloodaxe Books, 1986)
are reprinted by permission of Bloodaxe Books, Ltd., Newcastle upon Tyne.

Unless otherwise indicated, the Scripture references are taken from the *Holy Bible:
New International Version.* Copyright © 1973, 1978, 1984 by the International Bible
Society. Used by permission of Zondervan Bible Publishers.

Unless otherwise noted, all English translations of German text in this volume are
provided by the author.

For the people of the former Communist nations —
those who died because of their convictions,
those who were imprisoned, those who lived in fear,
and all those who have been freed by the grace of God

Contents

Contents

Acknowledgments

My heartfelt thanks to the many people who made this book possible. To Friedrich Hänssler, Professor Gerhart Niemeyer, and Dr. Kent Hill for their encouragement and advice. To Erwin Damson and Waldemar Zorn of Light in the East for opening doors in the former Soviet Union, and for the use of their archives. To Helmut Matthies for enabling me to make contacts in the former GDR and for use of the *Idea* archives. To Rev. Canon Michael Bourdeaux and Keston Research for their helpful information and the use of their archives. To the more than one hundred people throughout the former Eastern bloc who opened their hearts to tell their personal stories, many of whom opened their homes to me as well. And most especially to my husband, Peter, and my children, Tommy and Stephanie, who have carried the weight of this work with me. *In gloria Dei.*

Introduction

What was it that rumbled across the European continent, bringing Communist governments heaving and crashing to the ground in 1989 and 1991? Even the most astute political observers concede that there is no purely political explanation for the unexpected way this phenomenon occurred. It was a revolt of staggering proportions that freed about 400 million people — and it was remarkably peaceful. In the end, one of the earth's greatest powers simply groaned, staggered, and collapsed. But why?

When tanks surrounded the Russian parliament building in the attempted coup of August 1991, what gave a young woman the courage to walk up to a tank and speak to its driver, urging him not to fire? Why did a young border guard stationed at the Berlin Wall refuse to shoot at anyone attempting to escape? What motivated tens of thousands to risk their lives on the streets of Leipzig in the fall of 1989, armed with nothing but candles? All of these individuals contributed to the collapse of Communism.

To explain the collapse of Communism, most commentators have focused exclusively on the aspects seen comfortably through the conventional looking-glass of analysis: economics and politics. But, as George Weigel points out in *The Final Revolution*, what has been largely overlooked is the most important aspect of the collapse: it was a moral and spiritual revolution. It was not simply a clash of political realms; it was a clash of moral realms that triggered a political earthquake. Indeed, the conflict began long before 1989 as a revolution of the spirit in individuals who exposed the moral poverty of Communism and rejected it.[1] Christian involvement in the revolution was not peripheral; it was central. Key Christians provided moral leadership, and they were critically important in keeping the conflict peaceful.

The reason that most journalists missed the story altogether is that a clash of spiritual realms is not usually covered in daily papers and television news. Few observers have understood that it was not a coincidence that Solidarity workers knelt before the Black Madonna in Poland, that protesters gathered under the roofs of the churches in East Germany, or that people armed only with Bibles faced down the tanks in Moscow. These things do not fit through the grid most journalists use to define "news."

True, there were major figures in the news who influenced the course of history in the Soviet Union and Communist Europe as it culminated in the peaceful revolutions of 1989 and 1991. Several major players on the world stage filled critical roles at crucial moments, and credit is due them for their parts in these events.

If one takes 1980 as the beginning of the last act in the history of Communism, Lech Wałęsa and the Solidarity workers at the Gdańsk shipyards were the first to face down the Communist regime in a conflict that did not end with tanks and bullets. It had been otherwise before — in Berlin in 1953, in Hungary in 1956, and in Czechoslovakia in 1968. In fact, Soviet tanks did roll up to the Polish border twice during the conflict that ended with General Jaruzelski declaring martial law in Poland, but a new era began in Eastern Europe when the Soviet tanks did not fire.

The election of John Paul II as pope was an event that had a major impact — and not only on the spiritual world. He articulated a vision of human beings with rights and responsibilities transcending those of the state, moral agents with a God-given nature, a vision that challenged Communism at its very roots. The Catholic Church in Poland

---

1. Weigel, *The Final Revolution: The Resistance Church and the Collapse of Communism* (New York: Oxford University Press, 1992), pp. 3, 34.

had a long history of functioning independently from the state, and the growing movement away from Communism was validated by the pope's presence, as were the religious roots of the Solidarity movement. They galvanized resistance elsewhere in the Eastern bloc.

U.S. President Ronald Reagan made decisions that were to prove instrumental in blocking Soviet intentions to obtain what Churchill called "the fruits of war" without waging war. Military power can be converted into hegemony without a shot being fired, and that was the Soviet intention. But Reagan's decision to station the Pershing missiles in response to the Soviet SS20's and to initiate SDI (Strategic Defense Initiative) research thwarted this plan, forcing the Soviets into a corner they could not escape from economically. When Reagan referred to the Soviet Union as an "Empire of Evil," that statement was widely derided in the West at the time, but he was proclaiming a moral truth that resistance movements in the entire Eastern bloc affirmed as self-evident. Reagan, too, was to challenge Communism on a moral as well as a political and military level.

The West has touted Mikhail Gorbachev as the author of reform, the man whose *glasnost* and *perestroika* unleashed forces of change that revolutionized the entire Eastern bloc. One could also argue that the dynamism of these forces overwhelmed both his political career and the empire, forcing him to improvise when he found himself on ground that was already moving beneath his feet. There is no doubt that he was a key figure, if not *the* key figure, on the political stage, whether one sees him as merely permitting or actively implementing change. Actually, what he didn't do was at least as significant as what he did. As former U.N. Ambassador Jeane J. Kirkpatrick put it, "The most important event of 1989 was a non-event, the tanks that didn't roll and the Soviet troops that stayed in their barracks. This was the end of the Soviet empire, and it disintegrated faster than any other empire in modern history."[2]

2. Kirkpatrick, "Exit Communism, Cold War and the Status Quo," in *Man and Marxism: Religion and the Communist Retreat* (Hillsdale, Mich.: Hillsdale College Press, 1991), p. 162.

But none of these figures alone was responsible for the collapse of Communism.

* * *

There was something unique about the experiment of Communism. For the first time in history, man attempted to eradicate God fully, claiming that he held all potential within himself. And yet Communism drew "believers" in the same way as the Christianity it abhorred: both Marxist ideology and faith in Christ proved to have the capacity to fire man's imagination, to engender his loyalty, to inspire and to command a willingness to sacrifice. One belief system is based on a materialistic view of man, the other on a spiritual view. Whittaker Chambers, a man who knew the compelling attraction of both, claims that two faiths have been on trial in this century: faith in God and faith in Man. Communism is a manifestation of the latter. "It is, in fact, man's second oldest faith," he explains. "Its promise was whispered in the first days of Creation under the Tree of Knowledge of Good and Evil: 'Ye shall be as gods.' It is the great alternative faith of mankind. Like all great faiths, its force derives from a simple vision. Other ages have had great visions. They have always been different versions of the same vision: the vision of God and man's relationship to God. The communist vision is the vision of man without God."[3]

To understand Marxism, as Weigel points out in *The Final Revolution,* one must understand that it is an ersatz, secularized religion.[4] It borrowed the Christian vision, but stripped it of its source. Marxism adapted the biblical ideals of peace, the sharing of material wealth, and freedom from oppression, promising that they would mark the end-state of Communist man. It provided a vision of a transformed world, a compelling view of human perfection that inspired conviction and inculcated the willingness to sacrifice to

3. Chambers, *Witness* (1952; rpt. Washington: Regnery Gateway, 1980), p. 9.
4. Weigel, *The Final Revolution, Resistance Church and the Collapse of Communism* (New York: Oxford University Press, 1992), p. 11.

achieve it. Many Western critics do not understand Communism's ability to galvanize moral commitment. Many people who became Communists did so for moral reasons, earnest in their belief that following Communist ideology would produce the perfected state of man.

The reason that Communism collapsed is that Marxism is based on the false premise that the nature of man is inherently good and perfectible through human endeavor, that it is a product of his material surroundings, devoid of transcendence. But faith without transcendence often produces tyranny. Indeed, the march of Marxism-Leninism became a violent one, with the Gulag used as the last resort to silence those who rejected this new worldview. It is estimated that as many as 60 million people died in this century at the hands of the Communists. Stalin alone may be responsible for 50 million of these deaths, which would make him the greatest mass-murderer of all time. Even Hitler's atrocities do not approach his in scale. Some victims were shot; some were packed into freight cars like cattle and shipped off to Siberian labor camps, where they froze to death in the filth in which they were forced to live and work. Still other victims were abused by interrogators in the bowels of Lubyanka, the KGB's headquarters. And there were those who were injected with mind-altering drugs and left to languish in psychiatric prisons. Most of those who escaped death and overt abuses lived a cowed existence of subservience, conformity, and fear.

*   *   *

In this book I describe the conflicts and bold decisions of individuals who chose to resist because of their moral convictions. Many who resisted Communism did so because of their Christian faith, which demanded sacrifice. Those who chose to live by their convictions accordingly discovered that their decision was costly, not only for themselves but for their families. From childhood on, each person was forced to make decisions at every stage of his or her life that determined future opportunities for education, professional advancement, housing, and security. And those parents who made decisions on the basis of their convictions rather than on "proper political behavior" lost these opportunities, both for themselves and for their children.

Resisting Communism was dangerous. Informants were everywhere, so individuals who feared retribution from the regime were not paranoid. At best, those suspected of disloyalty suffered discrimination; at worst, persecution. They could never be sure what the consequences for noncompliance would be, because the enforcement of laws and expectations was enormously elastic. Some had their wills broken by interrogations and threats. Prison sentences and executions were also harsh realities.

But those who survived with their convictions intact experienced a revolution of the spirit, a fundamental rejection of Communism at the moral level that grew into a movement with political consequences. This was a truly amazing development. Somehow, individuals one by one found the courage to confront Communism, to say "No" on the basis of "a higher and more compelling 'Yes.'"[5] It was here, in the realm of the spirit, that the real revolution took place. It prefigured and enabled the political revolution that followed.

Theologian Józef Tischner has described *Solidarność* as a "huge forest of awakened consciences." This image aptly describes the movement that successfully challenged Communism not only in Poland but in all of Eastern Europe and the Soviet empire. When individuals with a heightened sense of the need to live with integrity dared to stand up for what they believed, they presented a challenge to totalitarianism at its very roots. As they stood, one by one, a forest of resistance grew.

There were many people who chose to resist because of convictions that were not Christian — and credit is due them as well. But what united the resisters — of whatever faith or political persuasion — was their commitment to waging a moral revolution. They attacked Communism at its core and built the cells of a civil society to replace it.

What motivated these individuals to resist? At some moment,

5. Ibid., p. 89.

a flicker of the spirit ignited the will. For many, faith overcame fear. Like candles in the darkness, these people bore witness to their convictions. And just as a few candles chase the night from a room, so these individuals illuminated their surroundings and made the darkness recede for others.

The stories in this book describe the awakening of conscience, the crystallizing of conviction, and the role these believers played in the revolutions of 1989 and 1991. A revolution of the spirit occurred first, with a spiritual, political, and economic earthquake following close behind.

* * *

On a personal note: My involvement with these people began in September 1989, as the first huge wave of refugees was released through Hungary from East Germany, headed for freedom in the West. It became clear through prayer that I should try to help them. I could not have guessed that the Berlin Wall would fall shortly afterward. In more or less blind obedience, a friend and I launched a private initiative to help provide food, clothes, and assistance with the transition to life in West Germany, including finding housing and employment. Many others joined us. Over the next three years, I had hundreds of conversations with people from the Eastern bloc that gave me a vivid picture of life on the other side of the Wall. It became clear to me what people there had suffered and, in particular, how different the fate of Christian believers had been. Those who had lived their faith had burned like candles behind the Wall.

When I traced their paths back to their hometowns, including Berlin, Leipzig, Warsaw, Budapest, and later Moscow, a story of the revolution emerged, a revolution that was spiritual as well as political. I discovered that in many cases the Christians were the moral leaders of the peaceful revolution: they set the tone for it, and they were decisive in keeping the confrontation nonviolent. Their courage and leadership galvanized a far broader movement.

Once I had begun to document the individual motivation of

those who resisted Communism for moral reasons, I discovered that there was a growing body of literature confirming the significance of the spiritual and moral aspects of the peaceful revolution. I am not the first or the only person to discover that these were central in the downfall of Communism. Accordingly, I wish to acknowledge the work of those who have preceded me. First of all, I acknowledge my intellectual debt to Timothy Garton Ash, who insightfully documented the revolution in the Eastern bloc countries in *The Uses of Adversity: Essays on the Fate of Central Europe* (Cambridge: Granta Books, 1989); *We the People: The Revolution of '89* (Cambridge: Granta Books, 1990); and *The Polish Revolution: Solidarność* (London: Granta Books, 1983). I am also indebted to George Weigel, whose book *The Final Revolution: The Resistance Church and the Collapse of Communism* (New York: Oxford University Press, 1992) gives a penetrating analysis of the spiritual aspects of the revolution in Poland and Czechoslovakia, and the role played by the Catholic Church. Kent Hill provides a thorough analysis of the role of religion in *The Soviet Union on the Brink: An Inside Look at Christianity and Glasnost* (Portland, Ore.: Multnomah Press, 1991). For years Michael Bourdeaux has followed religion in Communist countries through his association with Keston College/Keston Research. He has documented his findings in a number of books, including *Gorbachev, Glasnost and the Gospel* (London: Hodder & Stoughton, 1990), and *May One Believe in Russia?* (London: Darton, Longman & Todd, 1980). In *Revolution by Candlelight: The Real Story behind the Changes in Eastern Europe* (Portland, Ore.: Multnomah Press, 1991), Bud Bultman has chronicled the revolution of 1989 by dramatically recounting the experiences of individual Christian believers. And *Man and Marxism: Religion and the Communist Retreat* (Hillsdale, Mich.: Hillsdale College Press, 1991) is a thoughtful collection of essays by various authors. Many other authors and their works appear in the bibliography, and I am indebted to them too. Each of us has discovered aspects of the same greater truth; I am grateful to those who have gone before me.

These are the stories of courageous people who for moral reasons resisted Communism and willingly accepted the consequences.

Introduction

They come from individuals from throughout Central and Eastern Europe and the former Soviet Union. In my recounting, I have used their real names. Most of these individuals are still alive today.

While awaiting execution by the Nazis, Dietrich Bonhoeffer composed a simple but powerful prayer. The totalitarian order that ended his life was a different one, but the people who tell their stories here have lived the same prayer under the Communists.

> Restore me to liberty,
> and enable me to live now
> that I may answer before you and before me.
> Lord, whatever this day may bring,
> your name be praised.

BARBARA VON DER HEYDT
Cologne, July 15, 1993

PART I

Christians in Conflict
under Communism

CHAPTER 1

The Making of a Resister:
The Story of Rüdiger Knechtel

It was early summer in East Berlin, 1963. The man's hands trembled as he fingered the documents he had just sealed in cellophane. He shoved them into his briefcase, checking again to be sure they were watertight. In the distance he could see the border guard, but he was hidden from the guard's view. His hands moved as nervously as they had an hour before when he had gulped a schnapps to take the chill off the fear gnawing inside him.

As he waited for the guard to pass, he stared at the water of the Spree River, just a few inches from his feet. Five children were waiting for him on the other side of the river in West Berlin. Before the Wall had been built, his family had been together. But between the dark midnight hour of August 12 and the first rays of light on August 13, 1961, in a massive, unannounced action, armed men, police, and reservists had bisected Berlin with barbed wire and human walls of soldiers. Trains and subways had been halted; pedestrians had been turned back. The western sector had been surrounded. Overnight, West Berlin had become an island swimming in a red sea. And on that night, in a twist of random fate, this man and his family had been on opposite sides of the not-yet-visible line.

The man plunged into the cold water flowing before him. The first few strokes he took were easy, despite the weight of the briefcase he was dragging beneath the water. But suddenly the guard — who had now come back on his next round of surveillance — stopped and looked around, listening intently. Had he heard a splash? He froze. Then he saw the figure in the water.

"*Raus! Raus!*" he barked.

The guard ran closer to the river, shouting for other guards to join him.

"*Raus!* Get out!"

Panicked, the man changed direction. "Don't shoot!" he cried. In response, the first machine-gun round whizzed over his head. The bullets splashed into the water. He kept swimming. Then the guards opened fire from a second position, one round after another, sending bullets skidding across the water's surface. The man's inner rudder froze in fear, and he began to swim idiotically in a circle. As the bullets rained down, the river ran red.

A Soldier Refuses to Shoot at the Wall

Several days later, Rüdiger Knechtel opened a desk drawer in army quarters in East Berlin. He had been drafted into the East German army, and now, at the age of twenty-one, he was a border guard at the newly built Berlin Wall.[1] With intelligent eyes he studied the photo he had just gingerly pulled out of the drawer. He bent over the picture, absorbed, then looked up with disbelieving dread. "What is this?" he asked the officer standing nearby.

"A corpse."

"*Ja,* I see that myself. But who is it?"

"Someone who made the mistake of wanting to go to the West," the officer replied coldly.

The photo Rüdiger stared at showed a man who appeared to be about fifty, very wet and very dead, who had been shot through the eye.

A short time later, the officers in the 35th Border Regiment got their hands on a brown briefcase. It was the same briefcase containing

---

1. This account is based on the author's interview with Rüdiger Knechtel in Chemnitz on March 1 and May 11-12, 1991.

the sealed documents that the man had taken into the Spree. "Know who that belongs to?" one officer asked Rüdiger. He paused for effect. "The corpse," he said, and grinned.

Rüdiger recoiled. He watched in silent disbelief as the officers pulled out the contents and sifted through them, claiming what they wanted. The officers also passed around photos of the dead man; one commented that he had been the father of five children. Then they took his briefcase to go shopping. The callous way they joked about "the corpse" sickened Rüdiger.

How can they not care that this man was a father, a husband? he thought angrily. This experience made Rüdiger take a hard look at the orders that the border regiment had been given to shoot to kill those trying to cross the border at the Wall. He hated what he had just seen; his morality rejected it. What that meant crystallized Rüdiger's resolve at that moment: he decided then and there that he wanted no part of it. He would refuse to shoot.

Rüdiger was stationed directly across from Checkpoint Charlie on the eastern side of the Berlin Wall. At that spot, eighteen-year-old Peter Fechter had been shot by East German border guards on August 17, 1961, as he tried to escape. He had lain tangled in the barbed wire where he had fallen, visible to both sides, until he had bled to death, the first victim claimed by the Wall. A cross marked the site, and it seared Rüdiger's conscience every time tourists from the West photographed him standing there on watch. If there was no officer nearby, he and his fellow guard would call out, "We didn't do it."

Rüdiger maintained certain small contacts with the other side. Although it was forbidden, he would sometimes shout a greeting to the guards on the western side. And the American soldiers tossed over blue jeans, nylon jackets, and cigarettes to their East German counterparts like Rüdiger. Like many East German soldiers, Rüdiger also listened to AFN, the American military radio station in Berlin. One day he wrote a note to the station requesting the song "Rock around the Clock" by Bill Haley; in his closing line he called the Wall "scandalous." When he finished the note, he tucked it into a milk bottle and tossed it across the Wall. The note found its way to the station, and since AFN was celebrating its anniversary, it added Rüdiger's greetings to those it publicized from U.S. President John F. Kennedy, American Defense Secretary Robert McNamara, and West German Chancellor Konrad Adenauer. Then the press got hold of the story. "The most sensational letter was from a 21-year-old East German soldier, Rüdiger X," trumpeted the newspapers. The waves of interest that washed over West Berlin did not go unnoticed in the East. Authorities, having gotten hold of a copy of the letter, called in a team of handwriting experts to determine who Rüdiger X was.

Recently another man trying to escape across the border had been shot. But an Austrian sports car with people concealed in the trunk had made it through just one post farther down the Wall. Soldiers had shot at the car, but the passengers hadn't been hit. It couldn't be proven whether the soldiers had missed accidentally, because they were overexcited, or deliberately. Had they decided to refuse orders too? Rüdiger wondered. This incident further strengthened his resolve. He convinced the other guards in his company that the killings at the Wall were wrong, and the group of forty secretly pledged that they would deliberately miss or refuse to fire at defectors altogether. Only one of them balked at the pledge.

Because he had training as a draftsman, Rüdiger had been commissioned to do architectural renderings of the interiors of all the buildings directly on the border dividing Berlin. The Communist regime wanted to use the drawings to figure out where to plant trip wires along each of the potential escape routes. When Berlin had first been divided with barbed wire, scores of people had escaped by jumping from the windows of those buildings into blankets held out to catch them on the western side; that went on until authorities began sealing the division with mortar. Now that the Wall stood, potential escape routes through those buildings on the border had to be blocked. High-ranking officers took Rüdiger through each of these buildings, from their gables deep into their cellars, so that he could draw thorough plans for the regime to use in devising their alarm systems.

After Rüdiger completed these plans, he was reassigned to border duty at the Friedrichstrasse subway station. It was the only subway line that still connected the divided sectors of the city. Daring defectors sometimes sprinted across the platform from an eastern to a western train, trying to escape. More out of youthful bravado than heroism, Rüdiger and his fellow guards timed the intervals between the train arrivals and then during one of those intervals raced on foot through the dark tunnel to the western sector. When they crawled out of the tunnel with their guns slung over their shoulders, they were greeted by jubilant spectators who thought they had defected. If they had not had wives and children in the eastern sector, they would have done so on the spot — but they went back. Nevertheless, their stunt gave them an idea. Since they realized that it would be relatively easy to defect this way, they began concocting a plan to smuggle their families out via this subterranean escape route. Only one among them was excluded from their plans: Jakob, the one who had balked at making the pledge. He was rigid in his Communist convictions and was not interested in joining the "class enemy" on the other side.

Meanwhile, Rüdiger wrote a second letter to the Americans, this time with less innocuous content, again tossing it over the wall in a milk bottle. He asked the American forces to print up leaflets urging the East German soldiers not to shoot and to drop the flyers along the entire length of the border.

Only days later, an official car, a black Wartburg, pulled up a hundred yards away from where Rüdiger was standing on duty. Uniformed men jumped out of all four doors simultaneously. "Hands up!" they shouted at Rüdiger. "You're under arrest!" They yanked his weapon out of his hands and shoved him into the car. He was driven to the barracks, where, to his astonishment, his entire company was assembled. They were all under arrest — all except one. Jakob was conspicuous by his absence.

A bus stood waiting to take them away. Pale, bewildered, and perspiring nervously, Rüdiger put his hands on the side of the vehicle while he was frisked. The stunned soldiers piled into the bus with disbelieving stares on their faces. Some were weeping. *This can't be happening,* Rüdiger thought. *I'm supposed to be released from the army in twenty-eight days.* His reflections were brusquely interrupted by an officer. "If you try to get away, I'll shoot you." Rüdiger was pushed back into the waiting car.

Dusk was descending as they drove through the warm summer evening. Couples were sauntering under Berlin's linden trees, and the cheerful babble of children penetrated the closed windows of the car. Rüdiger thought of his son at home, a toddler now. *If they find out everything, I don't know when I'll see him again,* he thought in despair. *I'm finished.*

Eventually the car carrying Rüdiger and the bus carrying the others slowed and pulled onto Magdalene Strasse, stopping at a prison. Once inside, Rüdiger and the other soldiers were ordered to strip off their clothes, put on prison uniforms, and remove the laces from their shoes. Rüdiger was led down a long hallway, alone, and put into a cell. The door slammed behind him. He was in solitary confinement. It was August 1963.

The Wall's Last Victim

Twenty-eight years after his arrest at the Wall, Rüdiger Knechtel talked with Karin Gueffroy, the mother of the last victim of the Wall. Her son Chris was killed by border guards in the early morning hours of February 6, 1989. As many as 600 others before him had suffered the same fate.* Sixty-one shots were fired at Chris and his friend as they tried to escape. Chris was twenty years old. These excerpts from the published interview are telling:

"Four former border guards are accused of killing your son, while those bearing more guilt till now are left in peace. Are those lower being forced to take the blame for their superiors?"

"I hope that the people really responsible don't escape their punishment. But I can't share the opinion that these four border soldiers were just poor, innocent draftees. They were then 24 years old, and had

---

*On the basis of more recent information, it is now estimated that possibly as many as 600 people died trying to escape East Germany. See the article entitled "Three East German Aides Convicted in Wall Killings," in *International Herald Tribune,* September 17, 1922, pp. 1-2.

to know that shots aimed to kill defenseless human beings go against the principles of humanity. There was no compulsion to obey orders; there was neither war nor any extraordinary situation."

". . . Since September 1991 a trial against the four border guards has taken place in Berlin. Has one of the accused asked your forgiveness?"

"No, none of them seems to be capable of genuine remorse. Their standard reply to the questions is always, 'I didn't know that!'"

". . . In the hearings up until now, what has particularly shocked you?"

". . . I found out that the defendant Schmidt had shouted 'You pig, you swine!' at my son as he lay on the ground dying. And I was shocked by the unbelievable brutality with which then Major Romanowski, who was on duty on the night of February 6, abused Chris. He rammed his knee into his kidneys and as Chris stood up for the last time, Romanowski screamed: 'You're going to die soon anyway, you swine!'"**

During this trial it was decided that these border guards were morally responsible for their actions, and they were imprisoned. In 1992-93, Erich Honecker, the deposed Communist leader of East Germany, was put on trial. He admitted political responsibility for the orders to shoot at the Wall, but denied moral responsibility. While the convicted guards served their sentence, a cancer-ridden Honecker was released on "humanitarian grounds," and subsequently left for Chile.

Enduring Prison and Its Aftermath

Rüdiger was in solitary confinement for a full month before the authorities started interrogating him. The isolation was almost unbearable. He floated in a pool of suspended time with only fear as an occasional

**Taken from Rüdiger Knechtel's interview with Karin Gueffroy, "Es hat keinen Befehls-notstand gegeben" ("There Was No Compulsion to Obey Orders"), *Freie Presse*, December 14-15, 1991.

rudder. Days blurred into nights, a rotation of waking, thinking, eating, dozing, waking in fright, and sleeping again; Rüdiger felt his mental grip slipping. He knew that solitary confinement was a tactic to make him more likely to talk when he was finally interrogated, but even though he was aware of the device, it was working: his resolve was frayed by the uncertainty that gnawed at him in his isolation. *How much do they know? How many years will I be in prison?* There was no human voice, no glance from a fellow prisoner to cheer him. He was utterly alone.

When the day of interrogation arrived, officials led him down a hall to a room, all the while keeping him from making eye contact with any other inmates. A two-man team led the interrogation. One was restrained with him, even showing a hint of compassion. But the other was tougher.

"Knechtel, you're going to break," he said. "You're not going to get out of here for a long time. You've got only one chance — if you admit everything." They knew about the letter he had written to the Americans in which he had called the Wall "scandalous." But as the questioning wore on, there was no mention of the second letter, in which Rüdiger had asked the Americans to drop leaflets along the border. Was it just a tactic? Rüdiger didn't know.

Back in his solitary cell, Rüdiger waited for charges to be brought against him for the contents of his second letter. At Christmas, for the first time since he had been imprisoned, he was taken out of solitary confinement and put in a three-man cell. After five months of isolation, he was grateful to have a chance to talk.

"I'm scared to death they know what's in the second letter," he confided to another prisoner.

"What did you say in it?" the inmate asked sympathetically.

Despite his desire to open up to his new companion, Rüdiger kept cautiously quiet. Even so, a few days later, the interrogation team hit him hard.

"Well, Knechtel, how many letters have we written, then?"

"What do you mean?"

"You wrote a second letter," one of his interrogators said flatly. "Admit it. If you ever want to see your wife and son again, you'd better talk and talk now." He kept hammering away. Rüdiger had withheld this information for five long months, but now his terrible secret strained his nerves to the breaking point. How many years would he get if they knew the truth that he had buried and they had exhumed? *Ten years*, leered the corpse he saw in his mind's eye. Finally Rüdiger broke down. "All right. I wrote a second letter."

When he was led back to his cell, he noticed that the man in whom he had confided was gone. Rüdiger realized that he had told no one else of the second letter, and later the light went on: this inmate was an informer who got privileges for delivering information on other prisoners. He was sent from cell to cell to get what the interrogators couldn't. It was a system used frequently and successfully. A friend of Rüdiger's suffered the same fate with the same man.

Because Rüdiger's company had made a unified decision to refuse to shoot, Rüdiger's case received special attention. Officers from throughout the East German army were called in to underscore the severity of such mutiny. More than two hundred officers crowded the overfilled hall as Rüdiger faced the military tribunal. Fear seared him to the marrow. (For years afterward he would have terrible dreams about being led into the huge hall in handcuffs, nightmares that would replay the real nightmare just as it had occurred.) He was cleared of espionage charges, but he was convicted of "contact with criminal organizations," meaning those on the western side of the Wall. He was sentenced to two years in prison.

After his sentencing in 1964, Rüdiger was moved to a military prison near the Polish border, where he shared a cell with thirty prisoners, some of them rough criminals. His days were filled with work and weariness and punctuated by sporadic outbursts of violence among the inmates. Guard dogs stood watch, ready to attack, as he and the other men laid railroad ties. The letters from his wife were bright points of light in an otherwise dreary existence. The photo of her he showed the other prisoners proved that she had a model's beauty. Rüdiger wondered what their son looked like now. He had been a baby when Rüdiger was drafted; now he was almost four.

In commemoration of the fifteenth anniversary of the German Democratic Republic, a number of political prisoners were freed in the first political amnesty of the country — and Rüdiger was one of them. He was released just before Christmas. Prison officials paid him seventy ostmarks for his one-and-a-half years of labor, and with that, he was free. When he walked out of the prison, there was snow on the ground, and the anticipation of the holiday was in the air. He was almost bursting with joy as he made his way home, stopping to buy chocolates and presents for his wife and son.

With a bag bulging full of gifts, Rüdiger hurried down the street. He could have shouted. He leapt the last few steps to his apartment and rang the bell, shivering with excitement. When his wife opened the door, he threw his arms around her in a huge hug. She burst into tears. After he had gone inside and shaken the snow off his broad shoulders, he looked in on his sleeping son and took him gently into his arms. The tears again rolled down his wife's face. Next Rüdiger unpacked his bag of gifts and looked around their little apartment with grateful eyes, settling in for his first night of domestic comfort in years. The promise of the peace of Christmas buoyed his spirits. He was finally home. It was over — or so he thought.

But the next morning Rüdiger's wife was crying again, this time with shoulder-racking sobs. "What's wrong?" Rüdiger asked gently. Through her sobs he could only catch phrases.

". . . have to go . . . have to leave . . ."

"We should leave?" he asked.

"No, you."

"I should leave? After being gone all these years, and coming back, now I should leave?" Rüdiger was stunned and bewildered.

"We have to talk."

The words chilled Rüdiger. *What was going on?*

His wife looked down, abject. She told him that she had gotten involved with a man she worked with. The man had divorced his wife and left his children for her. "We thought we could give you some money in the transition . . ." she offered. He refused, furious and hurt. As bad as prison had been, this betrayal was even worse. He now believes that while he was in prison, the Stasi (the Ministry for State Security) had convinced his wife to divorce him. Subsequently he would learn, by talking with other political prisoners who also came "home" to broken marriages, that this was a common Stasi tactic.

A short while later Rüdiger's wife took their son and her things from the apartment and left Rüdiger for good.

*   *   *

Rüdiger's refusal to shoot at defectors at the Wall was a decision that had lasting consequences. It was a decision that sprang from moral conviction which later became Christian conviction, Rüdiger says in retrospect. In the years that followed, he thought more about the spiritual dimension. His spiritual interests grew over time, as he built a new life from his shattered situation. He met a woman named Eva and married again, had another son, and pursued a new field of study, becoming a geologist. When he and his wife asked the pastor of their church how they could help others, the pastor suggested they work with an organization called Blue Cross, which helped alcoholics in their transition to a normal life. Rüdiger and Eva assisted this organization for nearly ten years. As they see it, they were motivated primarily by social concern — but they were searching for something.

Having been through the experience at the Berlin Wall, Rüdiger spoke with natural authority on the issue of bearing arms for the Communist regime. The issue was discussed more frequently in the seventies, since by this time the church had successfully won a concession from the Communists permitting recruits to work in unarmed construction units. These *Bausoldaten,* or "construction soldiers," could fulfill their military obligations without bearing arms. As increasing numbers of East German youth opted for this alternative service, it became a source of consternation for the Communists. They had reason to silence anyone encouraging young people to become *Bausoldaten.*

Informant "Conrad" from the Stasi

One evening in 1980, Rüdiger Knechtel answered the ring at his door and was surprised to find a young man from his church standing there with a small spinning wheel in his hands.

13

"Excuse me, could I come in?" he ventured.

Rüdiger looked at the spinning wheel and nodded quizzically. Having become a self-taught expert in antiquities, he was often asked to estimate the value of various objects, and that's what the young man apparently was after — an appraisal of his spinning wheel. Once inside, the young man noted appreciatively the fine paintings on the walls and the exquisite pieces of antique furniture in the apartment. All the pieces were a testament to the hard work that Rüdiger and his wife had done over the years. They had scoured the country for overlooked treasures and had restored them.

Eventually the young man asked Rüdiger to take a look at his spinning wheel. Turning it over in his hands and inspecting it with a practiced eye, Rüdiger answered, "Maybe twenty marks, not a pfennig more, I'd say. It's perfectly new. You can see the varnish is still on it."

Not fazed in the least by this assessment, the young man asked Rüdiger more about his collection of paintings, curious to know how much they were worth. The young man then shifted the conversation from art to politics, asking Rüdiger how he sized up the situation with Solidarity in Poland. Recent developments there had captivated the attention and the hopes of many elsewhere in the Eastern bloc.

Since the young man went to his church, Rüdiger was inclined to trust him, although their previous contacts had not always been harmonious. When Rüdiger had addressed groups on the issue of military service for the Communist regime, this young man had stood up and said, "I'm a Christian too, but I think as a Christian you should be willing to carry arms for a state that does good for its citizens." Rüdiger saw the issue differently. "We should follow the example of Christ," he had argued, "and have the courage to use the means he did."

The issue of civil disobedience was a thorny one for Christians living in a Communist state. While the Bible instructs Christians to submit to the authorities of this world, it also instructs us not to kill without justification. If the worldly order conflicts with obligations of faith, what should Christians do? These questions troubled many young men, and they sought answers in the church. Should you follow orders to fire on your own countrymen? What do you do when you find yourself standing on the border of civil disobedience?

Having faced exactly that moral dilemma, and knowing what kind of consequences he had reaped, Rüdiger advocated becoming a *Bausoldat*. It was an option he had not had.

Previously Rüdiger had heatedly debated this point with the young man. But on this particular evening he was cheerful and agreeable; he stayed for three hours, spouting questions. After he had left, Rüdiger shook his head, puzzled. *What does a young fellow with a perfectly new spinning-wheel that's supposed to be old want from me?* he wondered.

~

Portrait of a Stasi Informant

Eventually it became perfectly clear what the young man with the spinning wheel had wanted. He was a Stasi agent, an informant for the secret police who had been sent to investigate Rüdiger. When the Communist government was toppled in 1989, Rüdiger was one of the first to conduct interviews with former Stasi agents, and this young man was among those he spoke with. The following are excerpts from the transcript:

"I reported on the Protestant Church for eight years. That was my main task. The MfS [the Ministerium für Staatssicherheit, or Ministry for State Security, known as the Stasi] wanted information from me about church gatherings and about people active in the church."

"What did that mean concretely?"

"For example, they wanted to know which vices these people had, I mean, problems with alcohol, how their marriage was, affairs, and things like that."

"What circle of people did you spy on?"

"From pastors to church staff, it depended . . ."

"And what about church functions?"

". . . The Stasi wanted reports on the mood, they wanted to know who was there and what was discussed politically."

15

"Could you give me an example?"

"Yeah, for example, what was discussed at a meeting about the draft. The Stasi wanted to know who spoke out against doing military service."

"You told me you were baptized as an adult. Are you a believer?"

"No. That with the baptism came from the Stasi. They said it would be better for my work for them."

"Didn't you have any scruples about standing in front of a baptismal font as a Stasi informant? Baptism is something sacred for Christians."

"It was a little strange for me . . ."

"Did you get recommendations from the Stasi on how you should behave as a 'Christian'?"

"Yes, I should cut my hair shorter, keep a low profile, not play the radio so loud . . ."

"Do you believe the Stasi had a special interest in the church?"

"That's certain. The church was completely covered with informants at all different levels."

"How and where did you give your information to the Stasi?"

"Mostly in anonymous apartments in Karl-Marx-Stadt or at home. And always orally, never in writing."

"Were you paid by the Stasi for your information?"

"Yes, but it varied and was irregular. You couldn't get rich from it. Sometimes it was 200 marks, sometimes less. Mostly I got something like a coffee service or something like that . . ."

"Were there other kinds of payment?"

"Often it was little advantages in daily life. When we wanted to go on vacation and our car needed to be fixed, the Stasi drove us. . . . Or when I needed an appointment for repairs, one call from the MfS would do it."

"What did the MfS call you?"

"My code name was 'Conrad.'"

". . . What effect did your work as an informant for the MfS have on your family?"

"You don't have a private life anymore. They wanted to know everything: who I slept with, who my friends and acquaintances were, who I talked to on the corner, everything! There wasn't anything that didn't interest them!"

". . . It didn't bother me as much as [it bothered] my wife, who did not work for the MfS, and suddenly had a persecution complex. She said she was being pursued by the Stasi. It went so far that she didn't know what she was doing. She wanted to jump out the window, ran around on the street half-dressed . . ."

"What happened?"

"She was a security risk for the Stasi. She had to disappear into a psychological clinic. For one year."

"Has she gotten over it today?"

"No, unfortunately not. She has to take medication regularly . . . and is still being treated by doctors."*

Succumbing to Flattery

Only a few weeks after the visit by the seemingly innocuous young man, Rüdiger received a phone call. "Herr Knechtel? Just a moment. Dr. Greim would like to speak to you."

Rüdiger recognized the name from the newspapers. Greim was the number-two man in the Liberal Democratic Party (LDP), and a director of a large porcelain manufacturing plant, a powerful man politically and economically.

Greim came on the line. "I'd like to meet you, Herr Knechtel. I'm coming to Karl-Marx-Stadt soon, and I'm taking over the region for the party. Your name has been recommended to me."

A question blipped on Rüdiger's mental screen: *What does he want from me?* "May I ask how you know of me?" he inquired.

---

*Taken from Rüdiger Knechtel's interview entitled "Deckname Conrad: Gespräch mit einem Informanten der ehemaligen Staatssicherheit" ("Code Name Conrad: Conversation with an Informant for the Former State Security"), *Die Union,* January 30, 1990.

"I attended a meeting of the LDP in Plauen, and I asked the leadership to recommend competent people. People who can think, who are engaged in what they do, who know what they're doing. You were recommended to me as just such a person. I need people like you."

Rüdiger was so pleased by the flattery that his defenses were half down. *I don't even know anybody in Plauen,* he mused idly. But that thought sparked a question. "Who in Plauen recommended me?"

"I've forgotten the name. But it doesn't matter. When could we meet?" They set up a day and time.

When Greim visited the Knechtels' apartment, he looked appreciatively at the collection of antiques and paintings they had collected. "It's clear to me that someone who can find these kinds of treasures is exactly the kind of man I'm looking for," he complimented Rüdiger. "Do you think you could help me find some paintings?"

The conversation moved from art to politics in such a smooth, friendly way that Greim suggested they continue talking over a glass of wine in a nearby café. "Bring your wife," he urged. "This isn't normal," Eva whispered to Rüdiger as they left together.

Poland's Solidarity movement had fired the hopes of some East Germans, including Rüdiger, and he warmed to this topic over drinks. He was critical of the Communists, but Greim topped him with his biting appraisal. "You're even more critical of the state than I am!" exclaimed Rüdiger.

"I know who I'm talking to. Listen. For years I've been only the number-two director in the porcelain business because I was in the LDP and not the SED [the Socialist Unity Party, the Communist Party]. I have my own problems with the state."

That sounded plausible enough. Rüdiger confided in his new-found ally that he feared he would be sacked from his job as a geologist for political reasons, and he asked if Greim could help him set up his own business. By the time they parted, they had forged plans as allies. Or so it seemed.

But after this single meeting, Rüdiger's attempts to contact Greim were futile. When he would call Greim's office, he would be told that Greim wasn't there, even if his voice was audible in the background. Rüdiger concluded that Greim had been sent to report on him — and indeed, that was the case. Twelve years later, Rüdiger was given access to the voluminous files that the Stasi had kept on him. Hartmut Greim had been a longtime Stasi collaborator, delivering reports to the MfS for 24 years. On March 6, 1981, Greim wrote a damaging evaluation of Rüdiger.[2]

"You're under Arrest!"

On July 28, 1982, at 6:30 in the morning, seven men appeared at Rüdiger's door and rang the bell. "You're under arrest," they told him when he answered the door. He was taken to an interrogation session that lasted, without letup, for the next seventeen hours. His wife, Eva, was also taken in for questioning. Once they had left their apartment, it was searched, and eight of their most valuable paintings were confiscated. Eva was told that she would be released if she would divorce Rüdiger. When that ploy failed, one interrogator offered to let her go in exchange for sexual favors. When she turned him down, he offered to lighten her husband's sentence in exchange for another painting or two.

The list of accusations against Rüdiger was long. Among other things, he was charged with making unauthorized contacts with Western organizations, including Amnesty International. He had indeed corresponded with a number of people and groups in the West, leading the regime to suspect him of being an intermediary supplying information to "enemy organizations," perhaps even guilty of espionage. Rüdiger was also accused of not paying a special tax on the objects of art he had acquired; records showed that he owed back payments amounting to 15,000 marks. The painful part was that this accusation was true.

While Rüdiger guessed that he had been arrested primarily because of his politics, the moral ramifications of the tax issue seared

2. "Dr. Hartmut Greim alias IMB Boysen, trotz Stasi in den Wüstenrot-Chefsessel; Buchautor Rüdiger Knechtel war sein Opfer" ("Dr. Hartmut Greim alias Informant Boysen, in Boss's Chair at Wüstenrot despite Stasi; Book Author Rüdiger Knechtel Was His Victim"), *Bild*, Chemnitz, March 25, 1992, p. 5.

his conscience as a Christian. Whether or not the system was corrupt, he still owed Caesar what was Caesar's.

In the end Rüdiger received a two-year sentence for tax evasion. While he was in prison, he had ample time to think about the moral implications of the decisions he had made. As painful as it was for him to acknowledge, justice was in one sense being served in his case. People in his church had warned him that his passion for collecting was in danger of becoming a pursuit of Mammon. He had laughed off their cautions then, but now he saw the truth in them. The salt on this wound burned. His collecting had become a powerful addiction, he realized, and he was getting a radical cure.

The most painful confrontation was with his interrogators. "You haven't paid your taxes," they taunted him, "yet you claim to be a Christian. What kind of Christian is that?" The question hurt because he knew the answer.

"It was a terrible feeling," he recalls. "Then it became clear to me how far from real faith I had lived."

When Rüdiger was given access to his Stasi files in 1992, there were shocks buried in the 1,500 pages. One of them was the revelation that George Brühl, who was reputedly the wealthiest antique dealer in East Germany, a man whom Rüdiger and Eva had known well and had counted as a friend, had been an informant who had compiled a detailed list on the Knechtels' collection.

The Stasi gained access to the Knechtels' apartment through a ruse involving the Knechtels' son Ralf, organized with Brühl's help. As Stasi reports document, an imprint of the apartment key was made from the key Ralf stowed in his sports locker at school. The Stasi used their copy to enter the Knechtels' apartment to confiscate eight paintings after Eva and Rüdiger were arrested. These were sold illegally in the West for cash; only one has since been returned.

When the story broke on Brühl's collaboration with the Stasi, he was on vacation in Morocco. When he was stormed by reporters, he admitted he had made the report on the Knechtels for the Stasi. Did he feel guilty? "Mr. Knechtel was a good friend of mine for a long time," he answered.

"You spied on him," said the reporter.

Brühl was unfazed by the accusation. "You know, anybody who knows my situation knows that you have to make accommodations."[3]

No More Compromises

When Rüdiger was released from prison, he was a chastened man. He had thought a great deal about the consequences of the decisions he had made. He understood the difficulty of living a moral life, but he was determined now to embrace that challenge. When he had vowed not to shoot at defectors at the Wall, he had suffered the consequences for that moral decision. And now he had paid for his moral lapse of evading taxes. Out of these experiences he forged his resolve to live in consistent harmony with his moral integrity, a resolve that was anchored in his Christian faith. Subsequently he boycotted elections, refused to make compromises with the regime, and took part in a risky distribution of leaflets urging others to do the same. He knew he was being closely watched by the secret police. Neighbors warned him that there were agents in nearby parked cars who were using binoculars to keep a constant watch on his apartment windows.

When the Knechtels' son Ralf decided he wanted to leave the country, Rüdiger understood, although he had decided that he should stay. Both Eva and Rüdiger supported Ralf's desire to risk being bought as a political prisoner. Because the West German government regularly intervened and "bought" the freedom of political prisoners, there was a chance — though no guarantee — that Ralf could enter the West this way. Still, when Ralf was willingly imprisoned, his parents were distraught. Only many tense months later was Ralf negotiated out, with the help of Josef and Irmgard Kneifel, friends of the Knechtels who had been political prisoners themselves and had been secretly traded into freedom in West Germany. The Kneifels knew how dangerous life in prison could be: Josef had been nearly tortured to death in Bautzen.[4]

3. "Brühl aus Morokko: 'Ich musste mich anpassen'" ("Brühl from Morocco: 'I Had to Go Along'"), *Morgenpost*, March 21, 1992.
4. The stories of Josef and Irmgard Kneifel are movingly rendered in the book

Surviving a Chamber of Horrors: Josef Kneifel

When Soviet soldiers marched into Afghanistan in December 1979, Josef Kneifel's cup of frustration was full to overflowing. In 1968 he had watched the tanks roll past his own house on their way to invade Czechoslovakia, and now the Soviets were demonstrating their willingness to use force again. Josef decided that the moment had come to protest.

In the sixteen years since he had been converted from a young Communist supporter to an opponent of Communism, Josef had tried peaceful means of resistance and change. But he had found himself frustrated at every turn. His attempts to found alternative parties had been shut down, his criticism of the system at public meetings had been squelched, and his refusal to cooperate with the party had blocked any pay increases or advancement in his work. In addition, his petition to emigrate from East Germany had been turned down. What could he try next? It was impossible to publish critical articles; a public speech of protest was a sure ticket to jail. He decided to make a statement of a different kind.

The Soviet tanks that rolled into Afghanistan gave him the idea. A monument of a tank stood in Karl-Marx-Stadt (now Chemnitz), and Josef decided to blow it up as a protest against Soviet militarism. Whether what he did was an act of terrorism or moral protest may be debatable. But the consequence was that although he was not identified as the perpetrator until several months after the deed, he was eventually arrested and sentenced to life in prison. His wife was also arrested and imprisoned for failing to report him. For most of his term, Josef was in Bautzen, reputedly the toughest prison in East Germany.

At Bautzen, Josef was nearly tortured to death. He was menaced not only by the prison guards but also by the other criminals, whom the guards allowed to abuse him. He was subjected to a wide range of horrors. They denied him adequate food, chained his hands together and beat him, ripped

by Rüdiger Knechtel and Jürgen Fiedler entitled *Stalin's DDR: Berichte politisch Verfolgter (Stalin's GDR: Reports of Politically Persecuted)* (Leipzig: Forum Verlag, 1991), pp. 94-130.

open his nose repeatedly, and put him into a padded solitary confinement cell. Sometimes they would leave him strapped to a metal frame for days on end in a cold cell, leaving him to urinate on himself and then nearly freeze to the frame. At one point he became so desperate that he slit his wrists, hoping that the doctor who treated him would recognize his plight and give him more extensive medical treatment. But the doctor simply ignored Josef's other obvious wounds.

Finally, after eight years of this abuse, Josef was rescued. Rüdiger Knechtel, who was a friend of his, brought his case to the attention of church authorities and human rights groups. During high-level negotiations conducted in 1987, the West German government bought his freedom as a political prisoner. To this day he remains bitter about the abuse he suffered at the hands of the Communists.

In the momentous year of 1989, as East Germany's resistance to the Communist regime coalesced into a movement, Rüdiger Knechtel was with the vanguard. In May he took part in an action urging people to boycott the farce of "free elections." Joining forces with the group that became *Neues Forum,* he was committed to change, but peaceful change. He was convinced that there was an acute need for truth. Wielding the power of the word, Rüdiger was one of the first to directly confront the Stasi with their abuses, interviewing them and publishing the results in East German newspapers. He also worked with an organization for the politically persecuted, documenting the personal stories of scores of victims of Communist brutality. He compiled the results, and shortly after the Wall fell he published them in a book called *Stalin's GDR: Reports of Politically Persecuted.*[5] In their stories the victims named real names and told the terrible truth. It sent a chill through a nation that had feared the worst and had recoiled when it was confirmed.

5. This book documents the stories told by the victims.

The Stasi were enraged, and vowed they would take revenge. Vicious responses hailed down on Rüdiger Knechtel — bomb threats, assassination warnings, poisonous letters. One caller warned him "not to go out in the dark alone." Another warned Rüdiger that if he didn't take back what he had written by Wednesday of that week, "you better get police protection by Thursday." The author of one letter made a chilling promise: "Now I know your address. I swear: By Dec. 31, 1991 I will not kill you. I will throw a cup of acid in your face. *You will be blind.*"[6] Menacing phone callers threatened to kill him. The police hooked up an alarm to his telephone, but warned that they could no longer guarantee his safety if he stayed in the country. In the next year, Rüdiger Knechtel received thirty threats on his life. But he kept on with the work he was doing, shaken but undeterred.

Shortly after this experience, Rüdiger reflected,

"As long as I could think politically, particularly after being imprisoned the second time, I couldn't stand the hypocrisy of [the socialist system]. . . . I admit that I am bitter about that, but console myself with Elie Wiesel's statement that hate is not the opposite of love, but indifference.

"Not long ago I asked a priest if it wouldn't be better to simply give a pardon to the Communist party and its functionaries for their misdeeds. He gave me his position as a Christian: forgiveness is important — and the recognition of sin and repentance are necessary. Then you can take a step toward each other."[7]

Today Rüdiger and his wife still live in Chemnitz, where he works caring for the sick and dying.

---

6. Sven Hadon, "Terror gegen Stasi-Aufklärer" ("Terror against Stasi Exposer"), *Bild*, January 19, 1991.

7. Knechtel, *Stalin's DDR*, pp. 78-79.

CHAPTER 2

"A Privilege to Suffer":
The Story of Alexander Ogorodnikov

One day Alexander Ogorodnikov was forced into a car by KGB agents and driven out of Moscow into a forest. As they drove farther into the woods outside the city, he couldn't recognize any landmarks; he had absolutely no idea where he was. When the car eventually rolled to a stop, he got out and faced seven large, muscular men. In an instant Alexander realized that his captors were clearly capable of beating him — or killing him.[1]

In the distance he could see a cottage, and in a moment several figures dressed in black came out and walked toward the group slowly. He waited tensely as they joined his captors; at that point one of the men in black indicated that he should move. The men encircled him so tightly that at first he couldn't get past them — but then he spied a narrow opening in the circle. Taking a chance, Alexander pushed through it, expecting to be shot in the back at any moment.

He had taken only several steps when he heard running footsteps behind him. Again he was encircled, jostled by the men who this time were talking. They debated what to do with his body if they killed him. Alexander spied the gun in one agent's hand as he cocked it. "Should we torture him first?" a black-clad man asked. "Let's get on with it," said another. "Where do you want to shoot him?"

---

1. This account is based on the author's interviews with Alexander Ogorodnikov in Moscow on March 12, 1991, and in Chicago on April 24, 1991.

As they debated, Alexander kept on walking, the men still jostling around him in a circle. He had no idea where he was, but he spied a path and followed it, hardly daring to hope where it might lead. When the men clumped around him again, he squeezed between their shoulders, pressing on. The path eventually led to the edge of the woods, where Alexander was grateful to see signs of a town. He broke away from his captors, running tensely, half expecting a shot from behind. Would they risk gunfire so close to the town? Without daring to look back, Alexander ran until he found the local train station. With heaving breaths he boarded the next train to Moscow.

But the men had followed him and had gotten onto the same train before it pulled out. When they found out where he was sitting, they crowded in beside him, squeezing him between their shoulders. He could feel their breath on his neck as clearly as their unspoken threat. When the train pulled into Moscow, he walked out of the station, but he could hear their steps echoing on the street behind him. Where could he go to escape them?

Trembling but trying not to panic, he mentally ran through the list of people who might possibly help him and settled on one. By this time it was late at night. As he picked his way through Moscow's dark streets, he was aware of his assailants shadowing his every step. He had decided to go to the apartment of Tatiana Hodorovich, a friend of Andrei Sakharov. Alexander was sure she wouldn't be afraid to help him. She was well enough known to Western journalists that the KGB agents would probably think twice about using overt violence if he sought her out. One thing they didn't want was coverage in the Western news. Alexander's hunch was right: when Alexander reached Tatiana's apartment, she quickly took Alexander in and slammed the door. The KGB agents tried to force their way in, but when they didn't succeed, they backed off.

But the next day the agents still surrounded the apartment. As Alexander peered out, he felt helpless. The forces against him were potent, and there was no one to stop them. *Wherever I go, they can find me*, he thought. *They have the power to do whatever they like with me.* He had no idea how he could escape, and despair threatened to undo him. But he decided he must do something, anything but give in.

Soon he walked out of Tatiana's apartment very slowly. He walked with deliberate steps, knowing that the agents were following him. He expected a confrontation at any moment, but he kept on walking. The agents tailed him for nearly an hour. When he sped up, they mirrored his tempo. When he walked slowly, so did they.

Eventually he saw a way to break free from them. He made a sudden dash between two buildings, running with a burst of strength. He raced into the courtyard behind the houses he had just passed, then panicked. *There's no way out!* he realized. It was a dead end, and he could hear the footsteps of the agents nearby.

Desperate, Alexander put his shoulder to the door of a back entrance to the next building and heaved it open. As he pounded up the stairs, he was sure he would be seized any second. When he reached the top of the stairs, gasping and out of breath, he prayed briefly and opened the small New Testament he carried in his pocket. His eyes fell on these words: "I write to you, young men, because you are strong, and the word of God lives in you, and you have overcome the wicked one" (1 John 2:14). A sense of quiet came over Alexander, calming him. He kissed his New Testament and put it back into his pocket.

He waited. Minutes ticked by, but he heard no footsteps behind him. He was sure the agents must be nearby — hadn't they seen where he had gone? Slowly he walked down the stairs and into the courtyard. There was no one there. The agents following him had disappeared. He was a free man — for now.

Driven Underground by the KGB

Alexander Ogorodnikov was being pursued by the KGB because he was a Christian, the founder of a group called the Christian Seminar. He looked the Russian intellectual and dissident that he was: intense eyes behind thin-rimmed glasses, luxurious beard, dark-brown hair pulled back into a ponytail. He had gathered together a group of young Russian intellectuals committed to putting their faith into practice, and in the Soviet Union, that was risky. In 1973 he had been expelled from Moscow's Institute for Cinematography for making a film about Christians. Even when Andrei Sakharov cited Alexander's case as an instance of unfair treatment in human rights hearings two years later, it did not change Alexander's fate.

The Soviet regime was engaged in a clear battle with all religious denominations, and the Russian Orthodox Church, with which Alexander was affiliated, was no exception. In order to be permitted to meet, each church had to be officially registered with the state authorities. The conditions of registration meant that the church was forced to abide by regulations and restrictions imposed by the regime. The church was only allowed to hold worship services; nearly all other overt manifestations of faith were not permitted. Public discussion of Christianity, Christian education of children, and all charitable activities were forbidden. The consequences of engaging in any of the forbidden activities could be severe — getting fired from work or expelled from school, being jailed or forced to pay stiff fines.

"They proposed that we could be Christians only in the church building, and that we leave our beliefs behind us like baggage when we live in the world," Alexander explains. "By the norm of Soviet ideology, it was impossible for us to live our faith."

This was precisely the goal of the Communists: to contain the practice of Christianity. Under the threat of persecution, the church made many compromises; as the church fathers saw it, it was a matter of survival. But the price the church paid was not being able to do many of the things the Bible instructs believers to do.

Alexander was determined to change this. "If the church cannot fulfill its mission of preaching, apostolic work, and missions, then we [as individual believers] are obliged to," he concluded. With his friend, Vladimir Poresh, Alexander founded the Christian Seminar in 1971. Together they read, prayed, and tried to help each other live as Christians should. Soon they had attracted a group of young intellectuals from several major Soviet cities. Together they formed a "nucleus of spiritual vitality"[2] that began to have an effect on others.

Not surprisingly, the Christian Seminar attracted the attention

2. Kent Hill, *The Soviet Union on the Brink: An Inside Look at Christianity and Glasnost* (Portland, Ore.: Multnomah Press, 1991), pp. 255-56.

of the KGB. It sent agents to infiltrate the group, then began threatening and trying to intimidate the group's members. The universities where they studied threatened to revoke their scholarships or expel them. Some were fired from their jobs; some were deprived of their residence permits. (Under the Soviet system, official permission to live in a given city like Moscow was granted by the state authorities. Accordingly, that right could be revoked, suspended, or denied, forcing an individual to leave the city or risk the consequences of staying illegally.) Others endured beatings by the agents. Eleven members were arrested, some of whom were put into Soviet psychiatric hospitals which served as prisons.

"The members had made a decisive step, [offering] a challenge to the world around them. And it had consequences," Alexander says now. Eventually he was expelled from Moscow, but the group fought back. Under an assumed name, they obtained a house for their living and meeting quarters, and they supported themselves by raising their own produce. On Easter of 1978, the high celebration of the Russian Orthodox Church, the house was filled to bursting with worshipers. In an attempt to intimidate the celebrants, thirty armed KGB agents surrounded the house. Alexander knew enough about the KGB to suspect that his arrest was imminent.

To protect himself, he decided to go underground. He was hidden by a monk in a monastery in western Ukraine. Using an assumed name and concealed by the monastery "uniform" of a cassock, he lived a clandestine existence, his identity hidden even from the abbot. He had already discovered that not everyone in the church could be counted on to help him. When he had earlier sought refuge in a monastery in Estonia, monks there had expelled him, fearing that his presence endangered them. He had been forced to leave in the night.

By the late 1970s the Christian Seminar movement had about 300 members in several cities, and Alexander was certain that he would be arrested soon. The monk who was sheltering him gave him some money, which enabled him to visit the far-flung Christians in the movement to help strengthen and organize them. Realizing that time was precious, Alexander traveled through the country to establish a network of communications between the members. He wanted to insure that even after he was arrested, the work would continue without him.

Specifically, he needed to help them establish ways to communicate with each other secretly. Because he had been constantly followed by KGB agents for the last several years, he was skilled at subterfuge in message passing. During a seemingly innocent conversation, for example, he could easily conceal a letter under a chair cushion with a casual move of his hand. Because his followers were now under surveillance, he taught them these techniques. They also developed a "language" of code words and code names, so that when their letters were intercepted — which they often would be — they could not be deciphered. In addition, the group developed a system for sending letters and a cache where communications could be hidden. A slash of lipstick in a symbol on the wall at an appointed spot meant a letter was waiting for pickup at a designated location.

KGB agents now set their sights on Alexander, who was on the run. They knew that he had perhaps twenty friends to rely on for refuge, so the agents made work of finding out about them, then trying to create a "dead zone" around Alexander by attempting to sever the relationships. The agents went to each of the friends in turn, employing the same pattern in each case. First they would familiarize themselves with the individual's character — and weaknesses. In some cases, simply forbidding contact was enough. If that didn't suffice, the agents might threaten to cut the person's phone line. Or to have him or her fired. Or to have his or her daughter expelled from the university. Sometimes the threat took the form of a beating. The goal was to isolate Alexander from even his closest friends.

Just as he had anticipated, Alexander was arrested in 1978. He was taken to KGB headquarters in Lubyanka, where agents told him, "We understand you want very much to be a hero. But we don't want to make new martyrs. We want to give you one more chance." They knew Alexander had been offered the chance to emigrate. They told him he had to go, and said they would give him one month to leave the country.

Alexander replied that he had no intention of emigrating. He said that they were the alien elements disrupting the country, and that they should leave instead. "You bring only fear, cynicism, and hate," he told them. Although he knew such remarks could send him to prison, Alexander was determined to speak his mind. The KGB agents were furious, unaccustomed as they were to hearing such criticisms. "One month, or you'll be arrested for good," they fumed.

Alexander took his dilemma to his friends in the Christian Seminar. Some urged him to accept the offer to emigrate and to carry on the work of Christian Russian emigrés. But Alexander countered that a new generation of believers had come into existence in Russia, and that they were charged to live by deeds and words that were equally convincing. "Great deeds start with victims," Alexander explained. "We have to prove our words are not empty, and we have to prove them with our blood and our flesh. It is a great privilege to suffer for Jesus Christ. Pardon me for these lofty words. But I cannot refuse this privilege." Clearly he was making a deliberate decision to remain in Russia and go to prison as a consequence. The room was silent as his friends listened to his decision. Then some began to weep, though they did not try to dissuade him. Others resolved that they would willingly face arrest too.

At the end of the month, in November 1978, Alexander was again arrested, as the KGB had promised he would be. A trial followed. Alexander's father, an old-line Communist who had been a loyal party member, expressed his bewilderment at the trial. "My son hasn't harmed anyone," he said. "He shares what he has with others, and he has worked hard wherever he was. People love him. Can you explain to me, as a member of the Communist party, what he is being judged for?" In response, he was told to be silent. This man who believed in the ideology now saw his son as its victim, and he was genuinely puzzled that such a thing was possible in the country he believed in. The trial concluded before year's end, and Alexander was convicted of anti-Soviet agitation, propagandizing, and "parasitism," and sentenced to one year in prison.[3]

3. Hill, *The Soviet Union on the Brink*, p. 256.

Witnessing to Criminals

During this year of incarceration, KGB officials hoped to break Alexander's will. They had him locked up with tough criminals in the prison in Moscow, who were physically able to — and, indeed, were expected to — abuse him. Prisoners of conscience were almost always locked up with criminals, a combination very likely to produce conflicts. But when Alexander began talking with these men, he proved so genuinely likeable that they became fond of him. They thought he must be a priest, although Alexander protested that he was not. When the jail administrators eventually moved Alexander from that cell, "it was very touching," he recalls. "The other inmates nearly cried, because we had become like brothers."

Alexander was then sent to a prison in the far eastern part of the country. He was made to travel day and night in a special train for prisoners, and conditions were extremely trying. Prisoners were permitted to use the toilets only twice a day. They were given no food, and they were sometimes denied water. When Alexander spoke up, telling the guards that this treatment violated the most basic human rights, he was beaten.

When the train finally arrived in Khabarovsk, Alexander was taken to the prison there and once again put into a cell with tough criminals. They assigned him to the spot nearest to the latrine bucket, the position given to all newcomers to prison cells. He still wore his suit, since he had not yet been given a prison uniform, and his cell mates, astonished, demanded that he give it to them. He told them he would be happy to give it to someone who needed it, but commented, half-jestingly, that it looked like they were going to be in prison for some time. This unexpected retort made the other inmates angry, and several of them moved into position to beat him.

But the tallest of the group, a large, tattooed, half-naked man who seemed to be the acknowledged boss, raised a hand and said, "I think this guy has something to tell us." The rumbling of the others subsided. Turning to Alexander, he said, "Are you a Christian?"

"Yes, I am," Alexander replied.

"We're here because we're being moved from one camp to

another. We know no one here. For several days we haven't had anything to smoke. If you are a Christian, prove it to us. Show us a miracle by getting us some cigarettes, and we will believe the Lord exists."

Alexander said, "I think the Lord will perform a miracle only if we all pray for it together." But he went on to say that smoking wasn't a good thing, and that the Lord probably thought so too, since it poisons the body. He explained that he thought the Lord would respond in such a situation only out of love and compassion for them as "lost people in miserable circumstances." Then he asked them to stand and pray. The criminals had intended their request as a jest to ridicule Alexander, but he took them up earnestly on their opening. "If we pray seriously," he said boldly, "the Lord will hear us."

Although he had been searched when he entered the prison, Alexander had managed to bring a small icon into the cell with him. Now he brought it out and began to pray. Some of the inmates began to smile, awkwardly eyeing the spectacle. But as Alexander continued praying for them and for their needs, it began to get quiet in the cell. For years the inmates had lived in a coarse atmosphere of violence, vulgarity, and brutality. Enmity and hatred were the norm. It was perhaps the first time they had heard words of prayer — gentle, good, uplifting. Alexander prayed for a full fifteen minutes. When he finished, there was absolute silence.

There was a small opening in the cell door, and suddenly two packs of cigarettes flew through it. The inmates caught them before they hit the floor.

At that moment the boss of the cell cried out, "God exists!"

* * *

Alexander was next sent to the prison in Komsomolsk-na-Amure, in the Orient. It didn't take long for the prisoners there to recognize that he was different. He talked to small groups of them about freedom, about what humankind is created for, about the Soviet system, about punishment, and about Christ. They quickly banded together to provide ways for him to move among them undetected.

One prisoner would exchange his uniform, which had his name on it, with Alexander's, a switch that allowed Alexander to enter other barracks.

All prisoners were obligated to fulfill labor quotas, and those who failed to meet the quotas would be put in the punishment cell. The other prisoners volunteered to fill Alexander's quotas for him, saying he should spend his time meeting with the inmates who wanted his counsel. At first he declined, but they insisted. So while the others quietly performed Alexander's tasks, Alexander slipped away to talk with inmates who wanted to ask him questions about God.

There were "endless meetings, giving great joy," in Alexander's words. These impromptu sessions were a mix of counseling, lecturing, preaching, and pastoral care, offered over cups of very strong tea brewed by the inmates. Priests were not permitted in the prison, so Alexander fulfilled the inmates' need for one. Some asked that he write a prayer for them; others wanted to confess to him or to ask his advice. Alexander even baptized some inmates who desired it, although he reminded them that he was not a clergyman.

"I never knew what I would tell them until I looked in their faces," Alexander says. "But then it would become clear." What he communicated in these talks lit a fire of revival in the prison. A number of inmates began an earnest journey to find out more about Christ.

Despite the subterfuge, prison officials eventually found out about what Alexander was doing, and they put him in an isolation cell. If they entered the cell while he was praying, they would shout at him to stand, but he would remain kneeling. These breaches of "prison regulations" earned him a vile form of punishment. Air pressure would be applied to the sewage pipes leading into the isolation cell, and raw sewage would pour out of the pipes, covering the bottom of the cell completely. There was a small cement post in the center of the cell on which Alexander could rest one foot — that was it. For several days he would be forced to stand day and night, with only this small post for a resting point and no way to lie down, in this pool of sewage. He could only wait for it to recede. "Remember this," he told the prison officials. "Your deed will accuse you. I will give witness of this."

The Consequences of Refusing to Collaborate with the KGB

Eventually prison officials offered Alexander a deal, saying they would release him if he would promise not to go back to Moscow. But he refused, saying that it was his duty to return there and continue his Christian work.

"You can do only one thing to stop me," Alexander declared. "You can kill me."

At that the officials angrily cut off the conversation.

Two months before Alexander's year-long prison term was to end, he was sent by jet to St. Petersburg, where KGB agents pressured him to "renounce his past deeds." They wanted him to sign a statement saying he would not participate in further work with the Christian Seminar.

"We don't want a new martyr," they said. "Why do you want to stay in prison? All you have to do is sign." They told him he was foolish, promising that if he would cooperate, they would give him an apartment and a good job. All he had to do was appear on television and renounce what he had done. If he refused, they threatened to extend his sentence.

The tactics that KGB agents used to try to pressure prisoners into recanting were always well thought out. They would try to coerce a priest by threatening to take away his congregation. If he agreed to the KGB's terms, he would be permitted to return to his parish. The threat typically used with laypeople like Alexander was an extended prison sentence. As Alexander explained, when you have been sentenced to prison for a year, as he was, all your hopes are centered on that date of release. All the deprivations you endure are bearable only because you know when the horror will be over. You count the months, the weeks, the days, and finally the hours. You dream of the day you will be released, when you will see your wife and child and your friends, eat a normal meal, see the sky. "All of your days are dedicated to this day," says Alexander. He had a fierce longing to be released on that day. But he refused the agents' offer.

Having failed in their first attempt, they tried another tactic to entice Alexander. He had written a manuscript called "Culture of the

Catacomb," which had not yet been published. The manuscript had been seized when Alexander was arrested. KGB agents told him that they could arrange to have it published. All he had to do was make a public declaration of his wrongdoing. They knew the bait of seeing his own words in print would be compellingly attractive.

But Alexander refused to take the bait. The grim consequence was that he was given a new sentence of five years. What he couldn't know then was that he would receive yet another extension of his sentence, so that in the end he would serve a total of eight-and-a-half years in Soviet prisons. Because the harshness of Soviet prisons was designed to change the convictions of the inmates, Alexander's unbroken resistance bewildered and perturbed prison officials.

Hunger Strikes, Hallucinations, and Help

In 1979-1980, while serving his new sentence, Alexander began a hunger strike for the right to have a Bible, a strike he continued for eight months. During that time he was force-fed, given liquid nourishment with a large syringe inserted through a pipe forced into his nose. But his strike was successful: he did finally receive a Bible. He waged other hunger strikes after this one, spending a total of two years of his eight-and-a-half-year sentence on strike. In this way he won other rights. He was the first prisoner to receive communion in jail (in 1980), and he successfully campaigned for the right of other prisoners to do so as well.

Meanwhile, two members of the Christian Seminar staged a demonstration in Moscow defending Alexander. They too were arrested. Ultimately, eleven members were sentenced to prison, and prison officials convinced one of them to recant and denounce his activities with the Christian Seminar. He was then permitted to visit Alexander to try to persuade him to do the same. But Alexander refused.

While Alexander was imprisoned, the KGB also embarked on a campaign to defame Alexander's character. Boris Razyeyev, who had visited the Christian Seminar, was induced to make slanderous accusations against Alexander. In a televised interview, this former friend described Alexander as a "new Rasputin," informing viewers that their "hero" was not what they thought him to be. The interview was shown on prime-time television in Russia and in America.

In these attempts to discredit Alexander and others like him, the KGB pressured a number of intellectuals and dissidents into writing public letters criticizing Alexander and other leading Christians. Indeed, fourteen letters defaming Alexander can be attributed to those dissidents and intellectuals manipulated by the KGB to discredit him. This sort of public slander continued well into the time of *glasnost.* Such letters were published in *Krokodil, Pravda,* and *Izvestiia* as recently as July and August of 1988.[4]

* * *

For Alexander, help in prison came from strange places. For example, he was permitted to read J. D. Salinger's *Franny and Zooey,* which proved to be the unlikely conduit that allowed the wisdom of an eighteenth-century Russian monk to reach Alexander in his cell. This was how he learned about the "Jesus prayer."

In Salinger's story, Franny is given a book for a course on Russian literature, the tale of an old Russian monk who was determined to know what it means to pray unceasingly, as the Bible commends us to do. According to the story, the monk retreated to the solitude of the country and prayed, "Jesus Christ, Son of God, have mercy on me, a sinner." He repeated the prayer as he walked, saying it in rhythm with his breathing and walking. He began by repeating the prayer a hundred times, then kept increasing his number of repetitions each day until the prayer was part of virtually every breath, whether he was waking or sleeping. He spoke no other words but these, and repeated them until they were truly unceasing. In Salinger's story, the tale of the monk makes a powerful impact on Franny — and it had a similar impact on Alexander.

4. An issue of *Argumenty i Fakty (Arguments and Facts),* no. 1 (January 1992) quotes KGB archives which indicate that efforts were made to discredit Alexander in both the Soviet Union and the West.

Alexander began to pray the "Jesus prayer" too, pacing off the steps in his cell, repeating it again and again. In Russian the words rolled musically off his tongue. Following the monk's example, he began reciting the prayer a hundred times a day, then more, until the prayer became ingrained in his consciousness. Alexander recalls the remarkable effect: "[You] make a spiritual journey from your mind to your heart. . . . After a while you don't feel cold or hunger. You are only in contact with Christ. It ignites a fire around your heart."

So Alexander paced his cell, which was small, dark, and cold, and prayed this prayer and smiled. Prison officials thought that he might be demented, and they tried to provoke him. But he simply told them that he forgave them. They didn't know what to think.

*   *   *

Others had joined Alexander in his hunger strikes, and under his influence began resisting prison policies. So Alexander was moved away from the political prisoners. He was also sent repeatedly to the punishment cell, which was dark and cold and harsh. He was denied books, adequate food, and human contact.

Because he had not been able to confess to a priest for some time, Alexander felt burdened. In the Russian Orthodox Church, the priest would touch a confessor with his cassock when he pronounced the absolution "By the power of Christ your sins are forgiven." Alexander longed for this experience of confession, so he prayed to Seraphim of Sarov, a Russian saint of the late eighteenth century, for help. As he prayed, Alexander felt that a cassock touched him — and he felt his burden lifted. When a priest accepts a confession, the confessor's sin is removed, and "you feel physically light," explains Alexander. "I felt the same feeling."

Alexander's imprisonment took a terrible physical toll. There were times when even the "Jesus prayer" couldn't lift him above his physical agony. Sometimes it was so cold in his cell that he felt his blood was scarcely moving through his body. His teeth were rotting from malnutrition. The hunger he felt was unimaginably fierce, the cumulative effect of years of deprivation, intensified by his repeated

38

hunger strikes. Sometimes he would imagine that he smelled a very good soup, that its phantom fragrance filled his cell. Sometimes he had hallucinations of cutting his veins to drink his blood, and of plucking out his eyes to fry them like eggs. Because he experienced so acutely the frailty of the human body, he nearly lost hope. There were times when he thought it was worse to go on living than to die. At one point his despair was so great that he wrote a letter that was smuggled out of prison: in it he begged authorities to let him die by firing squad rather than let him waste away in prison. He says that now he is ashamed of the letter, but hopelessness had overwhelmed him.

Alexander remembers one time that the fierce coldness of his cell was so piercing that he was desperate. There was no way to get warm, and no place to hide from the cold. So he prayed.

"I felt warm breathing, and the lovely touch of a brother's hand," he recalls. "I cried like a child, and understood it was a prayer for me. It helped me to survive."

The Power of the Cross

Next Alexander was sent to a prison for common criminals. One morning, during the check to insure that all 2,000 inmates were present, one of the prison officials ordered Alexander to remove the cross he wore tucked inside his prison uniform. Alexander refused.

"Take it off!" shouted the official. He was determined to make an example of Alexander in front of the assembled prisoners. Alexander refused again, saying politely but resolutely that it was a violation of his rights. When the official began to shout at him, Alexander replied, "I am a Christian. I must heed the Lord more than man."

"Take it off!" the official shouted again.

"I will never take it from my neck," Alexander said firmly. "You must understand that this is my belief. I confess it before these people. I want to warn you that the Lord will never be humiliated. I am nothing, but I am a son of the Lord. If you are against me, you are against him. I warn you."

With that, Alexander was dragged off to a special block of the prison. There a group of prison guards attacked Alexander in an attempt to remove his cross. But he put it in his mouth and clamped his jaws shut so they couldn't take it. Incensed, they beat him, raining down hard blows from all sides. As he was being struck, Alexander began to pray loudly. The official who had taken him from the assembly of prisoners shouted at him, "I am your Lord. Pray to me. I am your Lord!"

Unable to extract the cross this way, the officials sprayed Alexander with a gas. They intended to choke him, but they apparently hadn't considered that it would choke them too, since they were in the same closed room. When the gas failed, they brought out a pair of handcuffs, a special kind made in America that get tighter with increased pressure.

The officials put the handcuffs on Alexander and used their full body weight to jam them closed, jumping on his wrists with their feet. Again and again they jumped, crushing his arms against the floor. The handcuffs grew excruciatingly tighter. The pressure was strong enough to nearly break Alexander's wrists. Finally the pain was so severe that he passed out. At last the guards were able to take the cross from his mouth.

When Alexander regained consciousness in his solitary cell, his arms were so badly swollen that he couldn't move them. He had no sensation in his hands. (To this day the sense of touch in his left hand has not fully returned.)

The inmates in a cell near Alexander's knew what had been done to him. Although it was very cold, one of them took off one of his socks and unraveled it completely. Then he took the yarn and fashioned a cross with it. Next he took a piece of paper and made a tube from it, and then put the cross inside. Then he used the construction of the cell block to his advantage. Each cell had a small opening near the ceiling through which ran the electrical wires for the single light bulb in the cell. A small passageway connected the cells where the wiring ran from cell to cell. It was in this narrow passage that the inmate inserted his paper tube with the cross inside. Lifted up on the shoulders of two cellmates, he blew the cross through the paper tube like a blow dart toward Alexander's cell. The cross wafted down from the top of Alexander's cell and dropped straight into his lap.

He had been without a cross only three hours.

The prison official who had initiated the incident with Alexander disappeared two days after that. Later, guards came to Alexander's cell to tell him what had happened. The official had been a sportsman, strong, healthy, and proud of his physical prowess. But he had suddenly developed an acute bile disorder. The prison infirmary couldn't help him, and neither could the medical experts in Moscow who were put on his case. Two months later, Alexander heard the sound of a dirge as a coffin was carried to the cemetery nearby. The man had died.

"After that," says Alexander, "the prison officials were afraid to touch me."

Released: A New Beginning

As Alexander's prison term wore on, his poor health worsened. A letter to his mother describing his misery was smuggled out of the prison. Eventually it reached England and came into the hands of Athanasius Hart, a New Zealander who had become an Orthodox monk. To call attention to Alexander's plight, Hart built a cage in London to simulate the conditions of Alexander's imprisonment, and for thirty days he lived in the cage himself. He put on a prison uniform and took only the meager nourishment that Alexander would receive. He also fasted and prayed for Alexander.

The simulation had the effect Hart had hoped for. Many people came to see why a man would do such a thing, including a number of members of the British Parliament, and Alexander became the focus of both spiritual and political concern.

Finally, in 1987, Alexander was released. To mark the occasion, Athanasius Hart visited Alexander and gave him an icon that he had made while in the simulated cell. To thank this man for his extraordinary act of intercession, Alexander presented him with the cross of yarn given him by his fellow prisoner.

*   *   *

By the time Alexander was released from prison, he had served eight-and-a-half years. But his suffering was not over, as he was to discover. The people close to him had come under the crushing vise of the KGB, as KGB archives now document. While Alexander had been in jail, the KGB had exerted great pressure on his wife to leave him, claiming that he would never be released. She finally succumbed, and was granted a divorce without Alexander's knowledge; she married again the day Alexander was released from prison. His son had been turned against him too, having been told that his father was a lawbreaker who had spoiled his life and his mother's life. When Alexander saw his son again, his son told him, "You're not my father. I don't know you, but I know that you're a criminal."

Having survived prison largely on the strength of what he believed was waiting for him on the outside, Alexander was devastated. Both his wife and his son had deserted him, and he had no place to live. At this point he despaired. "The KGB ruined my family," says Alexander flatly. "It was very, very hard." For the first time he thought seriously about emigrating. But even more pain was in store for him.

Alexander's brother Raphael was also involved with the Christian Seminar, and he, like Alexander, had been warned to cease his activities. But Raphael ignored the threats — and reaped fatal consequences. On November 18, 1988, the 37-year-old priest died in a suspicious car accident. Alexander believes his brother was killed deliberately. "He received several warnings not to continue his work with me," he says in explanation.

*   *   *

Despite these blows, Alexander has gone on to live his life in service to others. He has developed charitable programs to serve the poor in Russia. He established the Christian Mercy Society, which feeds and clothes 7,000 needy people each month. Those who assemble at the door of the soup kitchens in anticipation of the hot lunch to be served inside — people who are toothless and dirty, with matted hair and tattered clothes — are a moving sight. The stories of their lives are written on their faces, harshness and despair etched deep.

Alexander has also founded a home for abandoned girls in St. Petersburg, where seventy girls who before were living on the streets are now cared for. The Christian Girls' Asylum hopes to rescue these girls, mostly teenagers, from a future of crime and prostitution. Drawing on his own experience of nearly nine years in prison, Alexander continues to help inmates as well.

In addition, Alexander responded to the clear need for a new political order by founding the first Christian democratic party in Russia in August 1989. Although Communism has since been toppled, Alexander is convinced that the battle against Communist ideology and its followers is not over. While many in the West believe that implanting democracy and capitalism will revitalize the country, Alexander believes that if those forces are not undergirded by faith in God, they will not succeed. He is convinced that there can be no meaningful growth or change in the former Soviet Union in the absence of a spiritual and moral foundation. He fears for the future of his country.

CHAPTER 3

The Tyranny of the State:
The Russian Orthodox under Siege

"The more you persecute us, the more we grow; the blood of the martyred is the seed of the church."

Tertullian, commenting on the
Roman persecution of Christians

The Unholy Alliance of Church and State

There may be as many Christian martyrs in the twentieth century as there have been in all the centuries of church history preceding it. What the Romans were unable to do by killing the Christians of the early church has proved impossible for modern regimes as well. Threats, imprisonment, hard labor camps, torture, mass executions — none has been able to extinguish the church. In this century the attempts to stamp out belief in Russia have been extraordinarily vicious — yet in many ways Russian culture has been, and remains, deeply religious.

Russia's religious roots go back centuries, dating back to before 988, the year Prince Vladimir descended the banks of Kiev's River Dnieper to be baptized; his courtiers and subjects also embraced his new faith. This was to leave a clear mark on all that developed in the culture thereafter. As Kent Hill points out in *The Soviet Union on the*

Brink, Russian literature, art, music, and architecture are all suffused with a sense of the spiritual, and would be incomprehensible without a knowledge of the framework of Christian values that shaped them.[1] Dostoyevsky without Christ is unthinkable.

But the trouble between church and state also stretches back several centuries. The relationship between the Russian Orthodox Church and the czar was to shape Russia two centuries before the Bolshevik Revolution. Peter the Great, who ruled Russia from 1689 to 1725, transformed the church into virtually a department of government. When the Revolution came, the church's subservience and ties to the state made it suspect, and also, according to Hill, "provided a historical precedent for not the Communists allowing the church to exist independent from the state." Although Lenin proclaimed separation of church and state, in 1917 he declared all church property to be public property. In addition, all bank holdings of the church were seized, and half the country's monasteries and 6,000 churches were confiscated early in the Revolution. During the terrible famine of 1921, Lenin outlawed the church's efforts to help famine victims while at the same time he began liquidating the clergy in a campaign to seize all church assets, ostensibly for the regime's Famine Relief Committee. In the next two years, 2,700 married priests, 3,400 nuns, and uncounted laymen were murdered.[2]

During this time, Soviet rulers began to require religious groups to register with the government. This was a tool that would be used to control and manipulate the church in the coming years, leading to conflicts and schisms, the effects of which are still felt today. The requirement was not implemented without a fight, however. Having detained Russian Orthodox Metropolitan Sergy in prison, the authorities tried to convince Metropolitan Kirill, his most likely

1. Kent Hill, *The Soviet Union on the Brink* (Portland, Ore.: Multnomah Press, 1991), p. 70.

2. Ibid., pp. 72-75. See also the following works: Michael Bourdeaux, *Gorbachev, Glasnost and the Gospel* (London: Hodder & Stoughton, 1990), revised and updated as *The Gospel's Triumph over Communism* (Minneapolis: Bethany House, 1991); and Jane Ellis, *The Russian Orthodox Church: A Contemporary History* (Bloomington: Indiana University Press, 1986).

successor, to accept the terms of registration. "You are not a cannon," Kirill responded, "and I am not a shell with which you want to destroy the Church from within." That same day Kirill was exiled to the Arctic; he died there seventeen years later. When Sergy was released from prison, he had been sufficiently broken to agree to the regime's terms.[3] Presumably he hoped the compromise would purchase some maneuvering room for the church — but he was to be disappointed.

Although Sergy had concluded that the church must acquiesce, others in the church disagreed strongly. A group of bishops formulated the Solovky Memorandum, which articulated a courageous position of resistance. These bishops were imprisoned on the Solovky Islands, one of the outposts of the Soviet labor-camp system that Solzhenitsyn described as the Gulag Archipelago. In the memorandum they drew pointed distinctions between church and state:

> The Church recognizes spiritual principles of existence; communism rejects them. The Church believes in the living God, the Creator of the world, the leader of its life and destinies; communism denies his existence. . . . Such a deep contradiction in the very basis of their *Weltanschauungen* precludes any intrinsic approximation or reconciliation between the Church and state, as there cannot be any between affirmation and negation . . . *because the very soul of the Church, the condition of her existence and the sense of her being, is that which is categorically denied by communism.*

On a single night in October 1929, 300 prisoners in the Solovky camps were executed. Some of the bishops who wrote the memorandum paid the ultimate price; some were spared but were denied positions of leadership in the church thereafter.[4]

By this time, Lenin had already stripped the church of its juridical status, making it impossible for the church to be represented in court. Then Stalin further confined the church in a new law on "religious cults" that he issued in 1929. According to that law, all

3. Hill, *The Soviet Union on the Brink,* pp. 76-77.
4. Ibid., pp. 78-80; the indented quotation reflects Hill's emphasis.

parish activities except regularly scheduled worship services in churches were banned. Each "religious association" had to consist of at least twenty people, and it also had to be registered with the government, which meant that it had to provide the names of its members, a ready tool for persecution. Minors could not attend church; all religious instruction had already been banned from the schools, but now the church was also prohibited from offering such instruction. Giving material assistance to church members in need was also forbidden. Local authorities were given the right to monitor parish activities and to remove individuals from the church's executive body and replace them with their own atheistic candidates.[5]

This law of 1929 and the decree issued in 1918 were to set the conditions for the church's troubled existence for the next sixty years. In addition, various unpublished laws came to govern religious bodies. What these restrictions meant was that anyone who tried to put his or her faith into daily practice ran the risk of breaking the law and was likely to be punished. Ironically, freedom of religion was guaranteed by the constitution, and Soviet authorities made massive public relations efforts at home and abroad to propagate this fiction.

The church was subjected to a prolonged assault. Between 1918 and 1940, an estimated 40,000 priests were put to death.[6] While there were reportedly 54,147 churches and 25,593 chapels in the Russian Empire in 1914, by the time World War II broke out, widespread closings had left only a fraction open: some sources claim there were no more than 4,225;[7] others say only several hundred. In 1943, in an attempt to garner needed support from the church for the war effort, Stalin promised to open some seminaries and churches, which he later did.[8]

In 1943 and 1944, two bodies were set up to control the Russian Orthodox Church and the Protestant denominations respectively. In

5. Bourdeaux, *Gorbachev, Glasnost and the Gospel,* pp. 65-66.
6. Hill, *The Soviet Union on the Brink,* p. 84.
7. Jane Ellis, *The Russian Orthodox Church,* p. 14. Russian Orthodox Archbishop Longin places the number of churches left before World War II at 500, while Michael Bordeaux claims there were only 100.
8. Hill, *The Soviet Union on the Brink,* p. 90.

1966 they merged to become the Council for Religious Affairs, the tentacles of the regime that were used to monitor and control the church for the remainder of Communism's tenure.[9] This development created a difficult dilemma for church leaders. If they ignored the laws and the council, they risked being suspended or having their churches closed. If they compromised, they sacrificed their integrity.

The dilemma was just as difficult for laypeople. If they did what the Bible commands them to do — show charity, give witness, or provide religious instruction — they were breaking the regulations. The consequences could be a fine, harassment, even dismissal from work. Being active in church life meant being blocked from certain professions and being discriminated against in others; this almost always led to a lower standard of living. It often meant sacrificing higher education for one's children, because they would be denied certain academic opportunities. Those who were married or baptized in the church were required to submit their identification to church authorities, who were to pass the information along to government authorities. The higher an individual's work status and responsibilities, the more likely it was that there would be punitive consequences. A government employee, an engineer, or a teacher would most likely be fired on the spot. Such risk of sacrifice made the church a communion of the highly committed.

Statements made by church leaders in this situation were sometimes surprising — and dispiriting. In 1930, Russian Orthodox Metropolitan Sergy told foreign journalists that there was no religious persecution in the Soviet Union. In the coming years, this was a fiction that was to be repeated by church leaders as obligatory fare for foreign consumption. Sergy justified his compromise by saying, "Our church was reminiscent of a hen-coop. Hens were driven inside it and trembled, not knowing which one of them would be snatched out next by the enemy."[10] Baptist leader Yakov Zhidkov claimed publicly, "Evangelical Christian-Baptists have full freedom, not only for their divine services but also to conduct the necessary activities

9. Bourdeaux, *Gorbachev, Glasnost and the Gospel,* p. 66.
10. Quoted by Zoya Krakhmalnikova in "Once Again about the Bitter Fruits of a Sweet Captivity" (Thomastown, Vic., Australia: Orthodox Action, 1989), p. 5.

embracing all aspects of our religious life."[11] Privately, he suffered on his deathbed for his duplicity. This mouthing of untruths was a problem that was intensified by the indiscriminate acceptance of these statements in the West.

Author Zoya Krakhmalnikova, a Russian Orthodox believer who was imprisoned for her Christian writings, blasted the hierarchy of the Russian Orthodox Church, saying, "We are commanded to be loyal to the state power, but we are not commanded to bear false witness to please the persecutors." Indeed, that is what some did. Russian Orthodox Patriarch Aleksy offered the following compliments to one of the greatest mass murderers of our time on his seventieth birthday: "Stalin is the first amongst the fighters for peace among all the nations of the world. . . . He is our leader, whose charming personality disarms any who have met him. [People are taken] by his kindness and attentiveness to everybody's needs . . . by the power and wisdom of his speech."[12] Patriarch Justin of the Romanian Orthodox Church paid similar compliments to President Ceaușescu:

> A warm word, coming from the heart, is also owed to the first citizen of the country, our highly esteemed President Nicolae Ceaușescu; as a brother of the holy soil of our Fatherland, he carries the torch of love for the nation, which warms the hearts of millions upon millions of people, in robust arms which fashion the image of a new Romania, the image of a free, independent . . . Romania. . . . Highly esteemed President of the Republic, that is why we all treasure you, why we all honor you, why we all love you.[13]

The lie had become an accepted part of life, even church life.

Between 1959 and 1964, Khrushchev launched an assault on

11. Quoted by Walter Sawatsky in *Soviet Evangelicals since World War II* (Scottdale, Pa.: Herald Press, 1981), p. 105.

12. Quoted by Gerald Buss in *The Bear's Hug: Christian Belief and the Soviet State, 1917-1986* (Grand Rapids: William B. Eerdmans, 1987), pp. 35-36.

13. Quoted by Kent Hill in his manuscript entitled "The Orthodox Church and a Pluralistic Society," p. 8, a supplement to the interview the author held with him in Moscow on March 14, 1992.

the church. He kept it sufficiently hushed so that he could continue to score points for tolerance in the West; meanwhile, he secretly closed down churches in a broad-scale sweep in the Soviet Union. During that time, he closed perhaps as many as 6,000 Russian Orthodox churches. He also cracked down on religious practice. Parents who were giving their children a religious upbringing faced having them forcibly removed from their care on the grounds that they were doing their children psychological damage. Church meetings were broken up with force. In one particularly grim incident, pilgrims on their way to a monastery were attacked, and the women in the group were raped, including one who had taken the vow of chastity. She was violated and then thrown out of her own attic window; she died hours later.[14]

Patriarch Aleksy was denied a personal audience with Khrushchev to protest such persecution. Yet he echoed Christ's declaration about the church when he stated publicly and unequivocally that despite the insults and attacks, "The gates of hell will not overcome the Church."[15]

These stark conditions are the backdrop against which individual dramas unfolded as Christians of different denominations expressed their faith in their actions.

Light and Shadow: Defenders of Orthodoxy

Some fifty million strong today, the Russian Orthodox Church has through the centuries provided an anchor of continuity, an oasis of retreat, and a sensual experience of liturgy, music, and art in its worship services. The faces of saints gleaming from icons, the sonorous singing of choirs, the candles and incense have atmospherically created what one bishop describes as a "momentary glimpse of heaven on earth." Critics have contended that the church, though a powerful institution, is irrelevant. Russian rulers have always sought

14. Hill, *The Soviet Union on the Brink,* pp. 95-96.
15. Ibid., p. 96.

to use it to further their own aims, while some clergy have misused their positions for self-advancement. The pressures and temptations to do so have been enormous.

In 1975, the so-called Furov Report, written for the Communist party's Central Committee by the deputy chairman of the Council for Religious Affairs, defined the three kinds of Russian Orthodox clergy. One sort was loyal to the regime, complying with its regulations and not involved in spreading Orthodoxy. The second sort was loyal to the state and complied with the laws on religion, but tried to activate the clergy and the church, to recruit for the priesthood, and to increase the church's role. The third sort tried to evade the restrictions on the practice of religion.[16] The ways in which the Council for Religious Affairs controlled the church is documented in this report. Clergy who were acquiescent had the advantage when it came to advancement. On the other hand, those priests who ignored the restrictions on religious practice were disciplined. From the local parish level to the top of the church hierarchy, the regime held the power to block and thwart those who were not accommodating enough. Following are the stories of some of those who dared to defy the regime.

Documenter of Persecution: Father Gleb Yakunin

Gleb Yakunin was a sandy-haired young priest ordained during Khrushchev's campaign against the churches in the sixties.[17] A believer in his youth, Yakunin had fallen away from the faith but eventually had embraced it again with renewed zeal. Yakunin was originally a student of forestry, but he became interested in studying theology when his belief was fired by Father Alexander Men, a major figure in the modern Orthodox Church. Although Gleb was exactly the sort of young man the state did not want in the clergy, a few brave bishops opened the way for his theological studies.

16. Ibid., p. 116.
17. This portrait is primarily based on the author's interview with Father Gleb Yakunin in Moscow on November 10, 1992.

He was a fearless preacher, despite the aggressive actions of the Khrushchev regime. People coming to his Moscow church from distant points in the Soviet Union brought horror stories of mass closings of churches, brutality against believers, rigged trials. Father Gleb began to collect such information, and the word soon spread that he was the man to see. When he asked other priests why no one did anything, he was told, "It's wiser to keep quiet. The storm will pass. Speaking out will only make things worse."[18] But he found the church's silence unbearable. "There was a triumph of evil in the church," he says now. "Communism had its hand on the church's throat." But what could one young priest do?

In 1965, he and Nikolai Eshliman, a fellow clergyman who joined him in compiling the growing documentation, sent an open letter to the Soviet government spelling out the abuses and pleading for justice. The two also wrote to the Russian Orthodox Patriarch, begging him to speak out. But the regime pressured the patriarch to deal with the two firebrands. As a consequence, both men were promptly stripped of their parish responsibilities as priests and ordered to be silent.

~

The Power of the Public Word

Although the open letter written by Father Gleb and Father Nikolai had harsh consequences for them, it had a powerful ripple effect. It came to Alexander Solzhenitsyn's attention, and he wrote, "I had been delighted to read the protest written by two priests, Eshliman and Yakunin, a courageous, pure and honest voice in defense of a church which of old had lacked and lacks now both the skill and the will to defend itself. I read, and was envious. Why had I not done something like this myself, why was I so unenterprising? . . . I must do something similar!"

18. Bourdeaux, *Gorbachev, Glasnost and the Gospel,* p. 7.

With this inspiration, Solzhenitsyn in 1972 penned his "Lenten Letter" to the patriarch in a similar vein, severely criticizing the church hierarchy for its acquiescence to the regime. He wrote, "By what reasoning is it possible to convince oneself that the planned *destruction* of the spirit and body of the church under the guidance of atheists is the best way of *preserving* it? Preserving it *for whom?* Certainly not for Christ. Preserving it *by what means? By falsehood?* But after the falsehood, by whose hands are the holy sacraments to be celebrated?"*

Although Father Gleb remained a priest, he was barred from any priestly activities and thus was forced to go from job to job to support himself. He had accepted the order of ten years of silence in obedience to his church superiors, but he remained committed to bringing the plight of believers to light, even if he had to wait. So he kept collecting information about atrocities — and many atrocities were still being committed. While the outright persecution of registered congregations had subsided, the members of these congregations still faced clear discrimination: Christians, for example, were routinely denied access to higher education. It was difficult for congregations to register in the first place — and unregistered congregations *did* face outright persecution. Virtually the only Christian activity permitted was a worship service held in a registered building; everything else was punishable by law. Churches were closed on flimsy pretexts, sometimes because of claims of "structural danger" after permission for building repairs had been denied. The farther a church was from Moscow, the worse the situation.

But foreign visitors to Russia were assured by church leaders that the country enjoyed religious freedom, obediently parroting the fiction that officials had told them to repeat. Any church leaders permitted to travel outside the Soviet Union were required to say the

*Quoted by Jane Ellis in *The Russian Orthodox Church,* pp. 294, 304.

same thing. The few churches and monasteries that were permitted to remain open were showcases of the "Potemkin village" sort for Western visitors. Westerners who returned to their homelands claiming they had seen no signs of persecution may have accurately reported what they saw. But what they could not see were the awful realities being hidden from them.

Boris Talantov, a layman, joined Father Gleb in chronicling the dire straits of Christians. In 1966 he wrote an indictment of the state control of the church, and in response he was blasted by both the regime and Russian Orthodox leadership. He was interrogated, and under the pressure of that ordeal, his wife died. He survived — and was severely punished. Neither his old age nor his frail health prevented his being sent to prison. Five years later, in January 1971, he died alone in a prison hospital.

In 1966, the *sobor,* the electing body of the Russian Orthodox Church, had convened to elect a new patriarch. Dissenting bishops were attacked, and some were physically prevented from taking part in the proceedings. The quiescent Patriarch Pimen, who had been found acceptable by the Soviet authorities, was the unopposed candidate who was "elected."

After ten years of church-imposed silence, Father Gleb broke that silence to become the catalyst for a coalition of different denominations that joined forces to document the persecution of believers in the Soviet Union. In 1975 they appealed to the Soviet government with carefully documented charges. That same year, Father Gleb, along with Lev Regelson, also appealed to the World Council of Churches. They were disappointed with the WCC's silence; support was not forthcoming.

Still, Father Gleb was determined to champion religious freedom as essential for civilization. "Religion is like salt which protects humanity from decomposition and disintegration," he explains. "Any attempt to banish it from social life invariably leads to a degradation of society."

To that end, in 1976 he founded the Christian Committee for Defense of the Rights of Religious Believers. This courageous group succeeded in smuggling to the West more than 400 documents, totaling about 3,000 pages, on religious persecution. It was a massive effort that was fraught with danger, both for those who authored the documents and for those who carried the forbidden information to the West. Michael Bourdeaux of Keston College, one of the preeminent institutions monitoring the state of religion in Communist countries, claims that it was one of the outstanding initiatives of its kind in this century. The vast network of contacts successfully evaded the ever-prying eyes of the KGB, a remarkable feat. Because of the courage of these individuals, the truth about the Soviet church in the twentieth century was revealed, despite all efforts to hush it. Unfortunately, few in the West took notice.

Nevertheless, the Soviet authorities were not pleased. Neither was the church hierarchy, which was unwilling to incur the wrath of the Soviet authorities on Father Gleb's behalf. The church's supine posture led Father Gleb to make what seemed to some a ludicrous proposal. He said that to escape the state-influenced control through the compromised church, believers should create their own unregistered (and therefore illegal) parishes, parallel to the Moscow patriarchate but independent of it. In fact, a catacomb church had been flourishing for some time.

On November 1, 1979, Father Gleb was arrested. Subsequently he was tried and convicted under article 70 of the criminal code for "undermining the Soviet power." He was sentenced to ten years, five in a labor camp and five in exile. His arrest and sentencing were part of a crackdown on leading believers and dissidents who were exposing the compromised church hierarchy and the persecution of Christians. Orthodox activist Alexander Ogorodnikov had already been in prison for a year. Vladimir Poresh, Lev Regelson, and Andrei Sakharov were arrested in the same wave as Father Gleb.

"Our motive was to let the world know the truth about the empire of evil, as it was correctly called," says Father Gleb. "This was the sorrowful burden of prophets of old who depicted the empires of the ancient world. This one was even more horrible. John the Baptist spoke the truth that Christ is the Savior, but he also exposed the social evil of Herod, since all the others were silent. We too had to speak with the same motivation."

Those who documented religious persecution were anathema to the Communist regime. "From the political side it is one of the greatest mysteries in this horrible system," comments Father Gleb. "How they feared truth! Although the KGB had massive power, they were afraid of the West hearing of any case of persecution. If we hadn't raised our voices in defense of these people, they could have done more evil."

Following Father Gleb's example, Deacon Vladimir Rusak wrote a history of the Russian Orthodox Church that was extremely critical of its passive and compromised stance in the face of the persecution of believers. In 1986 he too was sentenced to prison. He wrote a letter to the World Council of Churches, but it fell on deaf ears.

Father Gleb served more than eight years of his sentence. He was released in 1987 in the new *perestroika*. Shortly after his release, he joined others in appealing for the release of all prisoners of conscience. These individuals were bitterly critical of the passivity of the church, and the church struck back, warning that *glasnost* and *perestroika* should not lead to anarchy in the church. Ironically, the government at this point was far ahead of the church in reform. Nevertheless, the church did reinstate Father Gleb as a priest and allowed him to perform church duties. However, he was given the admonition "Go and sin no more."

By this time Father Gleb was known as a man of integrity and courage who had suffered for his convictions, and he became a political figure. He co-founded a Christian democratic party, one of several that have sprouted in the fledgling democracy. In 1990 he was elected to the Russian Parliament. In addition, shortly after the failed coup, he was appointed to a parliamentary commission to investigate the coup. The committee was given access to the KGB's files, and what emerged from KGB records confirmed Father Gleb's worst apprehensions about KGB collaboration with and control of the church.

The reports from the Fourth Department of the KGB's Directorate Z chronicle the top collaborators, who include nearly every member of the church's patriarchal synod. When one compares the names of the agents with press bulletins of the church, one can deduce who is who. KGB agent "Abbat" is Metropolitan Pitirim of Volokolamsk, head of the church's publications department. Agent "Adamant" is Metropolitan Yuvenaly of Krutitsy, the second highest church leader, who oppressed dissident clergy in the Moscow area. Agent "Antonov" is Metropolitan Filaret of Kiev, who, until being deposed for immorality, headed the Orthodox Church in the Ukraine.[19]

The KGB archives of Lubyanka reveal a strategy aimed at controlling the church that dates back to the early days of the KGB's predecessor, the Cheka. Its stated goal was to recruit and use the church leadership itself to accomplish its own aims. The means were spelled out: the Cheka used threats and inducements and tried to find people of weak character to accomplish the neutralization of the church leadership. In the words of the Cheka's 1921 report, the aim was to make the church the "eternal slave of the Cheka" by corrupting it slowly from within. Vyacheslav Polosin unearthed this document as chairman of the Russian Parliament's investigating committee. He notes that although the report is seventy years old, it chronicles the methods still used until recently by the KGB.[20]

The evidence indicates that the regime utilized both Orthodox leaders and other religious leaders to advance the agenda of the Communist party. Only those willing to promulgate the official line were permitted to travel abroad or meet with foreigners visiting the Soviet Union. Those who did not acquiesce were blocked or silenced. Some yielded to blackmail; some succumbed to other threats; some were jailed; some were killed. Agents were planted at all religious levels, from highest to lowest. In this way the church was compromised and controlled from the inside. General Nikolai Stolyarov, named vice chairman of the KGB by Gorbachev shortly after the attempted coup, acknowledged KGB interference in the church. In

19. Based on the interview between correspondent P. Vasil'ev and Gleb Yakunin, "'Abbat' Makes His Contact" ("'Abbat' vykhodit no svyaz"), in *Argumenty i fakty (Arguments and Facts)*, no. 1 (January 1992). The information on the KGB is based in part on documents made available by Kent Hill. See also Lawrence A. Uzzell, "The KGB's Agents in Cassocks," *The Christian Science Monitor*, April 28, 1992, p. 19.

20. Polosin, "The Eternal Slave of the Cheka," *Izvestiia*, January 22, 1992.

October 1991, with TV cameras rolling, he said, "I will not deny that in the past that was the situation."[21] Curiously, high-ranking officials of the Russian Orthodox Church still deny what the KGB openly acknowledges.

Metropolitan Pitirim, who has been identified as Agent "Abbat," denied knowingly collaborating with the KGB. "You have to understand the structure of our society, the system of social life," he explained. "The KGB was the organization concerned with intellectual life, the consciousness of people. Naturally it kept everything under its control, from the top echelons of power right down to the lowest levels. The whole society was under KGB surveillance and we were no exception."[22] Father Gleb estimates that 20 percent of the clergy collaborated with the KGB, while others claim as many as half of them collaborated. The situation elsewhere in the Eastern bloc was not much different, except in Poland.

The KGB files document that Soviet church leaders were forced to promulgate the state policy in all international meetings. Church leaders also provided intelligence to the KGB, watching and recruiting foreign religious leaders. In addition, KGB agents were routinely placed in the World Council of Churches — so miny, in fact, that the KGB reports list them by rank for each convention. Father Gleb claims that at certain meetings the number of agents exceeded the number of genuine delegates from his country. According to the report of the investigative committee, the KGB explicitly sought to "rule the internal life of the church in the USSR, particularly in choosing church leaders." The KGB's method was the "criminal and administrative persecution of priests and believers who did not acquiesce."[23] The files reveal that agents of all religious groups — including not only the Orthodox but

---

21. In 1992 a high-ranking official under Gorbachev claimed that Stolyarov resigned as KGB vice-chairman because he was discouraged about the prospects of reforming the KGB.

22. Quoted by Michael Dobb in "In Hard Times, No Time To Hunt Down KGB Agents," *International Herald Tribune*, February 12, 1992.

23. Taken from the summary of the findings of the Supreme Soviet's investigating committee, provided by Father Gleb Yakunin in an interview with the author in Moscow on November 10, 1992 (translation provided by Helen Mozgina).

also Baptists, Pentecostals, Buddhists, and Muslims — were used to further the aims of the Communist regime.

The results of the parliamentary investigation into the KGB files were compiled and sent to the patriarch and forty bishops of the Russian Orthodox Church. The information on the Orthodox Church was so damaging that, according to Father Gleb, the patriarch himself intervened to have the investigation halted — and he succeeded. After five months, on March 6, 1992, the special commission that had been given access to the KGB files was disbanded and forbidden to use the files.

Father Gleb's appraisal of the Orthodox Church is grim: "[Because] the patriarchy is absolutely incapable of revival of its own means . . . our church is in a deep crisis. . . . We have a very old church, but it has become a museum, fully incapable of influencing society." On October 28, 1992, Metropolitan John of St. Petersburg, under whose authority Father Gleb was placed by the church, threatened to strip Father Gleb of clerical authority. Clearly, the struggle for those who expose the truth is not over.

~

The Consequences of Refusing to Collaborate:
Alexander Borisov

Alexander Borisov was nervous as he walked into the school to take his examination.* He knew that what he was about to do could very well destroy his academic opportunities.

As examination time had approached, he had faced a moral dilemma. One of the subjects he was to be tested in was "scientific atheism," as the school called it. This troubled him, because he had made a commitment of faith and at nineteen had been baptized in the

---

*This portrait is based on the author's interview with Father Alexander Borisov in Moscow on March 10, 1992.

Russian Orthodox Church. He knew he was charged to speak truthfully about his faith, but he also knew full well that he could be denied a diploma from his school if he quarreled with the teachings on atheism. Students who gave the wrong answers had their grades docked and were not permitted to graduate.

What should he say? Like many students, he had mastered the material on Marxism-Leninism sufficiently to describe the Communist position while refraining from giving his own evaluation of it. But he decided before the exam that if he were asked a question about God, he would answer truthfully.

Now the moment of truth had come, and Alexander prayed. Once he was in the classroom, the teacher fired the question point-blank: "Does God exist?"

"Yes, of course," Alexander answered without hesitation.

A look of clear surprise crossed the teacher's face. Apparently taken aback by the conviction of Alexander's answer, the teacher let it stand unchallenged, shifting the questioning to Lenin. In the end, Alexander was given a passing grade.

He decided to become a biologist, specializing in genetics, and he worked in the field until he was thirty-three. But at that point he became convinced that it was more important to work on the spiritual health of humankind. In his country he could see the results of several generations having been deprived of faith. The rotting, both material and spiritual, indicated the sickness of the prevailing ideology. Alexander concluded that he should become a priest.

While he was studying theology, he received an "invitation" to meet with the KGB, a polite term for an interrogation. The interrogation lasted for three days, with ten hours of unbroken questioning each day. "You must help us," the KGB agent began smoothly. "You see many people go to church for many reasons. Some of these people are dangerous elements for our society. We need your help in spotting them, so we may prevent harm." This was a frequent tactic of the KGB: appealing to the civic virtue of those they hoped to win as informants, suggesting they would make a positive contribution to society by agreeing to report on dangerous, destabilizing tendencies and individuals. But Alexander refused to cooperate.

His decision was to have long-lasting consequences. For the next sixteen years, the KGB, working through the Committee for Religious Affairs, effectively blocked his ordination as a priest, and he was forced to remain a deacon. The Committee for Religious Affairs had the authority to influence decisions on the ordination of priests and bishops, and it favored those who collaborated with the state.

Today Alexander claims that it was impossible to avoid contact with the KGB. Its agents penetrated every level of the church organization, and the tentacles of their influence through the Committee for Religious Affairs touched every activity. The KGB kept files on all the clergy that included evaluations of their loyalty. A single negative notation in Alexander Borisov's file was enough to freeze his career for sixteen years — until the thaw of the Gorbachev years, when he finally could be ordained as a Russian Orthodox priest.

Conflict and Tragedy: Father Dimitri Dudko

No one epitomizes the conflicts and tragedies of the church under Communism better than Father Dimitri Dudko.[24] A gifted teacher and writer, he became the spiritual father of a generation of Russians. The attention he garnered led him into a struggle with the Communists that resulted in his imprisonment. Eventually he renounced his activities publicly before a stunned nation. Some see the dynamic man with sparkling blue eyes and flowing white hair and beard as a broken figure when they look at him today.

Father Dimitri is the kind of man who leaves an impression on everyone he meets. In a radio broadcast in 1979, Natalia Solzhenitsyn described the effect he once had: "After every encounter with him you are left with the feeling: how deep and joyful is his faith! He is

24. Information in this portrait is based on the author's interview with Dimitri Dudko on March 17, 1992.

a man of surprising integrity and simplicity, and his preaching finds a direct and accurate path to a person's heart."

Under Stalin, Dudko had been imprisoned for eight-and-a-half years for possessing religious poetry, an experience that may have left him with indelible spiritual and emotional scars. In his thirties he had become a priest in the Russian Orthodox Church. Despite the ban on discussions of faith, in December 1973 Father Dimitri initiated question-and-answer sessions after his Saturday-night worship services. Young people flocked to these sessions. There they could jot down their questions on pieces of paper they didn't need to sign and pass them to the front, and Father Dimitri would answer them in his lively and engaging manner.

These sessions electrified the youth of an atheistic culture in which religious literature was scarce and opportunities to ask questions were even more so. With his keen mind and winning manner, Father Dimitri began to draw people of all ages who were starved to hear more about God; they came Moscow and beyond in ever-widening circles. By 1974, Father Dimitri was well known. His question-and-answer sessions were developed into a book that proved enormously popular.[25]

Not surprisingly, the authorities were not pleased by his success. In the Furov Report, prepared in 1975 for the Central Committee of the Communist party, Father Dimitri was singled out for harsh criticism. He was described as a clergyman concealing his hostility and antagonism toward the government and charged with leading a struggle against it. The report also claimed that Father Dimitri had written libelous materials, preached slanderous sermons, trained young people in dangerous ideology, and collected and disseminated *samizdat* (self-made literature) and other publications from abroad. Father Dimitri reacted with equanimity, dismissing the claims as "products of their imagination" — but the committee found a way to act on its assessment. Father Dimitri was moved from his parish to another one farther outside of Moscow, a common maneuver

25. The English translation of the book is titled *Our Hope*, published by St. Vladimir's Press, Crestwood, N.Y., 1977.

employed with priests that the Council for Religious Affairs judged as too active.

In March 1975, Father Dimitri was involved in a suspicious car accident. The path of the car he was riding in was suddenly blocked by a large truck, and there was a collision. The other passengers in the car suffered concussions, and Father Dimitri was badly hurt. The bones in his legs were shattered, and his lungs filled with blood. Although doctors told him that he would be a cripple, in less than a year he was freed of the casts and crutches and stood again before his church. Father Dimitri believes that the accident was arranged by the KGB. (If that indeed was the case, it wouldn't have been an isolated incident. Throughout the Eastern bloc, a striking number of other Christians whom the Communists viewed as troublesome suffered similar "accidents," some of which proved fatal.)

Shortly after the accident, attempts were made to discredit Father Dimitri. Literary journals began to carry claims that he was anti-Soviet, opposing Communism and the government. The denunciations came in an orchestrated campaign to discredit a number of leading Christians. Along with Father Dimitri, Alexander Ogorodnikov, Lev Regelson, and Gleb Yakunin were attacked in the April 1977 issue of the *Literary Gazette,* a prominent journal in the intellectual community. The four of them joined forces to protest.

Father Dimitri was transferred again, this time to a parish in Grebnevo, which was far enough outside Moscow that the authorities thought his influence would diminish. But despite the two-hour travel time, many Muscovites boarded trains regularly to come and hear him. The trip became a kind of seminar on wheels, with the travelers talking about Christian teachings along the way. This was an alarming development for the regime. In response, KGB agents began boarding the trains and forcing passengers headed for the parish to turn back.

The pressure escalated, this time involving physical force. One day militia came and searched Father Dimitri's church, and then approached the building next to it, where he was staying. When he refused to open the door, agents took a log and battered it open. A search yielded no evidence that could be used to prosecute him, so Father Dimitri was not arrested. But the militia threatened to shoot everyone in the building, and they dragged one of Father Dimitri's young followers out into the snow and pistol-whipped him. The young man was forcibly taken to the police station, where he was detained for ten days of questioning.

Finally, Father Dimitri's day of reckoning arrived. On January 15, 1980, he was arrested by twelve KGB officers at eight in the morning and taken to Lefortovo prison. He had had a number of Christian books published abroad, and copies of these had been brought back into the country to be used as evidence of his "anti-Soviet activity." Prison officials made it clear that he could be given a stiff sentence, and he knew from the eight-and-a-half years he had spent in prison camps under Stalin exactly what that meant. A team interrogated him every day, trying to break him emotionally and psychologically by alternating verbal abuse with apparent friendliness.

Father Dimitri declined to reveal what occurred during the six months of his imprisonment; he would say only that he was not physically abused. But something happened that prompted him to reconsider and acquiesce to the Communists' demands. After half a year of resisting, he agreed to sign the statement the Soviet authorities put before him.

In the "confession" that was apparently written for him, Father Dimitri renounced his "anti-Soviet" activities. The full text was published on June 21, 1980, in *Izvestiia*, one day after he had appeared on television to make a public declaration seen by millions of people throughout the country. He claimed that he had been "arrested not for believing in God but for crime," that he had attempted to create conflict between the church and the Soviet state and had provided information to the West which discredited the country. "I renounce what I have done, and I regard my so-called struggle with godlessness as a struggle with Soviet power."[26]

Deciding whether to sign the declaration was the hardest decision he ever made, Father Dimitri said in retrospect, and much that he subsequently said and wrote indicates that he did so in anguish. Still, many friends and followers concluded sadly that he was broken in

26. Quoted by Ellis in *The Russian Orthodox Church*, pp. 430-31.

prison. This reaction grieved Father Dimitri. On July 27, 1980, he wrote a letter to his "spiritual children" in which he said, "I cannot forgive myself for my weakness, and my heart is torn asunder seeing your confusion and hearing garbled interpretations. I shudder at the thought of how I must appear to everyone, into what temptation I have led people, how I have disheartened those whom I had previously heartened. I prostrate myself before you and beg for your forgiveness."[27]

Father Dimitri indicated that he was somewhat puzzled that his friends had not read between the lines to try to understand why he had signed the statement. He said he had done so to avoid losing his congregation and to minimize conflict with the regime. Whether his moral authority was damaged in so doing is a question no one can answer for him. As his defenders have been quick to point out, not everyone is born to martyrdom. But his public recantation sent shock waves across the country. What disappointed people who knew his teaching was the contrast between the words he had spoken so forcefully and his eventual actions. In a sermon he delivered in April 1974, Father Dimitri had said, "Atheists are taking advantage of our fear of suffering. They oppress our spirit, our free thoughts and feelings. They abuse us. We must overcome our fear of suffering and then we shall be truly free, vital, active, and invincible." Had that been empty rhetoric?

His dilemma reflects the larger dilemma of the Russian Orthodox Church, as personified in Patriarch Sergy, who has been bitterly criticized for signing a statement acquiescing to Soviet power. Father Dimitri defended such actions, claiming that they saved the church from liquidation. "If you resisted, they had the right to kill you, and if you didn't, they gave you the right to live a little longer. Retreating in this way allowed us to maintain and save something."

When asked if the Russian Orthodox Church made too many compromises with the Soviet regime, Father Dimitri replied, "Do you ask a fish that has been taken out of water and been thrown into a hot frying pan if it has made too many compromises?" Then in the same breath he said, "When people were persecuted, their only hope was in the Lord. Persecution improved their life and made

27. Quoted by Ellis in ibid., p. 434.

it more pure. . . . Persecution has prepared the soil for the emergence and growth of the seeds of Christianity." Yet, when he was asked if the church should repent for the compromises of the past, he replied, "Will the fish in the frying pan repent for what it has done in jumping so high? There is nothing in the body of the church to repent for." Father Dimitri saw no apparent contradiction in these comments.

Modern Martyr: Father Alexander Men

Father Alexander Men was a dynamic Russian Orthodox priest with prodigious talent, a charismatic personality, and an inexhaustible capacity for work. He has been described as a beloved and gifted man, a spiritual giant with a formidable intellect who shaped a generation of Russians. He was the friend of both Alexander Solzhenitsyn and Andrei Sakharov. And he was a man of diverse gifts. Having been a painter in his youth, Father Alexander delighted friends with brilliant but wicked caricatures he could sketch in less than five minutes. He played the guitar and sang, and endeared himself to others with his spontaneous sense of humor. He read voraciously, and it is said he remembered virtually everything. He was the mentor of Alexander Borisov, who as a teenager sought Father Alexander's teaching. Borisov, a schoolmate of Men's younger brother who was in the Men home virtually every day, gave the following personality sketch, based on his intimate knowledge of the man.[28]

When Borisov was baptized in 1958 at the age of nineteen, Father Alexander was his godfather. Like Borisov, Men had first studied biology before entering the priesthood. While studying in Siberia, Men met Gleb Yakunin, with whom he became fast friends. Through Alexander, Gleb was led back to the faith he had lost as a child to the torrent of atheistic propaganda.

After his ordination in 1960, Father Alexander was assigned to

28. This portrait is based on the author's interview with Alexander Borisov in Moscow on March 10, 1992.

a church south of Moscow. Father Alexander's intellect and spiritual prowess attracted many, much to the consternation of the state authorities, and the congregation was soon transformed from a church of *babushkas* into a dynamic congregation of young people, scholars, and writers. Alarmed, the council saw to it that Father Alexander was transferred to another parish north of Moscow. But the seekers found him there too. Defying regulations that forbade spiritual teaching and all work with youth, Father Alexander continued to meet, preach, and speak with vigor. Young people flocked to him. In response, state authorities had him transferred yet again, this time to Novaya Derevnya, where he was to remain for the next twenty-two years. But this did not deter his followers.

A brilliant Christian apologist, Father Alexander wrote ten books, including a multivolume study on the search for truth in religion. In a country where there was almost no contemporary Christian literature, his books had a major impact on those who could obtain them. And though he had a formidable mind, he was not an aloof intellectual; his personal warmth endeared him to many. But for all his gifts and talents, Father Alexander was a flawed man, according to Borisov. He claims that Men was so convinced of his own rectitude that he carried his faith like a banner, doing battle with all who disagreed with him. "Such a bright person engenders great love, great hate, or great envy. There was no middle way possible with him."

His outspokenness proved fatal. On the morning of September 9, 1990, he was murdered on the way from his house to the train station. He was on his way to the church in Novaya Derevnya. Attacked by unknown assailants, he bled to death from head wounds inflicted with an axe. He was fifty-five years old. The nature of the assault indicated that it was a planned assassination. Police investigators claim that he was killed by a thief, but his briefcase contained nothing an ordinary thief would have coveted: notes for his sermon, a book, a pencil, his identification papers, reading glasses, and a few rubles.

Although no one knows who killed him, many people had reasons to want to see him dead. Because he had been an outspoken critic of the KGB and the way in which the Russian Orthodox Church had collaborated and compromised itself, there were those both in the KGB and in some circles of the church who would have welcomed his end. Beyond that, the regime would have been pleased to have the outspoken mentor of young people silenced. There is also the possibility that his killing was racially motivated. Because he was the son of a Jewish father and a mother who converted to Christianity as an adult, he was raised initially as a Jew. Father Gleb Yakunin believes that Men's death is related to growing anti-Semitism in Russia. Alexander Borisov confirms that there are certain reactionary elements in the Russian Orthodox Church that are virulently anti-Semitic and would possibly have welcomed Father Alexander's death. Borisov claims that a clandestine alliance between these elements and the KGB may possibly have figured in the assassination.

Michael Bourdeaux of Keston College offers yet another theory. He believes that Father Alexander's death was almost certainly the direct work of the KGB. He speculates that it was a way for them to assert that they were still in business, even though the Soviet Union was collapsing. The new law on religion, which abolished KGB control, was in its final draft and about to be presented to parliament. Bourdeaux sees the murder as an act of vengeance against the new order. To this day, however, there remain only theories about who is responsible for the death of Alexander Men.

In a country already rich with the history of martyrs, Father Alexander Men is perhaps the most recent one. When he was killed, there was a national outcry. Mikhail Gorbachev expressed "profound regret" at his death, and an article in *Izvestiia* commented, "He was the pastor to many human-rights champions, prisoners of conscience, those who were persecuted by the authorities. . . . His work in providing spiritual support to many intellectuals in disgrace brought him true friends, but also real foes."[29]

29. Quoted in "Killing of Rebel Soviet Priest," *New York Times*, September 15, 1990. See also "A Murder Most Unholy," *Chicago Tribune*, September 16, 1990.

The Price of Writing about Martyrs: Zoya Krakhmalnikova

Zoya Krakhmalnikova went to prison for writing about the Russian martyrs of the twentieth century. One day, when she returned to her cell from an interrogation session, she could feel the presence of the saints she had written about and for whose sake she was now suffering. She remembered God's words to Moses: "Take off your sandals, for the place where you are standing is holy ground" (Exod. 3:5). As Krakhmalnikova later wrote, "For me, this prison become holy ground, soaked with the blood of martyrs. . . . This feeling of nearness to the saints was so deep, so pure and strong that I will remember it for the rest of my life."*

Krakhmalnikova sees the conflict between Christians and Communists in her country as part of a far broader struggle:

> After October 1917 Russia [became] an arena where the destinies of the world were being decided. Because here was the tragedy of mankind which rose against God, repeat[ing] itself, though on a larger scale than at the beginning of the Christian era. Today the world witnesses for itself the fruits of this struggle against its Creator. . . .**

---

*Krakhmalnikova, "Hat Russland eine Hoffnung?" *HMK Kurrier, Stimme der Märtyrer*, 1/93, p. 4.

**Krakhmalnikova, "Once Again about the Bitter Fruits of a Sweet Captivity" (Thomastown, Vic., Australia: Orthodox Action, 1989), pp. 7-9.

CHAPTER 4

Uneasily Tolerated:
Soviet Protestants under Pressure

"[It] was a time of horrible persecutions. Exiles, arrests, fines, and beatings . . . rained down abundantly upon the audacious followers of the Gospel. Under continual fear of being caught by the police, the brothers nevertheless did not cease their meetings, holding them in basements, across the Dnieper [River], in the woods, in the cemetery, in ravines, and in the apartments of the more well-to-do brothers."

Quoted by Walter Sawatsky,
Soviet Evangelicals Since World War II

In this excerpt, a Baptist leader is describing the Russian czar's persecution of Protestants in the late nineteenth century.[1] But this is also an apt description of the situation of Protestants in Russia throughout most of the twentieth century. In a country that is overwhelmingly Russian Orthodox, the Protestant minority has wielded an influence disproportionate to its numbers. Sometimes that influence has been tolerated; at other times it has been greeted with persecution.

---

1. Sawatsky, *Soviet Evangelicals since World War II* (Scottdale, Pa.: Herald Press, 1981), p. 35. This book presents a detailed account of the Protestants' struggle under Communism. The factual information on the church here is also drawn from Kent Hill's *Soviet Union on the Brink* (Portland, Ore.: Multnomah Press, 1991), esp. pp. 80-82.

70

Strangers in an Inhospitable Land

Protestant faith came to Russia with the families brought from Western Europe to settle the country under Peter the Great (1682-1725) and Catherine the Great (1762-1796). Primarily Germans, these immigrants — Lutherans, Mennonites, and Pietists — brought their faith with them. The Russians, interested in harnessing the immigrants' industriousness, tolerated their foreign theology initially, if uneasily. But the Russian Orthodox Church did not view religious pluralism kindly, and its alliance with the czar eventually wrought havoc for the Protestants.

In a sense, the Protestants who came from Germany to the Soviet Union have since lived years of Babylonian exile. They have worked as clearly a lower class; they have been abused and often despised. Because their belief system taught them to be "in this world but not of it," they have shunned external contact and viewed diversity with suspicion, attempting to preserve their faith and ethnic identity.

One later swell of evangelical Protestantism entered the country via Russian POWs who were converted in Germany during World War I.[2] What Sawatsky calls a kind of "golden age" of tolerance lasted from the end of World War I until 1929, but under Stalin, terror was to follow. All religious leaders, including the Protestants, were persecuted. Large numbers of them were jailed; some of them were executed, and many more perished in labor camps.

In addition, the new law on religious affairs enacted in 1929 constricted the activities of Protestant churches in the years thereafter, just as it did of all other churches. In the face of such prohibitions, Christians suffered a conflict of conscience, and even the Bible did not offer unambiguous commentary on that conflict. In Romans 13:1, Paul says, "Everyone must submit himself to the governing authorities, for there is no authority except that which God has established." Elsewhere, however, the Bible clearly exhorts believers

2. The group called *Licht im Osten* ("Light in the East"), which distributed New Testaments in Russian to the POWs in Germany during World War I, is credited with about 2,000 conversions.

71

to instruct their children in faith, to visit those who are sick and in prison, to preach the gospel, and to live lives in which they openly profess their relationship in Christ. But these were precisely the activities that government authorities would object to and penalize.

Protestant evangelicalism experienced a modest revival in the first months at the end of World War II, but the decade that followed, marked by Stalin's crackdown on religion, was very difficult for Protestants. They were permitted almost no contact with foreigners, and unregistered believers could receive up to twenty-five years' imprisonment for "anti-Soviet" slander if they practiced their faith. By the mid-1950s, however, the situation had eased somewhat; believers had enough religious freedom to survive, if not altogether comfortably. After Stalin's reign of terror, it seemed that a more peaceful time might follow under Khrushchev. But appearances were deceptive. While reputedly "liberal," Khushchev's regime exerted extreme pressure on believers that went beyond atheistic propaganda: some believers were subjected to physical violence.

One grim example is Nikolai K. Khmara. A Baptist recently converted from a life of drunkenness, he had become a model father and husband and become active in the church. Subsequently he was arrested and imprisoned for his activities in an unregistered congregation. When he died, fellow believers were suspicious of the official ruling that his death was the result of illness, so they banded together and opened his coffin. They discovered a mutilated body with chain marks on the arms, scorch marks on the hands and feet, fingernails and toenails missing, signs of drug injections, and gaping wounds in the abdomen. According to Sawatsky, "the most revolting part occurred when someone pulled the cotton stuffing out of his mouth and discovered that Khmara's tongue was missing." It had been cut out, said other prisoners, because Khmara would not stop talking about Christ.[3]

Every believer had to decide where the greater obligation of loyalty lay, and be willing to suffer the consequences of his or her decision. As a result of their faith, Christians in all Communist countries suffered discrimination; in the most repressive, such as the

3. Sawatsky, *Soviet Evangelicals since World War II*, p. 143.

Soviet Union, they suffered true persecution. There were no casual Christians under such circumstances.

Heroes of the Protestant Faith

Georgi Vins and Mikhail Khorev

In this environment, governments exerted heavy pressure on church leadership to comply with the restrictions, and disagreements over how to respond produced strains and splits. In the Soviet Union, various Protestant denominations were joined under the umbrella of the All-Union Council of Evangelical Christians-Baptists (AUCECB). In 1960 the council issued a "Letter of Instruction" urging congregations to bring their practices in line with the prohibitions of the 1929 law. This provoked a bitter split among the Baptists, some of whom felt betrayed by their leaders' lack of courage. Those who banded together in protest were called the *Initsiativniki* (Initiative) group. They rejected the restrictions of 1929, including being registered with the government.[4] Many of their leaders were to pay for their convictions with repeated prison terms.

Baptist congregations faced difficult dilemmas. Some registered congregations decided to risk the forbidden activities despite the threat of stiff fines and potential imprisonment. Congregations attempting to register often discovered that they were turned down if their opinions on "church life" differed from those of the authorities. If they met without being registered, they were prosecuted for breaking the law.

In May of 1966, "over 400 persons representing 130 congregations converged on the Kremlin in Moscow and conducted an unprecedented demonstration on May 16, 1966." The demonstrators

---

4. Sawatsky, *Soviet Evangelicals since World War II*, pp. 139-40. The original "initiative" (in 1961) was to demand the convening of a free congress. The *Initsiativniki* became the Council of Churches of the Evangelical Christians-Baptists (CCECB). For brevity's sake, I refer to them as unregistered Baptists.

were not allowed into the building, "and on the second day they were forcibly dispersed and many of them were arrested."[5]

The church elders had prohibited their leader, Georgi Vins, from participating in this event, deeming it too risky. But Vins, desperate to know what had happened to the 500, came to Moscow two days later with another unregistered Baptist leader, Mikhail Khorev. Before they entered the building of the Central Committee of the Communist party, Vins turned to Khorev and said, "It's still not too late. It might be better if I go alone." Khorev began his answer by quoting John 15:13: "'Greater love has no one than this, that he lay down his life for his friend.' We are going to go in and say, 'Let our brothers and sisters go; take us instead.'" The two shook hands and went into the committee's building together, where they spoke with a regime representative. Immediately after they left, they were seized by KGB agents.[6]

They did not see each other again for three years, until they were released from prison in 1969. When they met again, Vins asked Khorev, "Aren't you sorry, Mikhail Ivanovich, that we went to the Central Committee to find out what happened to the delegates?" "Of course not!" Khorev protested. "That was an absolutely necessary step in protecting the kingdom of God in our country. And besides, I can tell you this: prison is a very useful school for . . . testing the authenticity of our faith."[7]

Gennadi Kryuchkov, another leader of the unregistered Baptists, had been arrested and tried with Vins in 1966, and had also served three years in prison. After the two were released, both were denied permission to work as pastors. Kryuchkov decided that the only way to continue was to go underground, and in an astonishing feat, he managed to evade the KGB for the next twenty years, visible only on "wanted" posters. Vins also went underground after his release from prison, leaving his wife alone at home with five children

5. Ibid., p. 148.

6. Georgi Vins in his introduction to Mikhail Khorev's book entitled *Ich schreibe euch, Kinder (I Write to You, Children)* (Gummersbach, Germany: Verlag Friedensstimme, 1986), p. 4.

7. Ibid.

to care for. But he was not as fortunate as Kryuchkov: after five years underground, he was arrested again in 1974.

The authorities deemed Vins punishable for the church's illegal activities, including a clandestine printing operation. The other charges varied in their degree of seriousness — one of them had to do with Scripture. Vins had written out the Twenty-third Psalm and his own commentary on it by hand. During his hearing, he was accused of composing this "anti-Soviet poem" himself. The line "prepare a table before me in the presence of my enemies" led the Soviet officials to conclude that "enemies" referred to them. "I'm not the author," Vins protested incredulously. "Don't you people know that that's from the Bible?"[8] The accusation was so absurd that it was almost comic, except for the gravity of the consequences.

Vins was also accused of playing a role in the case of Ivan Moiseyev. Ivan was a young soldier who in the summer of 1972 was asked to take the oath required of military recruits, swearing loyalty to the motherland and the goals of the Communist party. This oath was an important issue, because every Soviet young man was expected to take it when he was drafted for two years of compulsory military service at the age of eighteen. But because of his Christian faith, Ivan refused to take the oath, and he was subsequently tortured and killed. His death unleashed a firestorm of protest that caused state officials a great deal of trouble. Young Ivan was seen as a hero of faith, and his death motivated hundreds of other young men to refuse to take the oath. Many succeeded in resisting; some were killed, just as Ivan had been. As late as 1984, three young soldiers who refused to take the oath were beaten so severely that they died from brain injuries afterward. (Other resisters were later permitted to do their military duty in construction units, wielding shovels rather than guns, a kind of unofficial alternative service.) Some young men refused to do military service altogether on religious grounds, among them Pentecostals and Jehovah's Witnesses, and they faced at least five years in prison as a result. Young Ivan

8. Drawn from the author's interview with Jakob Janzen in Gummersbach, Germany, on January 19, 1992.

Moiseyev had been a powerful catalyst of all this unrest — and Georgi Vins was alleged to have influenced his decision to refuse the oath.[9]

Because of his alleged crimes, Georgi Vins was sentenced to five years in prison and five years in exile. But in 1979, when his prison term was up, Vins was exchanged, along with four critics of the regime, for two Soviet spies. So Vins, his family, and his mother were sent to the States, where they settled in Elkhart, Indiana.[10]

Mikhail Khorev was arrested again in 1979 for refusing to register his congregation under the existing stipulations. The official from the Council for Religious Affairs pressed him on his reasons. "We're prepared to register the congregation," Khorev said, "but we cannot abide by these so-called laws. That's why we are constantly in conflict with you."

"Your violations will be punished by the law," warned the official, "as you certainly know."

"Yes, I know," answered Khorev. "That's why I have been in prison twice. . . . Our church chooses to serve God regardless of the persecution."[11]

Khorev put his finger on the crux of the dilemma facing all believers: the conflict of conscience in deciding how to respond to an inherently unjust situation. If a believer fulfilled the obligations of faith, he or she broke the law. But that law conflicted with the country's constitution and international agreements on human rights. If ruling authorities ignored these guaranteed rights, and their laws contradicted the laws of God, what should a believer do?

Khorev had always known there was a price to be paid for religious conviction. He had grown up in Leningrad, where his father was a leader of a Baptist congregation. In 1938, church leaders were being arrested on a broad scale, and one day Mikhail had watched his father pack his few possessions, expecting to be jailed. In a backpack he put a shirt, a pair of thick, patched winter pants, boots he

9. Ibid.
10. Vins, *Wie Schafe unter Wölfen (Like Sheep among Wolves)* (Neuhausen-Stuttgart: Hänssler Verlag, 1989), p. 8.
11. Khorev, *Ich schreibe euch, Kinder,* p. 25.

had soled himself, some underwear, a bowl, a spoon, and a mug. Then he sat down with his children at the kitchen table.

"Children," he said, "I am going on a long trip. I don't know if I will come home again. Only God knows the way and what difficulties will be on the path, or how long the journey will be. But as I begin this long journey, I want to agree where we will meet, so we will not lose each other." He explained that when people went to the train station or to the market, they often agreed on a place to meet — perhaps at the entrance, or the information stand — in case they would get separated. He and his children should do the same thing in this situation, he explained. "We will be separated for a while. As soon as the heavenly Jerusalem comes, go to the white throne where Jesus will sit, and I will be there too. We will see each other there and never be separated again." Then he took a pencil and began to draw the throne. Mikhail's father did all this without a trace of pathos. For him it was a certain thing, like making an appointment he was sure every member of the family would keep.

Four days later he was arrested. On that day the "Black Raven," the wagon used to collect prisoners, stood outside the door of the house, waiting. The children watched as their father, his pack on his shoulder, got into the wagon, looking back at them. Though he was guarded by soldiers, he smiled and raised his hand to say good-bye. Then the wagon door slammed shut, and he was gone. Eight months later he wrote his last letter, and died perhaps an hour later. "When you hear that I have died," he said, "don't believe it, because whoever believes [in Christ] does not die but from death enters into life."[12]

Committed to *Samizdat:* Nikolai Saburov

Believers in Communist countries found it very difficult to obtain books to nourish their faith. In response, Christians in the West tried to bring Bibles

---

12. This experience is recounted by Khorev in ibid., pp. 67-68.

and Christian literature behind the Iron Curtain, and people like Nikolai Saburov on the other side tried to get the books or print their own.* Saburov is a bear of a man, his shaggy hair now white. He has an irrepressible sense of humor and boundless energy. He was a traveling evangelist in Russia for the underground Baptist church. When teams of couriers came over the Russian border from Czechoslovakia, Finland, and East Germany, he met them surreptitiously to pick up the Bibles they were delivering. As the main contact for this underground network, Saburov was the only man in central Russia who could decipher the letters he received in code from the Western partners. It wasn't possible to communicate via ordinary letters or phone calls, since these forms of communication were monitored by the Communists. This meant that clear arrangements for meeting times and places were tremendously difficult to make, but Saburov managed to find the pickup points with startling accuracy.

Although he didn't always know the couriers' names, he recognized their faces. Some of them drove cars or vans with double floors or internal cavities filled with books. Some of the women involved wore specially made dresses with scores of inside pockets just the right size for concealing thin editions of the New Testament.

The underground had a flourishing *samizdat* production of forbidden literature, although it was ferociously pursued by the Communist authorities. Since mimeograph machines and all other kinds of duplicating equipment were not to be used unmonitored by private citizens, anyone operating a clandestine printing press was breaking the law. Nevertheless, *Samizdat* presses were in operation throughout the entire Eastern bloc, employing a remarkable collection of improvised technical contraptions. A washing machine might provide the motor, while ink could be made from a mixture of moss, shoe polish, bark, and melted tires. Some printing presses were smuggled in one piece at a time from the West.

The underground group that Saburov worked with did printing as well as "receiving," and they had devised ingenious printing techniques. To produce their journal, they hand-printed the articles onto plates of glass, and then made copies with a home-concocted ink mixture. To print Bibles,

*Based on the author's interview with Nikolai Saburov in Moscow on November 12, 1992.

they used a machine that could be disassembled and put into a small suitcase. The printing process was both arduous and dangerous. A team of four to six people would arrive for a clandestine printing operation in a house prepared by another team, which had quietly laid in all the necessary food and supplies. Coming during the cover of night, the team would close and curtain all the windows and then set up the portable press. Once they got it operating, they could print 20,000 copies of the New Testament in six days. During that time, no one could go out of the house; they could only take a cautious whiff of fresh air late at night as the world around them slept. When they finished, they would disassemble the press, put it in its small suitcase, and in the darkness depart for the next printing site. By constantly changing locations, they hoped to evade the KGB. Those who got caught faced a prison sentence of at least three years.

The printed pages would be kept in the house for a full month, while all was quiet at that site. After this waiting period, the copies would be distributed, with perhaps 3,000 sets of loose pages sent to Moscow, 3,000 sent to Kiev, and similar shipments sent elsewhere. In each city, church members would then gather in one member's home to hand-bind the copies in clandestine all-night sessions. The finished volumes would subsequently be apportioned among churches according to the number of parishioners. Because the shortage of Bibles was so acute, it was not uncommon for twelve people to share one copy. Those who provided them — like Saburov — took great risks.

~

Yacov Dukhonchenko

Yacov Dukhonchenko was a man who believed that each individual had to make a personal decision about how to respond to the commands of two kingdoms in conflict.[13] As a young man, Dukhon-

13. This portrait is based on the author's interview with Yacov Dukhonchenko in Moscow on November 11, 1992.

chenko studied economics via a correspondence course. For that reason he was able to conceal his Christian identity until the final examination, when the institute gave him an ultimatum: either he denied his faith, or he couldn't complete his education. "Where does it state that you can't study here if you're a Baptist?" he asked. Because his grades were excellent, Dukhonchenko wasn't worried about passing the exam. About this time, too, the man who had blocked his advancement was transferred, and his replacement permitted Dukhonchenko to graduate.

Dukhonchenko wanted to become a pastor in 1960, precisely at the time that the Baptist Church was in turmoil over compliance with the restrictions imposed on congregations. He met with the Council for Religious Affairs, who told him that his congregation would be denied registration as long as he headed it, and sooner or later would be shut down. In response, he suggested that another individual be the head pastor, but made a simple request: "Can I just talk to the people?" The council said yes, noting that there was nothing in the law prohibiting that. So, for the next seven years, while he worked publicly as a chief accountant, he was an evangelist in private. His boss knew about what he was doing and was unnerved by it, but he was unable to find a legitimate reason for dismissing Dukhonchenko because he did his job well. Subsequently Dukhonchenko's boss was called in by the firm's top leader, who threatened to fire the boss if he didn't fire Dukhonchenko.

In 1967, Dukhonchenko became a pastor and was granted registration by the same official who had denied it to him before. Only one year later he was elected senior presbyter of the Baptists in the Zaborosz region of the Ukraine. Instead, he stayed to fight the restrictions head-on. The first issue he tackled was the submission of lists on baptismal candidates.

For each person baptized, a church was required to submit to the Council for Religious Affairs his or her name, passport number, address, and place of birth. This invariably resulted in families having problems with the local authorities, who would be hard on them because of their professed religious allegiance; sometimes individuals who had "declared" themselves would be in danger of losing their jobs. Dukhonchenko told his pastors that they were not to submit such lists, contending that demanding such information was an invasion of privacy which violated a clause of Ukrainian law. When the Council for Religious Affairs called him on the carpet, he told them, "You are breaking two laws — the law of the state, and the law of God." When KGB authorities threatened to take the lists from him, he refused to surrender them.

He also defied their ban on giving religious instruction to children, instituting classes in the parishes under his jurisdiction. The churches he oversaw also practiced charity despite the ban against it, keeping two sets of funds, one officially reported, the other not, which they would use to help people in need. He now admits that there was a "conflict between our convictions and the law. It was our calling, but it was forbidden. The law itself made us criminals."

In July 1974, when the chief presbyter of the Ukraine announced that church leaders had to abide by the existing laws governing church bodies, he was ousted. In the fiery debate that ensued, Dukhonchenko was surprised to find himself elected to head the registered Baptist church of the Ukraine. From this post he again railed against the lists of baptismal candidates, threatening to dismiss pastors who provided them to the government. He talked with parishioners who had been betrayed, and he put the question clear and hard to the pastors who had reported them: "Whom do you serve?"

Now that the Communist regime has collapsed, Dukhonchenko is free to speak openly in schools, hospitals, and prisons. "There is no place we do not preach," he says today with satisfaction. In the prisons where he ministers, thousands of convicts, many of them young people, listen to his words hungrily. He is familiar with the environment, having spent ten years in prison himself on two separate charges: the first time, when he was eighteen, he was convicted of refusing to provide information about a friend of his who was arrested for baptizing minors; the second time he was convicted of witnessing, accused of "anti-Soviet agitation." Today the gentle, white-haired pastor feels no bitterness toward those who imprisoned him. "It was God's chosen way," he says. "It was a good school for me. It gave me the ability to help those I visit in prisons now. . . . They must understand there's still hope."

During one of his recent visits to a prison, Dukhonchenko asked the inmates to stand if they wished him to pray for them — and every last one of them stood up, including the prison authorities. After he prayed, a twenty-year-old man, his face weary and lined with suffering, presented him with a bouquet of flowers on behalf of all the inmates. "We thank you for coming," he said. "We don't believe in God or the devil, and we don't believe in communism, but we have lost faith that there is goodness in this earth. You have warmed our hearts with the warmth in your heart. I don't know if we will ever be the people that you say we will become, but I know we will never be the same as before."

Ivan Fedotov

Ivan Fedotov, a young strawberry-blond man with a deep, gentle voice, was a carpenter by trade.[14] He was content with his work, particularly because he could do it without pressure to lie or steal, and this was not true of many other professions. But when the KGB asked him to provide information for them and he refused, he was threatened with dismissal.

The congregation he led — a group of 600 — was also in jeopardy. In all seasons, including bone-chilling winter, they gathered deep in the woods to avoid being discovered. As members of an unregistered Pentecostal denomination,[15] they had to be very secretive. Unpublished regulations had banned the group altogether (as Konstantin Kharchev, the former head of the Council for Religious Affairs, admitted in a surprisingly frank interview in 1988), and they were singled out for particularly harsh persecution.

14. This portrait is based on the author's interview with Ivan Fedotov in Kaluga on March 16, 1992.

15. In the Soviet Union there were Pentecostal congregations that were unregistered, that were registered with the AUCECB (All-Union Council of Evangelical Christians-Baptists), and that were autonomously registered. Fedotov is currently the senior bishop of the unregistered denomination in the Moscow region.

But even in the woods, Fedotov and his congregation were not safe. The KGB discovered them there, and secretly filmed their activities to produce a propagandistic "documentary" to discredit the group and its leader. Entitled "This Worries Everybody," this film, which was shot between 1957 and 1960 and shown on television, purported to prove that Fedotov was responsible for unexplained deaths. Among other things, he was accused of killing a young girl by throwing her in front of a train. (The charges were totally falsified.) He was also accused of the "crime" of providing religious education for children. The film showed children reading the Bible and praying and ridiculed those like Fedotov who "forced" them to engage in such activities. The young girls shown were the daughters of a couple belonging to Fedotov's congregation. They were three and five years old when they were later taken away from their parents and sent to a state-controlled orphanage; their father, Nikolai Voloshin, spent twenty years in prison. And this was not an isolated incident. Other Christian families were also robbed of their children.

The kind of character defamation employed in this film was a technique commonly used to discredit many Protestants. It was even rumored that they offered human sacrifices. In fact, the local newspaper claimed that Fedotov's wife told a neighbor that he must atone for his excessive drinking by sacrificing one of his daughters; the article alleged that she brought a knife and rope to assist him. This was pure fabrication, but it had dire consequences: she served a three-year prison term.

The consequences for her husband were even worse. Fedotov spent nine months in detention before he was sentenced for his "crimes" in 1960. During that time he was incarcerated in a psychiatric prison, where he was used as a subject for experiments with drugs. After he was sent to prison, he was ordered to do hard labor, made to dig in frozen earth and fell trees, often forced to work through the night in subfreezing temperatures. He shared cells with murderers, thieves, and rapists. After ten long years, in 1970, Fedotov was released from prison. But he hadn't seen a prison cell for the last time.

Subsequently he was arrested again, this time for opening a Sunday School for children, and was jailed from 1974 to 1977. By this time the Soviet authorities had changed their tactics. In the sixties, they used severe forms of coercion and persecution in dealing with believers; in the seventies and eighties, they tried to cajole and persuade with enticements. By promising Fedotov buildings for worship, a printing press, and the withdrawal of the charges against him, they attempted to win his agreement to register his congregation. But Fedotov said no. As a consequence, he was sent back to prison. Twice during his incarceration he suffered a heart attack, but doctors there were not permitted to treat him.

He was released from prison again, only to be convicted again, in 1981, of other "crimes" pertaining to practicing his faith. He was taken to a particularly harsh labor camp, a "camp factory for killing human bodies," as he describes it. His wife was denied permission to visit him; officials told her he would not come back alive.

Continuing to Document Repression: Boris Perchatkin

In 1980, Boris Perchatkin was elected secretary of the Moscow-based group that Fedotov had headed.* Perchatkin had become involved in trying to help Pentecostals emigrate from the Soviet Union, and he had contacted prominent dissidents Anatoli Sharansky, Yuri Orlov, and Alexander Ginzburg. Despite threats, Perchatkin documented the repression of the Pentecostals — and soon found himself in a labor camp like Fedotov. There he was threatened, beaten, and subjected to physical and psychological attempts at coercion. After his release in 1987, he was designated to emigrate and represent the denomination abroad.

In May of 1988, Perchatkin found himself in Moscow with a number of dissidents whom President Reagan wanted to meet. He was seated next to First Lady Nancy Reagan, who made a declaration that

---

*Based on Kent Hill's *Soviet Union on the Brink: An Inside Look at Christianity and Glasnost* (Portland, Ore.: Multnomah Press, 1991), p. 368.

must have sounded incredible: "You're here [in Moscow] because we are worried about you." There was reason to be. In Chuguyevka in eastern Siberia, persecution had been so severe that Pentecostals there renounced their Soviet citizenship in 1983 after a series of threats were made on their children. All of them were harassed, and many of them received prison terms of up to five years. But the group stood firm until they were permitted to emigrate in 1988. In another incident that occurred late in 1988, Grigory Kushin, editor of the Pentecostal church's underground religious journal entitled *Khristianin*, was nearly killed in a car "accident" near Rostov. He had been threatened with violence if he did not cease publishing the journal, and the accident was apparently an attempt on his life.

Fedotov managed to survive the labor camp. But shortly before he was to be released, he was informed that he would be detained for three more years because of infractions he had committed against prison rules. This was an insidious method that the KGB used to detain many prisoners for years, with no venue of appeal. A colonel in the KGB met with Fedotov and listed the names of clergy who had accepted the KGB's terms for registration. "Will you register when you get out?" he asked.

"It would be a sin," Fedotov answered. That response ended his audience with the colonel.

Finally, in 1986, after spending a total of eighteen years in prison, Ivan Fedotov finally was released — though he was then forced to accept a form of house arrest. But after about a year, a visiting delegation from the United States put his case to the Council for Religious Affairs, demanding to see him and to know the reasons for his detention. Apparently concern for maintaining the image of Soviet tolerance in the West was enough to pry Fedotov loose. After a flurry of phone calls on his behalf, he was released, one of the last Christian leaders in the Soviet Union to be sentenced for "crimes" pertaining to the practice of faith.

Only after the Communist regime toppled was the film that accused Fedotov unearthed in KGB archives and shown on television again. This time it was followed by a rebuttal that vindicated Fedotov.[16]

In the late 1980s, in one of the quirks of *glasnost,* tens of thousands of Pentecostals were permitted to emigrate by applying to emigrate to Israel under the new law primarily intended for Jews wishing to leave the country. When these emigrés reached Vienna, where their paperwork was processed, many of them — both Jews and Pentecostals — changed their destination; most of them chose the United States. Since virtually nothing was known about the Pentecostal denomination in the Soviet Union, the people at the processing centers were largely unaware of the extreme persecution these people had suffered.[17] And for some of them, the suffering wasn't over: many were denied refugee status or were blocked by major bureaucratic snafus in immigration processing in 1989, which left them stranded in the Soviet Union — without the jobs and apartments they had given up, but still unable to emigrate. In 1990 several thousand of them were airlifted out of the Soviet Union in a rescue operation organized by World Relief and U.S. Senator William Armstrong. Thousands more were permitted to emigrate in 1991 and 1992.[18]

Despite what he was made to endure, Ivan Fedotov has chosen to remain. The prison ministry that he is devoted to now is a continuation of what he was doing quietly behind prison walls for many years before. Because of this man who understands life on the other side, scores of inmates are becoming believers. Amazingly, when he speaks of his years in prison, it is without bitterness. He says those hard years

16. The film on Ivan Fedotov was broadcast in Russia in 1992 on "Maloyaroslavets Church Chronicle." A copy provided for the author provided additional documentation here.

17. Little was known in the West about this group until the incident of the "Siberian Seven," who gained notoriety by seeking asylum in the U.S. Embassy in 1965 in their unsuccessful attempt to flee the country. They tried again in 1978, staying in the Embassy for five years, until their case could be resolved by the authorities in 1983. Their plight drew attention to that of others of their faith who had suffered greatly. There has been a major exodus of Pentecostals since then.

18. This is based on an interview with Serge Duss of World Vision in Moscow on March 18, 1992.

may have prepared him for his current ministry. "My faith became stronger," he says. "I was undergoing stages of growth. . . . When I was very weak in body, I was very strong in spirit."

Alexander Firisiuk

The young dentist had been summoned to meet what the other doctors jokingly called the "unholy trinity."[19] The local leader of the Communist party, the head of the hospital, and the leader of the trade union had convened to decide what to do with this young woman who had been practicing in their clinic. The party leader told her what they had concluded.

"We've had a lot of wretched people in this clinic — alcoholics, thieves, and even prostitutes. But such a filthy thing as a Baptist — never. Get out of here!"

And with that, she was out of a job. The young woman was married to Alexander Firisiuk, who had suffered similar discrimination. He had been in his fifth year of study at a technological institute but had been expelled just before graduation when the authorities had learned that he was a Christian. Alexander subsequently became an engineer, but because he was a Christian, he was blocked from making any moves up the professional ladder. Pay was low, and even when his colleagues were granted raises, he was not.

This was the usual state of affairs for Christians in the Soviet Union, where they were systematically discriminated against. It was proof once again that even though the Soviet constitution guaranteed freedom of religion, in practice there was no such thing. Typically Christians had limited educational opportunities, and even those who managed to receive some higher education couldn't advance if they didn't belong to the Communist party or weren't approved by it. As a result, Christians became second-class citizens, undereducated and clearly disadvantaged professionally.

19. This portrait is based on the author's interview with Alexander Firisiuk (secretary and vice president of the Union of Evangelical Christians-Baptists in the [former] USSR) in Moscow on March 11, 1992.

Firisiuk had been secretly baptized at night. The brother of a friend, who had just been released from prison, performed the baptism but insisted on secrecy, because he was not eager to be jailed again for the "crime" of baptizing. As a pastor, Alexander performed this same secret ritual for others. Well into the 1980s, he baptized new believers in lakes and rivers he had driven to in secret. These people asked him to condone their clandestine following of Christ, afraid lest their faith become known. They had good reason to fear the unpredictable consequences of being "public" Christians. Those who were managers or teachers would most likely be fired; those who were political appointees certainly would be; those who were doctors and engineers might in some cases be allowed to continue in their professions.

To avoid detection, some congregations kept their meeting places a secret. Nikolai Kolesnikov, who grew up in Kazakhstan, attended such a clandestine church.[20] From week to week, its meeting place would change from one house to another; every week the host family would move to one side the furniture in their main room to allow all the worshipers to squeeze in. The leaders would decide on a location only two days before the planned gathering, divulging it to only the most trusted inner circle. When the evening for the service came, those who wanted to attend were to get on a specific bus, where they would be met by someone who would give them a signal at the stop where they were to get off. At that point they would be met by another person who would indicate what direction they should walk in, then yet another who would indicate which house to enter. But even with such precautions, there was no guarantee that they wouldn't be discovered and arrested. In fact, the pastor of Kolesnikov's church was eventually apprehended. He was threatened with the death penalty, but his sentence was "lightened" to ten years in prison and five years in exile.

"The KGB watched all Christians," Firisiuk claims. Anyone who

20. This is based on the author's interview with Rev. Nikolai Kolesnikov, vice president of the Union of Evangelical Christians-Baptists in the (former) USSR, in Moscow on March 11, 1992.

became a deacon or a pastor was visited by KGB agents, who attempted to persuade the individual to "cooperate." Specially schooled interrogators would alternate between cajoling and threatening to try to get what they wanted. "Frightened Christians agreed to cooperate," Firisiuk explains. "It doesn't mean they did so willingly — they did so out of fear. Some came to the church in tears later and asked for forgiveness."

But Christians under pressure often responded in exactly the opposite way that their persecutors intended. As Jakob Janzen, a member of an unregistered Baptist congregation, explains it, "They wanted to destroy the church, but during those times, the congregation was stronger than ever. They held together like never before. And they prayed more often than ever. At home our children didn't pray a prayer they had learned by rote; they prayed from the heart with their own words: 'Lord, give our father strength.' The result brought our children, and us, closer to God."[21]

*   *   *

The harsh persecution of Christians in the Soviet Union illustrates graphically the struggle of Christian conscience under Communism. Believers faced three options: accept the limitations imposed by the regime as a condition of survival; ignore them in practice while appearing to accept them, risking fines, loss of employment, and harassment; or refuse the limitations altogether, risking probable imprisonment. All three options presented serious problems.

It is possible that this is an issue for which there is not one clean, "correct" answer. In practice, defying Soviet-imposed restrictions demanded a willingness to sacrifice — one's career, good educational opportunities for one's children, and, in extreme cases, one's freedom or one's life. Arguably, not everyone is born to be a martyr. Credit is due those leaders who accepted registration but in practice defied it, carving out niches for the growth of spiritual

---

21. This quotation is taken from the transcript of the author's interview with Jakob Janzen in Gummersbach, Germany, on January 19, 1992.

and moral life. Those who broke the rules and gave young people religious instruction can be credited with nurturing the seedlings of the "forest of awakened consciences" that would later change the moral landscape of the country. And certainly deserving of credit are those who chose the stonier path of nonregistration and faced severe persecution as a consequence. These are the unsung modern heroes of faith.

Many Christians — Orthodox and Protestant, registered and unregistered — did not bow to the Communist monolith; they responded in critical, nonconformist ways, following their conscience. They were a source of strength in confronting Communism. The modest freedoms they carved out were costly — and the price they paid made their sacrifices spiritually potent.

Left: August 17, 1961: Eighteen-year-old Peter Fechter, first victim of the Berlin Wall, is carried away after being shot and left to bleed to death tangled in the barbed wire. © *Deutsche Presse Agentur GmbH, Germany*

Below: A section of the Berlin Wall near Check-point Charlie in 1963. The sign reads, "Victims of the Wall: 54 dead." *Courtesy of Rüdiger Knechtel*

Left: Rüdiger Knechtel (kneeling) and members of his company shortly before they were arrested and imprisoned in 1963 for refusing orders to shoot. *Courtesy of Rüdiger Knechtel*

Right: Protesting the unwillingness of the East Berlin regime to bring the abuses of the Stasi to light, Rüdiger Knechtel chained himself to the Ministry of Justice building in June 1990. *Courtesy of Rüdiger Knechtel*

Alexander Ogorodnikov, founder of the Christian Seminar movement in Russia, celebrating Easter at home in 1978. Later that year he was arrested by the KGB.

© *La Pensce Russe; courtesy of Keston Research Photo Archive, Oxford, England*

These two photographs clearly depict the neglect and desecration that many Russian churches fell prey to. These pictures are part of an unofficial exhibition that was to be held in Moscow in 1988 during celebrations to mark the Millennium of Christianity in Russia. But the photographer wasn't allowed into Moscow, so the exhibition never took place. *Courtesy of Keston Research Photo Archive, Oxford, England*

Some churches in Russia, like this one in Zagorsk, were allowed to hold services. Notice that all those in attendance here are women. *Courtesy of Licht im Osten, Germany*

Many believers in Russia had to worship in secret. Here a Russian Orthodox group worships in the woods during the 1930s.   *Courtesy of Licht im Osten, Germany*

Father Gleb Yakunin in 1980. After suffering years of imprisonment by the Russian government for documenting the persecution of believers, he was elected to the Russian parliament in 1990.
Courtesy of Licht im Osten, Germany

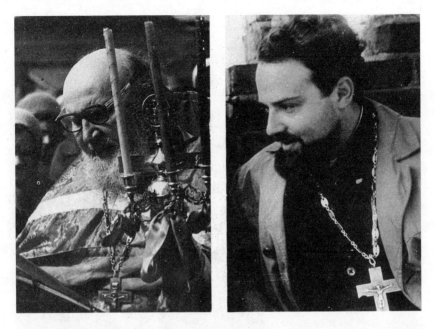

Left: In addition to being a teacher and a writer, Father Dimitri Dudko is a spiritual father to many Russians. Here he leads a worship service in Grebnevo, Russia.
Courtesy of Licht im Osten, Germany
Right: Father Alexander Men attracted many followers with his intellectual and spiritual gifts. He became a modern-day martyr when he was murdered on September 9, 1990.   © *Keston College; courtesy of Keston Research Photo Archive, Oxford, England*

Despite the potential negative consequences, these Russians, virtually all of them women, fill the room for a Baptist worship service held in Leningrad in 1974.
Courtesy of Licht im Osten, Germany

Right: The children of Georgi Vins, a leader in the underground Baptist Church, hold up his photograph after his arrest in 1966. *Courtesy of Licht im Osten, Germany*

Below: In Russia, Bibles and Christian literature were secretly printed in Christian homes on *samizdat* (clandestine) presses like this one. They could be easily disassembled and moved from place to place. © *Friedenstimme; courtesy of Keston College Research Archive, Oxford, England*

Russian authorities destroyed this family home in Alma-Ata after they discovered that it was being used to hold church services. *Courtesy of Licht im Osten, Germany*

Yacov Dukhonchenko, who defied orders to submit lists of baptismal candidates that went to the KGB, was once imprisoned for his beliefs. Now he ministers to prisoners in Russia. *Courtesy of Licht im Osten, Germany*

Trying to keep his outlawed congregation from being persecuted for gathering to worship, Ivan Fedotov leads a secret service in the woods. *© ARC; courtesy of Keston Research Photo Archive, Oxford, England*

Some young people resisted the pressure of the Communist system. Here a group meets at a Methodist youth camp in Estonia. Minutes after this photograph was taken, police raided the meeting. *Courtesy of Licht im Osten, Germany*

CHAPTER 5

Taking a Stand:
Tough Decisions for Young People

Early Indoctrination: Children and the Communist "Truth"

When Andrei Sakharov first married Elena Bonner, he held long discussions with her sixteen-year-old son Alyosha over whether the boy should join *Komsomol*, the Communist Youth League. For days the debate continued, with Sakharov promoting a kind of pragmatism. Bonner recalled his argument: "Andrei was teaching him conformism — that sometimes, a situation arises when a person must live in a certain way to achieve something. After all, a person has to get an education. And it's a pity for a gifted boy not to get the best. And so forth."

The debate ended when Alyosha raised a question that Sakharov later related to Bonner. "Alyosha taught me a good lesson. He said to me, 'Why [do] you, Andrei Dmitrich, think you can allow yourself to be honest, but not me?'"

"The only thing Alyosha didn't know," Bonner commented later, "was that unless you take part you won't be given an apartment, you won't get permission to travel abroad. That he didn't know, but all the rest he knew. By [this time], he knew all the rest, and he'd already made his choice."

"So in this case," Bonner continued, "a young man made the choice between conformism and nonconformism. Ninety-nine percent of Soviet youth are not stupider than Alyosha, but they join the Komsomol though it is meaningless — they do anything they must to assure themselves a Soviet career . . . [so] life is doublethink — Orwell!"[1]

Like Alyosha, most young people living in Communist countries had to make the most important decisions of their lives — the ones that would affect the rest of their lives — by the time they were sixteen. The regime was bent on shaping their intellect, their loyalty, and their convictions. Their membership in Communist youth organizations like *Komsomol* determined what paths would be open or closed to them from that time on. Although membership in these groups was never required, those who failed to join usually found higher educational opportunities blocked. Some refused to join because of their faith, others for reasons of political nonconformity. But the consequences were the same. Their refusal determined their careers, their earnings, their positions in life. Clearly, these young people were under enormous pressure in making these decisions, because the consequences were lasting.

Every now and again there would be an exception: a young person from a Christian family would be admitted to the university after all, and would then be used as an example of the state's tolerance. Sometimes they could pursue a degree over time in night school. But under Communism, Christians were often denied opportunities for higher education and consequently consigned to second-rate jobs with low pay, blocked from advancement, and denied responsibility. They became victims of an inverse system of advancement where competence, intelligence, and integrity were secondary to ideology. The Communist party was the ticket to advancement, and only those who joined it or otherwise received its blessing could be successful in worldly terms.

Parents who tried to raise their children to think independently were faced with a hard task because doing so was likely to bring their children into conflict with the world around them. Everyone was confronted with what Solzhenitsyn called "The Lie," but did one dare name it? To keep their children from experiencing the crushing con-

---

1. This incident is recounted by Kevin Klose in *Russia and the Russians: Inside the Closed Society* (New York: W. W. Norton, 1984), pp. 169-70.

sequences of resisting the regime, most parents raised their children with a double persona, one for the public world, and one for the private world. Truth became relative, dependent on whoever was listening.

Indoctrination with the party line began early. The Communist educational system began drilling its worldview into kindergarten children. Teachers were ordered to present state-controlled lesson plans; their goal was to instill loyalty to socialist ideals and the Communist party. Everything — curriculum, grading, and evaluation of the students — was centered on this premise. Teachers graded students partly on their loyalty to socialism, and were told to lower the grades of critics.

Two kinds of truth were anathema to the Communists: historical truth and religious truth. The schools propagated their Marxist-Leninist revisionist version of history, which painted all historical events as the result of class struggle. In East Germany in 1988, for example, seventh-grader Christine Gohlke read in her textbook an explanation of World War II at least as fascinating for what it doesn't say as for what it does. In Germany in 1933, the text claimed, "out of fear of organized labor, the ruling major capitalists elected the openly fascist dictator. With bloody terror, the fascist powers wanted not only to eliminate the communist party and all labor organizations, but all other democratic forces. Everyone should understand how the German major capitalists prepared this catastrophe."[2]

The next significant date that Christine's class learned about was May 8, 1945, "The Day of Liberation," which is presented as a Soviet achievement. A passing reference to "American and British bombers that no longer demolished German cities" is the only indication of the involvement of England and America in the conflict. Nothing is said about the annexation of Poland. The word *Jew* does not appear anywhere in the text; concentration camps get one passing mention. In light of these omissions, it's conceivable that some of the young people who went through school systems like this one never learned what really happened.

2. *Staatsbürgerkunde 7* ([East] Berlin: Volk und Wissen Volkseigener Verlag, 1983), pp. 15, 20.

When East German teenager Gabi Anger asked her teacher why the Berlin Wall was built in 1961, she was told it was a "wall of defense" — in Orwellian newspeak, "protection against western aggression." When she asked what had happened on June 17, 1953, she was told a counterrevolution was put down. The standard school textbook for eighth graders offered this explanation of the events of 1953 and 1961:

> In tough, intensive work, "Day X" [June 17, 1953] was planned in West Berlin, in Washington, London and Paris — the day on which the GDR was to be destroyed. Acts of espionage, diversion, and sabotage had increased, counter-revolutionary forces were prepared militarily and ideologically. . . . The western radio stations broadcast falsified reports of strikes in the GDR and tried to incite volatile laborers. . . .
>
> A second attempt of world imperialism to penetrate the socialist world-system was withstood through the security measures of August 13, 1961. NATO had made detailed plans for an invasion of the GDR. In a Blitzkrieg, the GDR was to be conquered, after counter-revolutionaries smuggled in from West Berlin were to organize a putsch and call for a "new government."

According to the text, it was through the building of the Berlin Wall that a world war was avoided and peace in Europe was saved.[3]

When Gabi's mother learned what her daughter had been taught, she told her daughter the truth about those events. She explained that the Soviets had intervened on June 17, 1953, to crush an uprising of the East Germans sparked by labor protests over raised work quotas, an uprising that had turned into a general revolt against the Communists; it ended with Soviet bullets flying and protesters lying dead on the streets. Over the next several years, the exodus from East Germany into the West produced a hemorrhage that the Communists sought to block with the Wall, which was built on August 13, 1961. It was a desperate act to keep the citizens from leaving,

---

3. *Staatsbürgerkunde 8* ([East] Berlin: Volk und Wissen Volkseigener Verlag, 1984), pp. 98-100.

painful evidence of a failure the Communists wanted to erase. Parents like Gabi's mother who gave their children history lessons at home had to teach them to deal with such truths carefully. It was like handling dynamite.

The schools promulgated the view that socialism and imperialism were the two world orders, and that socialism, as the superior order, had to protect itself against imperialism. In her textbook, Christine read, "The citizens of the state of the German Democratic Republic, through their daily work on machines, at the plow, at the drawing board, in labor and at the schooldesk can and must contribute to strong socialism, to strong peace. It is a part of that duty to protect socialism with a weapon in the hand against the aggressive imperialistic powers." It went on to say, "Through daily diligent work, creativity and continued learning our life will always become better and richer."[4] But Gabi, not taken in by official rhetoric, made these observations: "Food was cheap, but the stores were empty. Rent was low, but the houses were crumbling. Health care was paid for, but the quality was poor. Public transportation was cheap, but if you wanted a car, you had to wait fifteen years for it. Women worked not because they were emancipated, but because you couldn't live on one income."[5] If socialism was supposed to be so successful, why did it look otherwise?

The clear message sent to children was that it was better not to ask. What was taught in school was undergirded by what was taught in the Communist youth organizations. Because belonging to these groups was so critical to future success, 99 percent of all children in Communist countries joined up, participating in the series of organizations that would take them from early childhood into adulthood. In East Germany, children first joined the Young Pioneers, then the Thälmann Pioneers, then the *Freie Deutsche Jugend* (FDJ) or so-called Free German Youth, in which they participated until their mid-twenties. The Soviet Union had a similar track: children started with the young Octobrists (who wore sashes displaying Lenin's picture), next went on to the Pioneers, and then the *Komsomol*. From

4. *Staatsbürgerkunde 7*, pp. 6, 8.
5. Taken from the author's interview with Gabriele Anger in Köln in June 1991.

there the next step was into the Communist party. Other Communist countries had similar series of organizations.

Parents whose convictions ran contrary to Communist ideals were held hostage by the threat to their children's opportunities. Many discovered that even if they were willing to make sacrifices themselves, it was extremely difficult to sacrifice their children's future on an altar of convictions, even religious convictions. Children's decisions had consequences for their parents too. A hard question pressed them all: What are you willing to risk?

Standing Up for Their Beliefs

Harald Thiermann

It was 1969, and Harald Thiermann, a young boy from East Germany, was being pressured by his teacher and his school's director to take part in the *Jugendweihe,* the Youth Dedication Ceremony, which was the secular alternative to confirmation in the church.[6] Since Harald was a Christian, this involved a conflict of conscience. He was only thirteen, but he was absolutely resolute, even though he was speaking to adults.

"I'm not going to do it, and that's that."

After six months of trying to convince him to participate in the *Jugendweihe,* the teacher and director were getting exasperated with Harald. The pressure had been intense: Harald's teacher had asked him every few days if he had changed his mind yet, threatening not to recommend him for higher education. The problem Harald had with the ceremony was the vow that all the students were supposed to take at the end of it, a vow of loyalty to the socialist system and its ideology — that stood in clear conflict with his convictions as a Christian. And that meant no ceremony.

Harald's Christian faith was new, and he was being instructed

---

6. This story is based on the author's interview with Harald Thiermann in Köln on December 14, 1990.

in it by a young priest in the Catholic Church. "You must be a light in the darkness," the priest had urged him. "As a Christian, be an example, so others can see that you are different — not so much by what you say as by how you live. You are a light, and the darkness will try to extinguish you. But you are never alone." With the encouragement of this young priest, Harald determined to live his faith.

He was not alone in his resistance. Six other students out of the thirty-one in his class had said that they didn't want to take part in the *Jugendweihe*. When school officials heard this, they summoned the parents of all seven children to the school and told them that their children's refusal to take part could have serious consequences. The father of one of the students was a teacher, and he was threatened with dismissal from his state-granted job. He gave in to the pressure, and after the united front crumpled, two more families caved in. Four were left.

Harald's parents were summoned again and asked if they were certain they stood by their son's decision; they said they did. What happened then Harald found out about only years later. Shortly thereafter, Harald's father was summoned to his boss's office. There he faced the four top directors of the plant, who informed him that due to this decision, his wages would be cut by more than a third. That reduced the family's monthly income to the point that the five of them could barely survive on it. They had no second income, because Harald's mother had become so ill that she could no longer work. After four months, without explaining why, Harald's father told him that he had changed his mind — Harald should go through with the *Jugendweihe*. Harald protested, but his father insisted.

Harald was crushed, angry, and bitter. He didn't understand why his father had changed his mind. He went through with the ceremony, but he felt as though he had betrayed his faith. It was at that point that he became determined to push back against a system that had pushed him into moral compromise.

With the help of the same young priest, Harald learned more. "You have to study your enemy to be able to use his own weapons against him," the priest told him. The two of them studied Marxism-Leninism and party propaganda together, so that Harald could learn how to respond to the Communist accusations against Christianity. It was a strategy that would later allow him to disguise himself as a sheep in wolf's clothing. Although he had considered becoming a priest, Harald decided that he wanted to become a teacher instead. He wanted to help shape the next generation in East Germany by absorbing some of the pressure intended to force young minds into the Communist mold.

Two teachers he dubbed his "guardian angels" concealed his nonconformity, shielding him despite the fact that he disagreed with the party line. In 1972, one of them let stand an essay Harald wrote claiming that Communism could never succeed because it is inconsistent with human nature. Instead of failing Harald, the teacher gave him an A and didn't report the inflammatory nature of his topic — a definite risk. Another teacher who had refused to dock students' grades for ideological reasons was made to undergo psychological examination and "treatment."

In East Germany's two-track educational system, the recommendation of the school's director determined which students were sent to trade schools and which were sent to the university. Academic qualifications counted, as well as the student's "socially useful activity," such as participation in the Free German Youth organization. During the recommendation process in the fall of 1973, Harald also submitted an essay about his values. While his grades placed him at the top of his class, his essay set off rockets when it reached his advisor. She called him in for a private conference and closed the door.

"Harald, you've got to take this statement out."

"What do you mean? It's perfectly honest."

"It's perfectly impossible — that's what it is. Read it out loud." She handed him his essay.

" 'I am a Christian,' " Harald read. " 'As Christianity and socialism have significant common goals, such as the equality of man and peace in the world, insofar as it is possible to pursue the goals consistent with my philosophy of life, I will give my best efforts to shape the development of socialist society.' "

"Do you want to become a teacher?" she asked penetratingly.

"Yes."

"Look, you have to think this over very carefully. You say that you're a Christian. I don't believe in anything myself. But if you say your beliefs are important to you, you should know that as a teacher you're going to get a terrific amount of pressure from the system to do things you won't want to do. As a Christian, you are most certainly going to face enormous difficulties. They're going to try to force you to do things you abhor. You're going to have to make compromises to survive. If you think you can stand the pressure, then do it. But if you want to get there, you have to take this statement out. Think about it very hard."

Harald sat in silence for five long minutes.

Am I betraying my faith if I do it? he wondered. *But if I don't, how can I ever teach? Is my advisor right — will I be unable to become a teacher if I openly confess to being a Christian? If I compromise, will I be able to bear the consequences?* Finally Harald decided to take the two sentences out. For the second time he was making a compromise — and he hated it.

In the end, Harald was recommended for university training.

Harald began attending the university in 1974. In 1976, after he had studied for two years, Harald was given another student as a partner to help him with the research on his thesis. He was not unhappy to discover that she was pleasant, intelligent, and very attractive. The two research partners began to discover love between the bookstacks. Harald and his beautiful companion spent endless hours discussing everything in the universe, debating in high spirits the nature of man. So what this woman eventually revealed to him a few years later left him flabbergasted.

"Harald, you should marry me. Then you can go with me when I'm sent to the Soviet Union."

"What? What do you mean 'sent to the Soviet Union'?"

"I'm being sent there for training. It will take three years. After I'm finished, I'll be deployed in Sweden, Switzerland, or West Germany. Harald, you have to come with me," she finished insistently.

"What on earth are you talking about? Deployed as what?"

"As a Stasi agent."

Harald's world exploded.

She explained that she had been sent by the secret police to keep a close watch on Harald's ideological development, to find out if he had a clean bill of health as a future teacher. It all became clear to him then — the penetrating questions about his views, the grilling about his faith. It was so obvious. And when he thought about it, he realized that there had been clues that she was "well connected." She had always had more money than he and access to stores not open to ordinary people. He remembered the spirited debates they had had, and her saying with a laugh, "Harald, with your views, there's no way you should be permitted to become a teacher!"

Probably because she had fallen in love with him, she had not reported what she had discovered about him. If the Stasi would have known the truth, he would have been bounced from the university promptly and banned from ever setting foot in a classroom as a teacher. So, despite his bitter discovery, his dream to become a teacher remained intact.

Harald's intellectual ability was to serve him well in perfecting his cover as a sheep in wolf's clothing. His tutorials with the young Catholic priest allowed him to debate so convincingly on Marxism that the university faculty singled him out as a future propagandist to train young people in the FDJ (the Free German Youth organization). But when he took on this task, instead of teaching them socialism's virtues, he talked to them about why dissidents had been expatriated from the country.

In 1978 Harald became a teacher of math and physics in a high school in Strausberg. The students knew he was a Christian, and their contact with him chipped away at their resistance toward faith and the church. What most of them had rejected was a caricature of Christianity. They had been told Christians were backward, superstitious, and "unscientific." But Harald's obvious intellect didn't fit the preconception.

In 1979, when the director of the school was preparing to be transferred, she tapped Harald to become her successor. She called him into her office and told him that his work had been exemplary and that he would make an excellent director.

"There's only one small problem," she said. "You'll have to join the party."

"That's out of the question," he replied quietly but firmly.

"What do you mean?" she shot back.

"I'm a Christian, and I cannot in good conscience join the party."

"What!" she roared.

She became determined to change his mind or ruin him. But her strategy was interrupted by Harald's being called up for the standard eighteen months of military service in late 1980. After he was released from the army in 1982, Harald returned to teaching, and his clear ability won him two attractive career offers, including perks like international travel. But he was again faced with the same problem: to take advantage of these offers, he would have to join the Communist party. The school directors, board members, and party members all promised that he could still go to church on Sunday, and assured him that membership was "only a formality." It became clear then what a No would mean: there would be no opportunity to advance now — or ever. He had to make a decision that would have lasting consequences for his life. Looking back, he says, "I decided then that if having a successful career depended on being in the party, then I wouldn't have a successful career. If I had done it, I would have been an absolute traitor to everything I believed. I would have felt like I had sold my soul."

But the Communists were not content to leave it at that. They embarked on a campaign to break Harald. In 1984 they assigned him to a hardship post teaching juvenile delinquents. When he returned to his school a year later, he was stripped of authority and blocked from assemblies. When he protested manipulation of grades on ideological grounds, the school hit back, demanding that he submit minutely detailed plans for each hour of instruction he intended to give. His classes were monitored, and he was reprimanded for niggling things. All of these were obvious tactics of harassment. It was a war of nerves, and Harald's frayed under the cumulative burden of the next four years of conflict that followed. He asked to resign, but his request was turned down. When his health failed, he asked to leave on medical grounds, but again he was turned down. After that he suffered a physical and mental collapse, and in October 1988 he stopped teaching. He says that if he hadn't been a Christian, he would have committed suicide.

On July 4, 1989, Harald defected to West Germany. Today he teaches computer programming in Bonn.

Anatoly Rudenko

Anatoly Rudenko discovered that Russian universities don't welcome professing Christians. When repeated expulsions didn't silence him, he found himself locked up in a psychiatric prison.[7]

Anatoly was born in the Urals in the town of Ufa to a family of nonbelievers. Growing up, he knew no Christians, but as a contemplative schoolboy, he had reflected on the need for a supreme being and later prayed to this "something" he could not define. In 1976, when he was a teenager, it was extremely difficult to obtain Bibles in the Soviet Union, but Anatoly begged a monk at the Zagorsk monastery so convincingly that the monk gave him a New Testament with the admonition not to show it to anyone. The more Anatoly read, the more he understood. Eventually, when he was a university student, he committed his life to Christ.

Immediately he was faced with a conflict: he knew that he should speak of his faith, but if he did, he risked being expelled from the university. He had to choose. For a young man from the provinces, this was no easy decision. Since childhood he had wanted to study at a major university, and being admitted for advanced study in economics was a rare privilege.

"Christianity is more precious than higher education," Anatoly concluded. "If it costs me my education, then that's all right. It's worth it." He began to witness among the students, and he asked to be expelled from *Komsomol*. Many tried to dissuade him, suggesting there must be "a softer way." But he said no.

The consequences were swift. Although Anatoly had always

---

7. This story is based on the author's interview with Anatoly Rudenko in Moscow on March 12, 1992.

received the highest grades, he was suddenly informed that he was "academically inadequate." He knew the arguments of Marxism-Leninism seamlessly, but his professors told him that if he was to pass the exam on the political economy of socialism, he had to do more than simply know the material — he had to believe it. And on that basis, Anatoly was failed four times. His professors couldn't give him a passing grade if they concluded that he didn't believe the ideology, and Anatoly couldn't lie and say he did. The result was a commotion intensified by the fact that he had been hand-picked for a politically oriented field of university study. To have a "defector" in the ranks was an event that caused ripples in the Communist party itself. In the end, because he wouldn't say he believed what he knew about Marxism-Leninism, he was dismissed from the university.

Anatoly returned to his province in 1978. After working with a geological team, he decided to pursue a new field of study, geology and geography. He was admitted to a university in Tomsk, Siberia. When the university administration asked him why he wasn't a member of *Komsomol,* Anatoly responded that if they wanted him to, he would give a public explanation. Several hundred people attended the event that grew out of that question. Anatoly told the assembled audience that he wasn't a member of *Komsomol* because he was a Christian. This public profession of faith was too much for the city's Communist officials, who demanded that he be expelled from the university. The administration asked him to leave "voluntarily" to preserve the appearance of propriety. The official reason was to be "academic inadequacy" again. "You were aware of what it meant to witness openly," said the vice rector.

Having been expelled from a university for the second time, Anatoly went back home again. At this juncture, as a matter of survival, he took on three jobs, working as a locksmith, an electrician, and a refrigerator repairman. Besides holding down these jobs, for the next five years he completed study in three professional trade schools. But the Communists wouldn't leave him alone: for a year and a half they made Anatoly the object of an investigation, attempting to discredit him publicly for propagandistic purposes.

"If you've read *1984,* you know that the Communist regime always needs an enemy," Anatoly explains now. Public trials would often be instigated to discredit those deemed disloyal by the regime, trials in which people were forced to give evidence against themselves. "First they break a person psychologically," Anatoly explains. "And then after he 'confesses,' they pull out of him everything they want, all the missing strokes in the picture they want to paint." The KGB wanted Anatoly to confess that he had spread anti-Soviet propaganda, that he was involved in a clandestine printing operation, and that he had contacts who were involved in Western subversive agencies. He refused.

Consequently, Anatoly was put into a psychiatric hospital and told point blank, "Here you will be more cooperative." Anatoly was told that the first month of his incarceration would be a test period during which doctors would assess his "sanity." If at the end of that time he were judged to be mentally ill, he would be "treated."

What he saw at this hospital was Dante's hell on earth. Alexei Nikitin, who pleaded for safer working conditions, ended up incarcerated in just such a hospital, where perfectly sane inmates were "treated" with pain-inducing and mind-altering drugs. His record of what he saw there gives a grim picture of such institutions all over the Soviet Union, including the one where Anatoly was kept:

> Some of the inmates had fragile frames made even weaker from years of inactivity. Some chewed their tongues, drooled through slack jaws, or made licking and swallowing motions. Some stood hunched and swaying, hands moving spasmodically, fingers curling or rolling imaginary ball bearings or other objects across their palms. There were murmurs, sobs, groans, sighs, and, here and there, snatches of furtively spoken words. Some men lay on their stomachs on their beds and could not turn over. Others seemed possessed by devilish spirits that caused them to roll and turn incessantly or pace back and forth like crazed animals, while some lay in dazed stupors, inert and uncaring.
>
> A heavy, musky odor laced with the sharp smell of urine and the stench of vomit and excrement permeated the air.[8]

8. Klose, *Russia and the Russians,* pp. 76-77.

Among the others incarcerated in such institutions were men and women whose "crimes" included baptizing their children, pleading for free speech, and writing to people in foreign countries. Some were workers who, like Alexei Nikitin, had protested against unsafe factories and corrupt bosses.

The psychiatric hospitals, which also functioned as prisons, were run by the Ministry of Internal Affairs, together with the KGB. The behaviorist theories of Ivan Pavlov coupled with the political application of Communist ideology guided the Russian concepts of psychiatry. Pavlov maintained that mental illness was a consequence of a chemical imbalance in the brain and nervous system, and influenced by his theories, Soviet psychiatrists used drugs to control, to alter, and to punish. According to Kevin Klose, author of *Russia and the Russians,* the determinations of who was mentally ill and what constituted derangement reflected Communist ideology, "which emphasizes the needs and goals of the collective ahead of the individual. Since the party was inseparable from nationhood and a well-adjusted Soviet citizen was loyal to the motherland," it was disloyal — and possibly a sign of derangement — to reject the party. A psychiatrist evaluating a religious believer saw a citizen who rejected "scientific atheism," and had no trouble concluding that he was mentally ill.[9]

Anatoly elaborates: "The line of argument was this: If you do not believe in Soviet values, you are mentally insane. If you are insane, you must be treated. If the treatment has no result, you must be eliminated." Every day Anatoly was subjected to sessions lasting up to five hours with doctors and psychiatrists. The psychiatrists alternated low-key psychological pressure with aggressive verbal bullying. The doctors worked more with hints and insinuations, but the message was the same. Anatoly was warned that his refusal to give in could result in his execution. His parents were also given that news, and they were desperate.

Anatoly had not yet been given any drugs, but he could see the awful consequences of "treatment" all around him. The drugs used included a powerful tranquilizer that caused some inmates to com-

9. Ibid., p. 78.

mit suicide when they were given an overdose of it. According to Klose, another tranquilizer was given to those diagnosed with "severe schizophrenia": an overdose of it causes "depression, weight loss, low blood pressure, skin pigmentation changes, and sensory distortions." Another tranquilizer that was administered in massive overdoses causes "severe disruptions in muscle control that will bring on head-rolling, swallowing, stammering, lip-licking, convulsions, and other Parkinsonian-like side effects."[10]

The drug that stood at "the pinnacle of pain" was Sulfazine, a form of sulphur suspended in peach oil that induces high fever, nausea, mental disorientation, and severe muscle spasms. Alexei Nikitin describes its properties:

> People go into horrible convulsions and get completely disoriented. Their body temperature rises to 40 degrees centigrade [104° F] almost instantly, and the pain is so intense they cannot move from their beds for three days. Sulfazine is simply a way to destroy a man completely. If they torture you and break your arms, there is a certain specific pain and you can somehow stand it. But sulfazine is like a drill boring into your body that gets worse and worse until it's more than you can stand. It's impossible to endure. It is worse than torture, because, sometimes, torture may end. But this kind of torture may continue for years.[11]

And the drugs were supplemented by other atrocities, according to Nikitin. In these institutions, convicts who functioned as orderlies were given special tasks. These "orderlies" would drag a drugged patient into a punishment cell, spread-eagle him, and pummel his stomach and kidneys. Afterward he might be trussed to a bed frame and "left for days, defecating on himself and trying to feed himself with hands tied to the bed." He might be thrown into "a tiny, unheated cell with a steel pipe bed frame, without mattress or blankets." Or he might be disciplined with the "wet pack" or "roll-up," "wrapped

10. Ibid., pp. 81-82.
11. Ibid., pp. 80-81.

like a mummy in wet canvas strips that shrank as they dried, grinding the body like some medieval torturer's machine, compressing the joints. The victims shrieked with pain."[12]

Seeing what was taking place around him, "I just prayed," Anatoly says. "I tried to behave reasonably and calmly." Anatoly insisted on receiving a Bible, and after the first week of his confinement, the authorities granted his request. Unbeknownst to him, his parents had contacted the general secretary of the Baptist Union in Moscow, Alexei Bychkov, to protest Anatoly's incarceration. Bychkov, who by merit of his position had contacts with international churchmen, in turn approached the Council for Religious Affairs and the KGB. This apparently prompted a call to the hospital, warning that Anatoly's case might become known about in the West. Anatoly noticed the change in his treatment without knowing what was behind it. Only later could he piece events together to figure out why the hospital officials had backed off.

At the end of his month of "assessment," Anatoly was released from the hospital, and the case against him was closed for lack of evidence. He believes that the threat of making his case public in the West contributed to his release. He was grateful, but he also knew that unknown numbers of others still languished in those hells on earth.

Today Anatoly is the director of the Bible Society in Moscow, which provides Christian literature and teaching in Russia.

The Gohlkes and the Toasperns

"For Peace and Socialism, be prepared — always prepared!" shouted the children. This was the standard greeting every morning as class began. After saluting, the Young Pioneers with their blue kerchiefs sat down. And so did Matthias Gohlke, who stood out as the only first-grader in the school in Leipzig not wearing the blue neckerchief.[13] From the wall of the classroom Lenin's portrait stared down

12. Ibid., p. 80.
13. This story is based on the author's interview with Ute and Manfred Gohlke and their children — Christine, Annedore, Beate, Stephan, and Matthias — in Leipzig on February 26, 1991.

at him; the motto below it read, "Learn, learn, and learn more." Matthias wondered why so many of the lessons in his schoolbook addressed the Young Pioneers, telling them how industrious and intelligent they were. "Young Pioneers learn well," said his lesson for the day. *What about kids who aren't Pioneers?* he wondered.

It was 1989. Like all first-graders, Matthias had been given the application forms to take home to his parents so he could become a member. Although membership in this Communist youth group was, technically speaking, voluntary, it was so automatically expected that hardly anyone considered not joining. For the youngsters, being a member was equated with virtue. The organization even had its own version of the Ten Commandments. On the face of it, it was hard for a young child like Matthias to see why he shouldn't join.

But his parents wanted nothing to do with the Communist system — and they didn't want any of their five children to have anything to do with it, either. So Matthias wasn't the only one who felt like an outsider because of their decision. His two older sisters, Christine and Annedore, had often felt the sting of being different as they went through the school system. Their teachers mocked Christian faith, saying people who believed such things were simply stupid, although the academic performance of these girls contradicted that assertion.

The Gohlke family had already been branded as untrustworthy by the regime because Manfred Gohlke, a neurologist and psychiatrist, had protested publicly against the misuse of psychiatric institutions for political purposes. He had locked horns with the authorities in the hospital in Leipzig where he worked, with local authorities, and ultimately with the Communist party. One way that the regime got back at him — and at his children — was by denying the family permission for adequate housing: for nine years the seven of them lived in an apartment that measured only 525 square feet.

*　　*　　*

Years earlier, Johannes Toaspern was one of just two children in his class in a school outside Berlin who, like Matthias Gohlke, hadn't

joined the Young Pioneers.[14] Many of the school activities were organized around the Pioneers, and whoever didn't belong couldn't go,
even if it was an integral part of what was being studied in class.
Johannes didn't mind missing the class excursions that much, but it
was clear that he was an outsider. In some cases non-Pioneers didn't
appear in class pictures. It was as if they simply didn't exist.

For Johannes's parents, there could be no reconciliation between Marxism and Christian faith, all debates of church hierarchy
aside. Consequently, none of the seven Toaspern children were allowed to join Communist youth organizations. Because they were
outsiders, teachers had ways of making their lives miserable, and
other children were predictably ruthless in razzing them. Paul
Toaspern was a man who lived his Christian convictions: he was a
pastor from West Germany who had willingly gone to minister in
the East before the Berlin Wall was built. And his children paid a
price for his belief that one had to be perfectly consistent in staying
clear of the Communist system. But Johannes understood his father's
position. When the time came for him to join the FDJ, the *Freie
Deutsche Jugend*, Johannes refused, just as he had refused to join the
Pioneers. Subsequently his father received a letter informing him that
his son would not be admitted for university study because his "entire
attitude toward society does not fulfill the expectation we have of a
future cadre of state and economic leadership." Johannes's A-minus
record in all his school subjects was irrelevant. In his letter of protest,
Paul Toaspern pointed out his son had not done anything wrong by
not joining the FDJ, because the East German constitution guaranteed freedom of religion and conscience. But his protest was in vain.

One year later, Maria, Johannes's younger sister, found herself
in the same situation. Her straight-A grades seemed likely to
guarantee that she would be admitted to the university to pursue
pediatric studies — her dream since childhood. But her parents were
sent a letter much like the one assessing Johannes: "Maria shows the

14. This story is based on the author's interview with Johannes Toaspern in
Potsdam on May 27, 1991, and on her interview with Paul and Ursula Toaspern in
Hohen Neuendorf bei Berlin on February 12, 1991.

necessary academic achievement, but has not reached the necessary degree of socialist personal development which would justify her being admitted."

Most Christians in Communist countries who tried to live their faith consistently paid a hard price for it. Asking those nearest, youngest, and weakest to pay it too must have made it even harder.

Giving Young People an Alternative Message: Theo Lehmann

Because Communist ideologues were committed to shaping the minds of young people in accordance with their views, they didn't look kindly on anyone who successfully reached young people with a different message. And there was scarcely a category of people they liked less than successful youth evangelists.

Since the 1970s, Theo Lehmann has been East Germany's best-known youth evangelist,* a man with a gift for reaching young people through music and teaching as piercing as a two-edged sword. Young people have flocked to see him: sometimes as many as 5,000 have attended a single performance. Predictably, his success made him a target of the East German regime, which attempted to silence him and destroy his credibility.

Theo collaborated with Jörg Swoboda, a singer and songwriter; Jorg composed the music, and Theo wrote the lyrics. Together they made a powerfully effective team, reaching young people with songs that were modern but had a Christian message. As Theo traveled throughout East Germany, young people often asked him if he thought it was possible to be a Christian and also a member of the FDJ. In response, he would pull out two little books from the inside pocket in his jacket: the bylaws

---

*This portrait is based on the author's interview with Theo Lehmann in Chemnitz on February 28 and March 1, 1991.

of the FDJ and a copy of the New Testament — two worldviews in confrontation. In explaining the difference between the two, he would quote Marx's rejection of religion. The gist of his message was very simple: either one view or the other was true, but not both. Waves of resignations from the FDJ rippled in Theo's wake.

In a retributive strike, the Stasi waged a smear campaign against him in his hometown of Karl-Marx-Stadt (now Chemnitz). They canvassed every home, distributing leaflets with allegations that called Theo's morality into question. The claims were such a skillful blend of truth and lies that it was clear that someone very close to Theo and his family must have provided information to the Stasi. But who? Theo was distraught and angry.

Theo knew full well that his telelphone was bugged and that his mail was read — that was routine under Communism. But where had such specific information come from? Theo discovered that the one youth who he thought was above suspicion and trusted the most was the one who had divulged the information. This was a boy who had lost his mother and whom Theo and his wife had subsequently taken in as a foster child and raised themselves. "He was the one — my Judas, the one I trusted," says Theo. "He was like our child. It was terribly painful when we found out."

The boy, distraught over what he had done, got drunk one night and confided in another friend, who then told Theo. Soon after that, when the boy came to the Lehmanns' house to pick up his guitar, Theo handed it to him and uttered only three short words: "Save your soul." Why did the boy do it? Theo never found out. But today he says, without bitterness, that he has forgiven him.

Besides this betrayal, there were other ways in which Theo was a visible target of discrimination and manipulation by the Communists. None of his three daughters was permitted to study at the university. He was denied permission both to travel outside the country and to publish, privileges that other East German pastors were often granted. Three times he prepared a final manuscript for a book on Christian teaching, and three times the regime blocked publication at the last minute.

Throughout all this, Theo remained unwavering in his commitment. Orders to close the doors of his church did not intimidate him. Smear campaigns had not sullied his integrity. When these methods failed, the

Communists decided to make him an offer they thought he couldn't refuse. They told him they would get visas for him and his entire family if they would be willing to leave the country and go to the West. But Theo turned them down. "My place is here," he said.

Since the fall of the Wall, Theo is able to reach many more in both the East and the West with his music and his preaching — and his books, which he is now permitted to publish. But his enthusiasm for his newfound freedom is qualified. "In some ways, being a pastor under Communism was clearer," he says frankly. "You knew where you stood, and what you were opposing. In a secularized Christian society, that's not the case."

Wilfried Gotter

Teenagers were confronted with critical decisions at an age when resisting the status quo was almost unthinkably hard. They stood at the threshold to the rest of their lives, which could be altered by a single "incorrect" response. Wilfried Gotter of East Germany was confronted with such a decision when he was just fifteen years old.[15] He was summoned to a conference with the school superintendent, members of local government, and Communist party functionaries. Seating Wilfried in a closed room, five men began to wield their verbal tools of persuasion to extract a commitment from him.

Not only did they want him to join the Free German Youth and the German-Soviet Friendship group, but they also wanted him to agree to serve as an officer in the army. Agreeing to do this would mean serving beyond the term of the typical draftee. The school system also pressured all young men like Wilfried to try to get them to agree to an extended stint in the army by making it virtually a prerequisite for advanced study afterward. Many male teenagers

15. This story is based on the author's interview with Wilfried Gotter in Chemnitz on February 28, 1991.

joined the "right" groups, and those with ambition agreed to the extended military service as well, hoping it would be a ticket to better opportunities later.

But Wilfried wanted no part of this kind of deal-making. Since his confirmation, he had become deeply committed to his Christian faith, and he was determined not to carry arms in military service for a regime that was at odds with what he believed. He knew that if he made this declaration he would not be allowed to pursue university studies, and he could only guess at the further consequences. Still, he decided he had to honor his commitment to God. But how to communicate that to a panel of interrogators who were bent on extracting a different commitment from him? What on earth could he say to convince them?

"To sit there as a youngster and defend yourself against five men sitting opposite you who try to overwhelm you and intimidate you with arguments is not so easy. My heart was pounding," Wilfried recalls. At first he had no idea how he would present his case. But then he prayed, and he knew what he would say.

"I was given a word from God," Wilfried says. It was Colossians 2:8: "See to it that no one takes you captive through hollow and deceptive philosophy, which depends on human tradition and the basic principles of this world rather than on Christ."

When Wilfried quoted this verse in his defense, he was surprised to see how disarming the effect was. The men interrogating him had age, rank, and numbers on their side — yet this simple retort from the fifteen-year-old left them stymied. The interview halted, sputtered to an end, and they decided to let him go. They made no more attempts to change his mind.

"In that moment," Wilfried recalls, "I really experienced what it says in the Bible [Luke 12:11-12] — that when you are led before the authorities, you shouldn't be concerned about what you will say."

Through this incident, some of Wilfried's friends also found the courage to resist. Unfortunately, there were just as many others who yielded. Wilfried is not self-congratulatory about his ability to resist. "It was really a gift from God," he explains. "To have such words in such a situation wasn't due to my quick-wittedness or anything — I was only fifteen." And he remains grateful. "These are the practical experiences of faith in the everyday. They have a lasting effect when you experience them and realize that what's in the Bible is true."

Marsha and Vera Borisov

Marsha and Vera Borisov faced their moment of truth when they were interviewed by a commission to determine their eligibility for higher education.[16] They knew they had to answer to a higher power than the commission.

Father Alexander Borisov's twin daughters were on their way to becoming surgeons. Like their father, who had become a Russian Orthodox priest after a career as a biologist specializing in genetics, they had a deep interest in science, and they pursued their studies diligently. They both had excellent grades. When they applied for postgraduate study, they were required to appear before a commission. This body of thirty examiners decided the future of all the students who came before them.

Marsha and Vera each met individually with the commission. In each session each of them was asked why she wasn't a member of *Komsomol.* "Maybe it's because you're a Christian believer?" one of the examining professors ventured probingly.

Both girls had read the Bible since their childhood, and they knew well the passage where Jesus said, "I tell you, everyone who acknowledges me before others, the Son of Man also will acknowledge before the angels of God; but whoever denies me before others will be denied before the angels of God" (Luke 12:8-9, NRSV).

As Marsha stood before the committee of thirty, all of whom were waiting for her answer, she remembered this verse. She imagined the company of heaven looking on at that moment to see

16. This story is based on the author's interview with Alexander Borisov in Moscow on March 10, 1992.

how she would answer the question. She knew what answer she had to give, regardless of what the commission thought. "Yes," she said. "I am a Christian." Interrogated separately, her sister Vera gave the same answer.

"Don't you think your faith will be an obstacle to your future work?" one of the committee members asked Marsha.

"No, on the contrary," Marsha countered. "It will be a help."

"Do you suppose God will make you a professor immediately?" one examiner remarked sarcastically.

The result of the committee's examinations of both girls was predictable: they were rejected. But the committee rejected them in a surreptitious way, to avoid the appearance of blatant discrimination. It required them to take another academic examination — but instead of receiving the high grades they had always deservedly gotten, they both earned Cs. So under the guise of "insufficient academic achievement," they were blocked from further study. When protests came from the university, the committee reluctantly upped the grades to Bs, but that still wasn't enough to get the girls into a postgraduate program.

Under ordinary circumstances, it would not have been possible for the twins to advance in the career they had chosen. But a family friend recommended to the director of a medical institute that he take them on as students, despite the fact that their father was a priest and that they were not members of the *Komsomol*. The director took the suggestion, and the twins were able to pursue their studies in this alternative way.

Although they have not had an easy journey professionally, Marsha and Vera have succeeded, in part because a friend was willing to help them despite the risk involved. And they have persevered with their spiritual integrity intact.

*   *   *

These are just a few of the many stories that could be told about individuals who, in the face of grave consequences, took bold stands for what they believed.

PART II

The Revolutionary Years

© Harald Kirschner

Prologue in Poland

When the electrician with the droopy moustache clambered over the twelve-foot wall to address striking workers in Gdańsk at the Lenin shipyards in August of 1980, there was nothing inevitable about the outcome of the confrontation. Lech Wałęsa and *Solidarność* were to wage a showdown with the Communists that would end just at the brink of Soviet military intervention. It would be the first time in Eastern Europe since the post–World War II agreement at Yalta that a revolt of this magnitude was not put down with Soviet tanks. Poland was the first country to begin breaking free in birth pangs that would last about ten years, a separation process that eventually would be repeated by other countries throughout the Eastern bloc. The character of the Polish breakaway would set the tone for those to follow: it was based on moral precepts, anchored in the church, marked by restraint, and astonishingly free of violence. This was in marked contrast to virtually all the revolutions that had come before it.

The Polish pope, John Paul II, and the Catholic Church were critical in these developments because, in the words of Polish theologian Józef Tischner, "Revolution is an occurrence in the realm of the spirit."[1] On his first pilgrimage to his homeland in 1979, the pope

---

1. Quoted by Timothy Garton Ash in *The Polish Revolution: Solidarność* (London: Granta Books, 1983), p. 292. This book provides an insightful history of the birth and triumph of Solidarity.

articulated the vision of human beings as moral agents with responsibilities linked to freedom, with God-given rights (beyond those conferred by the state). In so doing, he challenged authoritarianism at its deepest roots, not only in Poland, but in the entire Communist empire. He also delivered a simple but powerful message that may have unlocked the fetters of decades of submission: "Be not afraid!"[2] The pope's presence and his message moved the country in a striking way. Since then, many Poles as well as outside observers mark this pilgrimage as the event that galvanized the country with hope for a changed future. It was the first hour of the revolution.

The demands of the striking workers in Gdańsk give evidence that their concerns were more than material. The document they produced was a litany of human rights: workers pled for the right to organize freely, for freedom of speech and freedom of religion, and for the release of political prisoners. By its own definition, Solidarity's vision was a moral one. In *The Polish Revolution*, Timothy Garton Ash records their credo: "What we had in mind was not only bread, butter and sausage but also justice, democracy, truth, legality, human dignity, freedom of convictions and the repair of the republic. All elementary values had been too mistreated [for us] to believe that anything could improve without their rebirth."[3]

The pope and the Catholic Church guided Solidarity by providing the moral precepts for its aspirations and defending its legitimacy, while sometimes reining in the movement when it careened toward confrontation with the Communists. Indeed, faced with possible invasion of the country in December 1980, the church issued a conciliatory communiqué and urged that Solidarity show restraint.

When General Jaruzelski declared a "state of war" a year later on December 13, 1981, he apparently did so under extreme pressure from the Soviet Union.[4] A defecting Polish officer claims that a plan for

2. George Weigel offers a brilliant analysis of the role of faith, the pope, and the Catholic Church in the revolutions of Poland and Czechoslovakia in *The Final Revolution* (New York: Oxford University Press, 1992); the quote is from p. 102. For the impact of the pope in Poland, see pp. 93-102 and 129-36, as well as Ash's *Polish Revolution*, pp. 31-33.

3. Quoted by Timothy Garton Ash in *The Polish Revolution*, p. 232.

4. Based on the author's interview with General Jaruzelski in Warsaw on April 8, 1990.

martial law began as early as August 1980, but that for the next year Jaruzelski sought a political rather than a military solution; reportedly the military alternative was implemented in late October 1981.[5] Today Jaruzelski says that he "deeply regrets" his decision to impose martial law. If he had to make the same decision again, he claims, "I'd rather shoot myself in the head." Yet, he says, "I still believe I couldn't have acted any other way."[6]

Of the 50,000 Solidarity activists, it is not known how many were imprisoned. By January of 1982, the number was reportedly down to 5,000. But at this juncture the struggle was far from over, and it was to claim more lives. Between December 13, 1981, and March 1985, 78 people reportedly died at the hands of the Polish police and secret service.[7] Thousands more in the movement were jailed, beaten, threatened, and intimidated. Among the victims was Father Jerzy Popiełuszko. On October 19, 1984, he was stopped in his car by state security officials, who beat him to death and dumped his bound body into the Vistula River.

An attempted murder may also be linked to the Communists' attempt to maintain their power in the Eastern bloc. When Mehmet Ali Agca attempted to kill Pope John Paul II on May 13, 1981, he presumably did so under the orders of Bulgarian intelligence. It is hard to believe that the Bulgarians would have dared order the assassination on their own. As George Weigel concludes,

> If John Paul was indeed the key to the rise of Solidarity, and if Solidarity challenged the post-Yalta order in Poland, and if Poland was *the* domino in the Yalta imperial system, then Agca's assassination attempt in St. Peter's Square does look like an attempt to decapitate the leadership of the social and political resistance within Poland.[8]

What is striking about the reporting on Poland's revolution and on Solidarity both then and since is that it has focused almost ex-

---

5. Col. Ryszard Kukliński worked for U.S. intelligence and defected to the U.S. in November 1981; he is cited by Ash in *The Polish Revolution*, pp. 357-58.

6. "Jaruzelski Rethinks," *International Herald Tribune*, March 6-7, 1993, p. 6.

7. Ash, *The Polish Revolution*, p. 360.

8. Weigel, *The Final Revolution*, p. 144.

clusively on the economic and political aspects of the movement, to the exclusion of those of morality and faith. These aspects were central. While not all Solidarity members shared Wałęsa's staunch Catholic faith, they did share an understanding of their movement as one of moral revolution. It is worth noting that a number of Solidarity leaders who went through extremely trying times during the birth of the movement emerged in later years as political leaders. Lech Wałęsa and Tadeusz Mazowiecki are the two best known, but there were scores of others. They spoke with authority because of their integrity, and later were granted power when the movement became politically significant. This was a process that was to repeat itself throughout the Eastern bloc in the coming years.

In the conflict with Communism in Poland, a certain kind of person was forged, morally and spiritually. Wałęsa put it this way:

> If you choose the example of what we Poles have in our pockets and in our shops, then . . . communism has done very little for us. But if you choose the example of what is in our souls, I answer that communism has done very much for us. In fact our souls contain exactly the opposite of what they wanted. They wanted us not to believe in God, and our churches are full. They wanted us to be materialistic and incapable of sacrifice: we are anti-materialistic and capable of sacrifice. They wanted us to be afraid of the tanks, of the guns, and instead we don't fear them at all.[9]

Over a decade, that fearlessness was to succeed in breaking Poland free of Communist domination in a gradual, restrained, and, in the end, largely peaceful transfer of power. It was the first great contraction in the birth of a new Europe.

---

9. Wałęsa, quoted by Ash in *The Polish Revolution,* pp. 291-92.

CHAPTER 6

Glass Houses, Glasnost, and Gorbachev

When Mikhail Gorbachev was elected General Secretary of the Communist Party of the Soviet Union in March 1985, he took the helm of a rudderless ship. Between 1982 and 1985, the Soviet Union had four leaders, three of whom died. Following the death of Leonid Brezhnev, the short tenures of Yuri Andropov and Konstantin Chernenko made it clear that a younger and more flexible man was needed to try to overhaul the Soviet system, which was creaking in deterioration. According to Gorbachev's own description in *Perestroika*, the Soviet Union was in dire straits:

> The country began to lose momentum. Economic failures became more frequent. Difficulties began to accumulate and deteriorate, and unresolved problems to multiply. Elements of what we call stagnation and other phenomena alien to socialism began to appear in the life of society. A kind of "braking mechanism" affecting social and economic development formed.[1]

Since the 1970s, economic growth had evaporated, national income-growth rates had declined by more than half, production quality had been lagging, and personal consumption had dropped to Third World levels. A former major supplier of steel, raw materials,

1. Gorbachev, *Perestroika* (New York: Harper & Row, 1987), pp. 18-19.

fuel, energy, and grain had shortfalls due to inefficiency, mismanagement, and waste.

Gorbachev introduced *perestroika,* or restructuring, as "a policy of accelerating the country's social and economic progress and renewing all spheres of life."[2] Two aspects of that change were to be fostered by *glasnost,* or openness, and *demokratizatsia, or* democratization. But he also made it clear that what he envisioned did not mean moving away from socialism: "There is the view that [*perestroika*] has been necessitated by the disastrous state of the Soviet economy and that it signifies disenchantment with socialism and a crisis for its ideals and ultimate goals. Nothing could be further from the truth." Gorbachev concluded that "the potential of socialism had been underutilized."[3] He did not envision replacing it with a different system. As dissident Vladimir Bukovsky put it, "He wants to save it, together with his skin."

Gorbachev's economic program was greeted with enthusiasm, although he had rejected a faster-track 500-day plan. Gorbachev introduced certain kinds of privatization by selling state properties, abolishing many price controls, and permitting greater decentralization to republics. But he still balked at allowing genuine private property and an open market system. Despite his attempts at change, things did not get better. Several years into his restructuring efforts, *The Economist* tartly observed that the Soviet economy "has not merely stood still, it has moved briskly backwards."[4]

According to Alexander Zaichenko, who was a senior economist at the Soviet Union's Institute of U.S. and Canadian Studies and later an economic advisor to Gorbachev's Council of Ministers, Gorbachev found himself forced to improvise but scarcely able to. "The construction of the economy was as rigid as a house made of glass. If you tried to rebuild it, it would shatter," Zaichenko claimed. The system "did not evolve organically, but was constructed by force, and it could only remain with force." Gorbachev's first efforts proved to

2. Gorbachev, *Perestroika,* updated ed. (New York: Harper & Row, 1988), p. xii.
3. Gorbachev, *Perestroika,* 1987 ed., p. 10.
4. "Russia Meets the Market," *The Economist,* September 15, 1990, p. 13.

be "very ineffective," in Zaichenko's appraisal. "He wanted to reform step by step. It was like a game of giving up. He was brave enough to start this reformation, but he had no plan to reform [the country] completely to a democratic society. He wanted to reshuffle it, and make it 'socialism with a human face.' I don't think he had a plan. [He made] desperate attempts to remold the Soviet Union according to the situation."[5]

Along with two other analysts, Zaichenko prepared a report in 1986 that may have had an impact on Gorbachev's strategy. The three examined the effect of the arms race on the Soviet economy, claiming that the U.S. government under President Ronald Reagan planned to isolate and financially strap the Soviet Union by opening a new frontier in the arms race with the Strategic Defense Initiative, or SDI. Competing with SDI would impose such a massive financial burden on the Soviet Union that it would be unable to productively restructure itself, either economically or technologically, Zaichenko concluded.

The Pershing missiles had been stationed in Western Europe in response to the Soviet SS-20s. In his report, Zaichenko claimed that the Soviet Union was already spending 20 percent of its GNP on military materials and research; on the other hand, the U.S. was spending only about 6 percent of its GNP, and Europe, 3 to 4 percent. Even if the Soviet Union could hold its military expenditures to 20 percent, further decline of its economy was inevitable because of this heavy financial burden. And if the Soviets tried to compete with SDI, they would be ruined economically by the year 2000. According to Zaichenko, the problem with SDI was clear: "The military superiority of the U.S. and their allies would be so great . . . that there would be no way out but to follow their ultimatum."

Zaichenko explains that he and his colleagues chose their language carefully. "In order to be accepted from the Kremlin side, this idea had to be [presented] as a pre-designed plan from Americans to ruin the Soviet economy," he says. "We did it purposefully to

<hr>

5. These comments and the subsequent profile are drawn from the author's interview with Alexander Zaichenko in Moscow on March 11, 1992.

frighten our authorities." Did he personally believe there was such a plan? "Not necessarily. There were some centers, like the Heritage Foundation, which had offered such ideas. But there were phrases from Reagan which indicated his thinking, like 'We will see communism on the ash-heap of history.'" The report documented that likelihood for Mikhail Gorbachev.

Gorbachev reacted quickly. Zaichenko says that Gorbachev called his top advisors and told them in so many words, "We must put an end to the Cold War and especially the arms race. There is no way out." With a brave face, Gorbachev put a different spin on the policy change when he later explained it to the outside world. As he wrote in *Perestroika*, "Some people say that the ambitious goals set forth by the policy of perestroika in our country have prompted the peace proposals we have lately made in the international arena. This is an oversimplification. . . . We in the Soviet leadership have come to the conclusion — and are reiterating it — that there is a need for new political thinking. Furthermore, Soviet leaders are vigorously seeking to translate this new thinking into action, primarily in the field of disarmament."[6]

Gorbachev: Recognizing the Importance of Morality

Gorbachev had his hands full. With whole segments of the economy already heaving and crashing, he desperately needed a way to jumpstart the country. Other analysts have dealt with the ramifications of Gorbachev's political and economic policy in great detail. For that reason, this book will not. But one aspect of the changes he introduced has been largely overlooked: the human aspect. He concluded that what was necessary was a policy that not only was ideologically correct but also took human motivation and morality into account. As he wrote in *Perestroika*,

> Unless we activate the human factor, that is, unless we take into consideration the diverse interests of people, work collectives, pub-

6. Gorbachev, *Perestroika*, 1987 ed., pp. 11-12.

lic bodies, and various social groups, unless we rely on them, and draw them into active, constructive endeavor, it will be impossible for us to accomplish any of the tasks set, or to change the situation in the country.[7]

What he recognized was that the malaise in his country was not only economic but also moral. Indeed, in *Perestroika* he wrote that the erosion of moral values was one of the key problems in the Soviet Union, and he called for renewal: "Our main job is to lift the individual spiritually, respecting his inner world and giving him moral strength."[8]

Gorbachev has said that he values the inner spiritual world of individuals. That may explain why he was willing to reverse the policy of the previous regimes and open the door for dialogue with others who he knew had moral strength. It was at his initiative that Christians were invited to become partners in *perestroika*. It is one of the least-known aspects of his plan.[9]

No doubt Gorbachev's background provides at least a partial explanation for his willingness to open the doors to Christians. He grew up in the 1930s in the Stavropol region of southern Russia, the son of a tractor driver wounded in the war. His mother was a devout Russian Orthodox believer, and he was baptized as an infant. His grandparents on his father's side are said to have hidden icons behind pictures of Lenin and Stalin.[10] Another of his relatives was an active Baptist. As a child, he probably attended church and was told about religious persecution.[11]

His interest in the spiritual welfare of the Russian people may have been partly fueled by pragmatism. From his exposure to this community of Christians in his childhood, he knew that they could

7. Gorbachev, *Perestroika*, 1988 ed., p. 15.

8. Ibid., p. xii.

9. Bourdeaux, *Gorbachev, Glasnost and the Gospel* (London: Hodder & Stoughton, 1990), pp. 40-41. This book gives a detailed and thoroughly researched account of the ways in which Gorbachev's *glasnost* affected the Christian churches.

10. Kent Hill, *The Soviet Union on the Brink: An Inside Look at Christianity and Glasnost* (Portland, Ore.: Multnomah Press, 1991), p. 400.

11. Bourdeaux, *Gorbachev, Glastnost and the Gospel*, pp. 23-24.

be a potent element in the workforce. Reliable workers who didn't steal or come to work drunk were sorely needed to make *perestroika* work. Gorbachev hoped that he could harness their energy to help implement his plans for restructuring from the grass-roots level upward. There were tens of millions of unmobilized religious people — perhaps as many as 100 million, or a third of the population, including the Muslims — working at the lowest levels of the economy. Michael Bourdeaux, author of *Gorbachev, Glasnost and the Gospel,* explains the potential these believers represented — and what Gorbachev realized he needed to do in order to tap it:

> If challenged in the right way, Mr. Gorbachev must have reasoned, could they not be persuaded to move *perestroika* in at the bottom rung and start reforms at the local level, while above people still deliberated or even actively resisted?
>
> If this was to happen, serious and genuine reforms in favor of religious liberty must come first.[12]

More recent interviews with Christians have confirmed Gorbachev's openness to people of faith — something he himself has expressed in a way that reveals both his frankness and his shrewdness:

> Let me be honest with you — I am an atheist. Even so, I have profound respect for your beliefs. This time, more than ever before, we need support from our partners, and I value solidarity with religion.
>
> But I must say, for a long time I have drawn comfort from the Bible. Ignoring religious experience has meant great losses for society. And I must acknowledge that Christians are doing much better than our political leaders on the important questions facing us. We welcome your help, especially when it is accompanied by deeds.[13]

12. Ibid., p. 40.

13. Quoted by Philip Yancey in "Praying with the KGB," *Christianity Today,* January 13, 1992, p. 19.

Gorbachev knew he needed the help of Christians to make the economy work. He also knew that he needed the support of the West to stay in power — and getting that support meant changing the harsh treatment of dissenters and believers of all denominations in Russia, including Jews and Christians. Possibly with that as one motive, Gorbachev had already shown his willingness to deal more leniently with prisoners of conscience, having released human rights activists, including Anatoli Sharansky. He also personally called dissident Andrei Sakharov, who was in exile in Gorky, and permitted him to return to Moscow.

Under Gorbachev, the fetters on the Christian church were also being slowly undone. Piecemeal changes in legislation during the late 1980s opened up new opportunities for Christians to meet, to speak, and to do charitable works. Gorbachev was aware of the practical advantages of such changes. During the crisis in Chernobyl, when radioactive contamination spewed across the countryside from the disabled nuclear reactor, Christians had been willing to set up hospitals to care for the victims. This incident showed him that it could be beneficial to loosen the restrictions on Christians.

This was an abrupt turnabout. According to the *Moscow News*, between 1958 and 1988, a total of 3,000 Christians had been sent to labor camps or psychiatric institutions. But under the new policy, most of them were to be freed. Among others, Gorbachev chose to permit the release of Irina Ratushinskaya, the young Christian poet, just before the 1986 Reykjavík summit. It was a move calculated to generate maximum coverage of the gesture, an apparent bid to validate Gorbachev's new image of tolerance.

~

Protest in Poetry: Irina Ratushinskaya

Irina Ratushinskaya's critical survey of the Russian landscape and her explicit Christian convictions produced passionate verse that garnered both the attention and the wrath of the Soviet regime. The result was that she was convicted of "anti-Soviet agitation and propaganda." In March 1983, on her twenty-ninth birthday, she was sentenced to seven years in a prison camp and five years in exile for the poetry she had written.

Irina is a slender, intense woman with sweet features, a sparkling sense of humor, and an iron will. Born in 1954, a child of Polish gentry who escaped Soviet occupation of their country, she was raised an atheist but became a Christian. She was trained as a teacher of mathematics and physics, but she had been writing poetry secretly since her childhood, and in her twenties she began to write in earnest. She married Igor Gerashchenko, the human rights activist, who, like her, had become a believer despite an atheistic upbringing. Together they wrote to Soviet authorities to protest the exile of Andrei Sakharov. This, coupled with their petition to emigrate, began a round of interrogations and repression in 1980. The KGB insisted that Irina stop writing poetry. She refused; the hand-typed copies of her poems kept making the rounds among friends and admirers. Some poems were even smuggled out of the country and published. This helped seal her fate, as her husband explained: "If literary works circulate in *samizdat* and are published abroad, their author already has one foot in prison. . . . We were well aware, of course, how the Soviet regime defends itself against its own citizens. By then we had read *The Gulag Archipelago*."* Because Irina had read Solzhenitsyn, she knew what to expect. She recalled his admonition: "Never fear them, never trust them, never ask them for anything." She was arrested on September 17, 1982.

One of her friends, Ilya Nykin, had this to say about her arrest. "Irina was not a political activist. She didn't choose poetry for a weapon of struggle — whatever that means. She was just too talented. . . . And she wouldn't relinquish her right to honesty even when writing about her country. . . . Her offense was considered criminal rather than political, for of course there can be no political offenders in the land of victorious socialism."** Another friend made this observation: "What

*Gerashchenko, "About the Arrest of Irina Ratushinskaya," in *No, I'm Not Afraid* (Newcastle upon Tyne: Bloodaxe Books, 1986), p. 20. This book provides factual information on Ratushinskaya as well as her books, *Grey Is the Colour of Hope* (London: Hodder & Stoughton, 1989) and *In the Beginning* (London: Hodder & Stoughton, 1990).

**"Irina Ratushinskaya: A Memoir by Ilya Nykin," in *No, I'm Not Afraid*, pp. 24-25.

can one say about a government that is forced to kill [or imprison] poets in order to maintain law and order? Why is our poetry time and time again subject to such frenzied attacks? A true poet can not lie. To be silent, or to be reluctant to see the world in which one lives in its true colors — that is also a lie! The calling of a poet is to speak the truth."***

Shortly after she was imprisoned, Irina went on a hunger strike and suffered a concussion while she was being force fed. In the winter of 1983-84, she spent 39 days in an unheated punishment cell and suffered pneumonia as a result. Over time she suffered ailments of the heart, liver, and kidneys, and was striken by ovaritis, angina, and severe bronchitis. In the prison where she was held, 135 women prisoners died, 34 by suicide. When she was transferred to another prison, Irina suffered another concussion, and she was beaten unconscious by prison wards, who then stripped her and dragged her down a corridor, leaving her in a heap in her cell. She was beaten repeatedly, and in 1985 she engaged in another hunger strike to protest the beatings and to demand that her cell be heated. In 1986 she was taken to the KGB for "reeducation" and was told that she must sign a statement admitting her "guilt." She refused.

Despite her suffering, Irina continued to write, and her letters and copies of her poems were smuggled out of the prison. They reached the West sometimes on cassette, sometimes as memorized works. Keston College in England passed along information on her failing health, and when Dick Rodgers, an Anglican minister, heard about her trouble, he took action. He helped publicize her plight by spending Lent of 1983 in a cage, living in the same conditions she did and eating only the kind of food she would get. This dramatization may have saved her life. It garnered international attention just before the Reykjavík summit in 1986. Gorbachev seemed determined to present to the world a Soviet Union with a different face, and with his intervention, Irina Ratushinskaya was released on the eve of the summit. She was then permitted to emigrate with her husband to England.

~

***"The Calling of a Poet Is to Speak the Truth," in ibid., p. 27.

In 1988 it was opportune for Gorbachev to make a further gesture. That year the celebration of the millennium of Christianity in Russia was being planned. In April the Russian Orthodox patriarch Pimen met with Gorbachev — a landmark meeting of the estranged church and state. Although the formal request for the meeting came from the Russian Orthodox Church, reports of the meeting indicate that Gorbachev set the agenda. This occasion provided Gorbachev with an opportunity to make concrete promises for the celebration, including the return of churches, the reopening of monasteries, and the implementing of a new law on freedom of conscience. Presumably he hoped to gain the Christians' support for *perestroika* in return.[14]

Gorbachev may have unleashed more than he bargained for. Millions watched when President Reagan visited the magnificently restored Danilov Monastery and spoke of embracing religious liberty. The Monastery of the Caves in Kiev was also reopened in a symbolic act reversing the campaign to eradicate religion. Christian leaders from throughout the world descended on the Soviet Union for the millennium, and across the country church bells pealed and jubilee concerts celebrated old truths and new freedoms. The sweeping changes of a new era were illustrated in a festival concert attended by Raisa Gorbachev and Andrei Gromyko: seven choirs and six orchestras presented alternating secular and Christian performances. Surprised Soviet citizens found the airwaves of television and radio full of a message that had been banned for as long as they could remember.[15]

Unofficial programs celebrating the millennium proliferated. The few Westerners who joined the Christian dissidents, former prisoners, and representatives of the catacomb Orthodox Church, the outlawed Ukrainian Catholic Church, and the persecuted Pentecostal Church were able to participate in memorable events that brought the word "ecumenism" to life. As the official delegations were entertained in the state palaces, hundreds of unofficial partic-

14. Bourdeaux, *Gorbachev, Glasnost and the Gospel*, pp. 43-45.
15. Ibid., pp. 45-46, 49, 61, 63.

ipants, including clandestinely ordained and practicing bishops in full regalia, crammed into upstairs Moscow apartments. Alexander Ogorodnikov and a group of others organized the unofficial jubilee committee in January 1988. They called for "the release of all prisoners of conscience, the abolition of Stalin's laws on religion, the reopening of the Monastery of the Caves in Kiev. . . , the right to hold a Christian seminar during the Millennium celebrations, putting on a photographic exhibition to mark the darker side of the church's history, and the canonization of modern martyrs." Astonishingly, all of their requests except the last one were granted.[16]

On June 18, thousands of believers, primarily Baptists from all over the Soviet Union, converged on Kiev to celebrate the millennium at the site where Prince Vladimir had been baptized in the year 988. There were many more celebrants than the main Baptist church could hold, so believers who were inside were asked to go outside so that nonbelievers could come in. In the spontaneous worship that followed both inside and out, dozens of participants converted. Five days later, thousands more gathered in an assembly that shouted down the policemen who tried to end it. Marching in a column to the center of the city, they came to a halt at the statue of Lenin, where they prayed until late into the night. These experiences had great spiritual power. As Michael Bourdeaux observed, "Not a few of those present who were familiar with the Acts of the Apostles felt that they were witnessing a twentieth-century recreation of those biblical events."[17]

In August, thousands assembled in Moldavia for eight days of celebrations. Crowds packed into a rented movie theater to hear the evangelist Iosif Bondarenko, a pastor from Riga who had been pursued by the authorities for almost thirty years. In Belorussia, only a fraction of the 10,000 people who came to hear the American Christian radio broadcaster Earl Poysti could get into the service. During this highly charged summer, hundreds were converted to Christ, most of them young people. Something powerful had been unloosed.[18]

16. Ibid., pp. 92-93, 91.
17. Ibid., pp. 111-12.
18. Ibid., pp. 112-13.

An Unusual Advisor: Alexander Zaichenko

People within Gorbachev's regime were affected as well. While it was axiomatic that a member of the Communist party could not be a Christian, there were key people who became believers later, once they held positions of influence. They had tremendous potential to be instruments of change; at the same time, their careers were at risk.

Alexander Zaichenko, the economic advisor to Gorbachev who authored the report on the SDI, is one example. His personal story is one of a Russian Nicodemus who was searching for truth, but didn't dare to do it in the daylight.

It had begun years earlier when Alexander was a philosophy student. He remembers the day in class that he posed the question "What is the sense of human life?" The Marxist professor asked Alexander to stand up. "Look, students," he said. "Here is an example of an incorrect question. It is false because [Alexander] made the idealist assumption that life must make some sense. No Soviet student should pose such a question."

Still, Alexander continued to search for an answer, scouring the libraries for pre-Revolution works. He got excellent grades in the history of "scientific atheism" because he was sincerely interested in finding out what it meant. He turned to the philosophical works of the eighteenth century — treatises by Hegel, Nietzsche, and Schopenhauer — in search of an "absolute spirit." In 1979 a friend gave Alexander a Bible that had been smuggled in from the United States. He was told to begin with the New Testament, which he did. By the time he had reached the fifth chapter of Matthew, he was sure that he had found the book with the answers he was seeking. To his analytical mind, Scripture rang true.

He began to relate the Christian teaching of Scripture to the behavior of the Baptists he had seen as a youngster in his grandmother's village. They had been diligent, hard-working people. Although he was unable to obtain books about religion — they were classified — he discovered that if he read between the lines of the publications of the Institute of Scientific Atheism, he could glean a great deal of factual material about Christians. Among other things, demographic studies documented that Protestants were more disciplined and economically productive than others.

It took Alexander seven years to get to a church. During that time, although he was not a member of the Communist party, he had become a senior research fellow at the Institute of U.S. and Canadian Studies — so he knew that attending a church would mean risking his career. He had found out that there was a Baptist church somewhere in Moscow by reading an atheist journal. Using his title as a front, he called the Intourist Agency, which dealt with foreign tourists, as if to ask for the address for a visiting delegation of prominent Americans. After a consultation, they gave it to him. The street on which the church was located was not on the official map of Moscow. Like a sleuth, Alexander searched the city systematically, driving in increasingly smaller concentric circles until he found it. When he went in, he took a seat on the last bench in the back.

After discreetly attending the church for half a year, Alexander sought out one of the pastors and explained his desire to confess and to make a commitment. He also told the pastor about his work. The two men knelt together and prayed.

"It is very good that you have come," began the pastor. Then he asked point blank, "Are you a Communist?"

"No," Alexander answered, "I'm not a Communist."

"But then why are you working at the Institute?" the pastor asked — but then softened his response. "Even if you are a Communist, the Lord will forgive you."

Alexander assured the pastor that he really wasn't a member of the Communist party, despite the position he held. The pastor warned Alexander that he should remain inconspicuous in church because it had been infiltrated by KGB agents. If they were to find out who Alexander was, he could be fired. "And there is no need for you to make such a sacrifice," the pastor explained. "Do not be open." Alexander followed his advice.

A year later, Alexander wanted to be baptized in the Moscow church, but the pastor suggested that he go to the church in Leningrad instead. He explained that Alexander's name would be put on the officially registered list of baptismal candidates, which would ultimately end up in KGB hands. If his baptism were to be known about in Moscow, his job would be at great risk. In the end, Alexander decided to be baptized secretly at home. Until recently, he and his wife had lived with their two small children in a one-room apartment, sharing a kitchen and bathroom facilities with four other families, which was common. But in 1986 they had finally received an apartment of their own. Since the family had newfound privacy, Alexander and his wife decided to be baptized in their bathtub. He muffled the doors to the apartment with blankets to prevent anyone from hearing the secret ceremony.

Alexander was a clandestine Christian until 1989. In September of that year he became an economic advisor to Gorbachev's Council of Ministers, the first non-Communist to be put in such a position. What they didn't know about him was an even bigger surprise. The news of his faith was broken in an unexpected way: on television in 1990, when Alexander was interviewed as an author.

Before the show went on the air, he and the host had reviewed the questions he was going to be asked. But during the interview, which was live, the host asked a question that hadn't been on the list: "Are you a Christian?"

Somewhat taken aback, Alexander hesitated for a moment. The cameras were rolling, and viewers across the nation waited for his answer.

"Yes, I am," he said deliberately.

"Aren't you afraid that you'll be fired from your job?" queried the host. Alexander said no, perhaps with more bravado than conviction.

The host asked Alexander what role he as a Christian played with the Council of Ministers, where he was on the staff of the committee for economic reforms. He answered that he believed economic reform wouldn't be possible unless a significant portion of the population was guided by Christian morality and ethics.

His colleagues at the Council of Ministers seemed not to know how to respond to the revelation. "Are you really a Christian?" they asked him afterward. "They expected me to be embarrassed," he says now. But soon they began coming to Alexander's office one at a time, closing the door and asking if he could get a Bible for them. In the next three weeks, he distributed thirty Bibles to high-level consultants working for the Council of Ministers.

Since then, Alexander Zaichenko has founded the Association of Christian Businessmen. He is convinced that economic growth can best be fostered in a society with a moral foundation built on its members' personal relationship with Christ. Others who share the same belief have joined him.

A Man Transformed: Konstantin Kharchev

One of the key figures in Gorbachev's regime responsible for making decisions about religious matters underwent a fascinating change himself. Just months before Gorbachev came to power, Chernenko had appointed Konstantin Kharchev chairman of the Council for Religious Affairs. Raised in an orphanage in Gorky, he had risen through the ranks to become first a local party secretary and then a Soviet ambassador, a party member with credentials of loyalty. In the early years of his tenure, he was a brusque defender of the status quo — in fact, he seemed personally hostile toward religion. Asked if he preferred dealing with the Protestant or the Russian Orthodox Church, he replied, "The only thing I'd prefer would be not to have to deal with Christians at all."[19] Oddly enough, he would become the man who would open the door to their freedoms.

By 1988, Kharchev was sending mixed signals. Sometimes he encouraged Christians to ignore the legal restrictions on teaching children and doing charitable works; at other times he blustered at those pointing out abuses against Christians. In that same year, he acknowledged that over the last twelve months he had received 3,000 complaints from believers, most begging for churches to be reopened. Although he bristled at questioning from Westerners who monitored the status of prisoners of conscience in the Soviet Union, he agreed to talk with them.[20]

19. Quoted by Hill in *The Soviet Union on the Brink*, p. 241.
20. Bourdeaux, *Gorbachev, Glasnost and the Gospel*, pp. 74-79.

In less than two years, his stance toward the church changed remarkably. In March 1988 he gave a speech to the teachers of the Higher Party School in Moscow, and according to notes made of the speech that were smuggled out of the country, he admitted that seventy years of trying to eliminate the church had failed: "The Church has not only survived, but has begun to experience a revival. And questions arise. Which is better for the Party? Someone who believes in God, someone who believes in nothing, or someone who believes in both God and Communism? I think we must choose the lesser of two evils." Kharchev concluded that the Russian Orthodox Church had been successfully controlled, the Catholic and Protestant churches less so. He was convinced that since religion could not at present be eliminated, it should be co-opted by the government and put to good use.[21]

Only several months later he was making very different comments that surprised many. In December 1988, in a public dialogue printed in the pages of *Ogonyok,* Kharchev was interviewed by the journalist Alexander Nezhny. Kharchev declared that he supported religious liberty and advocated a lesser role for the Council for Religious Affairs. (Later he suggested abolishing it altogether.) He said that the 1929 law on religion should be revised, and that the state printing presses should be producing theological works. Astonishingly, he also claimed that the registration of churches should be abandoned. When asked about the myriad believers traveling to Moscow to ask that closed churches be opened, Kharchev took an unexpectedly open slap at his superiors, saying that "an indifferent executive, a cold functionary" might refuse their requests. "There's no justice," he sniped; "don't look for it." He did, however, partially vindicate himself, claiming that during that year his office had reversed 83 decisions by local authorities who had refused to reopen churches.[22]

In March 1989 he made an even bolder statement. Clearly crossing over the line of *glasnost,* Kharchev told an Italian journalist, "The state must have nothing to do with religious belief, nor with atheism, and propaganda of the latter must not be financed by the

21. Hill, *The Soviet Union on the Brink,* p. 241.
22. Bourdeaux, *Gorbachev, Glasnost and the Gospel,* p. 79.

state budget."[23] Kharchev criticized not just the state but the church. He charged that the Russian Orthodox clergy were slow to implement *perestroika* and were financially corrupt.

When Kharchev said that it was time to start publishing audited accounts of the church's financial records, he apparently went too far. Church leaders struck back, urging his removal. Twice that year, in fact, Kharchev had been summoned by Vadim Medvedev, then a member of the politburo, and told to resign. Medvedev told him that all the highest officials of the Russian Orthodox Church had complained about him to the leaders of the Supreme Soviet. Party ideologues and the KGB had had their own reasons for wanting him fired, because his intervention in church affairs stymied their intentions. The handwriting was on the wall, and in May of 1989, Kharchev was sacked as chairman of the Council for Religious Affairs.

Although one can only speculate about what prompted the decision to terminate Kharchev's career, the speed at which Kharchev experienced a change of heart may have outstripped that of the old Communist guard and those in the church they still controlled.

A Determined Evangelist: Peter Sautov

As new opportunities opened up during the final days of Communism, the church ranks were divided on how to respond. Before the fall of the regime, Peter Sautov was one of the first to seek dialogue with the Communists. He had been imprisoned by them twice, the first time for his participation in an unregistered congregation, the second time for printing *samizdat* documentation of persecution. Despite that, Sautov took to the streets with his Christian message, preaching on Moscow's Arbat in 1987. The increasing crowds he drew proved that the time was ripe to open an evangelization center — so Sautov founded one. He

---

23. Quoted by Hill in *The Soviet Union on the Brink*, p. 243.

organized showings of a film on the life of Jesus, taking it to the police, members of Moscow's government, and the cadre of trainees for the *nomenklatura*, the party's ruling elite. The response of his Baptist congregation was to excommunicate him in 1989; they accused him of having ties to the Communists. "It was a bitter time for me," he admits. "As a believer I have been taught that I should be obedient to the church. But . . . God encouraged me to evangelize. It was a great conflict."*

New Freedoms, Old Violence

After the seminal changes in the late 1980s, a transforming wave swept swiftly over the Soviet Union. In 1990 a new law on freedom of conscience was passed, and there were numerous other changes as well. The emigration process for victims of religious persecution of all communions, including Jews, was sped up. Numerous political and religious prisoners were released. Christians were permitted to work in psychiatric hospitals and nursing homes to offer sorely needed care. Churches were reopened in waves. Mandatory instruction in atheism in the schools was abolished, and Christian instruction in the churches was permitted.

But there was a darker side to this wave of change. Harassment of believers continued well into 1989, along with confiscation of Christian literature. Worship services were broken up with force; tents and buildings used for meetings were bulldozed; hired thugs broke into Christian camps for children. Unexplained deaths and beatings continued among Christian activists. Human rights activist Sergei Savchenko was struck and killed by a car in a suspicious accident in October 1989. An advocate of religious and political

* Drawn from the author's interview with Peter Sautov in Moscow on March 19, 1992

freedom, he had championed the causes in Russia, Lithuania, and Latvia. Between the time he was struck and the time his death was announced, his entire photo archive of desecrated churches was stolen, circumstantial evidence of foul play. Another human rights activist, Merab Kostava, a Georgian Orthodox believer, was killed just ten days earlier than Savchenko in another suspicious car accident in Georgia. He had received death threats for several months, the last one on the day before he died. In February 1986, Father Juozas Zdebskis, a Lithuanian Catholic priest, had been killed in another car "accident." The founder of the Catholic Committee for Defense of Believers' Rights, Zdebskis had been threatened by the KGB before. According to the *Chronicle of the Lithuanian Catholic Church,* the collision that took his life was "a carefully planned and executed act of violence."[24]

And the list goes on. Estonian Lutheran pastor Harald Meri, who investigated the Soviet deportation of Estonians to Siberia, was reported missing when his house was destroyed by arson on April 5, 1990. When his body was discovered later in the month, it was evident that he had been severely tortured. The church charges that he was buried alive. Armands Arkentins, a young Latvian pastor, was killed in a car accident near Riga. The autopsy revealed multiple stab wounds in his back and evidence of repeated blows to his head with a metal rod. The ID card of a KGB officer, who was hospitalized with a concussion and abrasions shortly thereafter, was found in the car. Father Ivan Kupts, a Russian Orthodox priest from the Ukraine, was murdered in November 1990. Father Alexander Men was murdered on September 9, 1990, not far from Moscow.[25]

The Baltic States and the Ukraine Catch Fire

During the 1980s, resistance to the Communists coalesced throughout the Eastern bloc. The churches provided a focal point for this resis-

24. Hill, ibid., pp. 331-32.
25. Ibid.

tance, allowing people a place in which to distance themselves from the regime. In some cases they trod a thin line between religious and national interests. What had begun in Poland and Czechoslovakia was not limited to their boundaries. A revolution in thinking had its genesis in morality, and leaders who articulated the need for truth — many of whom were Christians — sparked it. Encouraged by the new freedoms permitted under Gorbachev, movements of resistance flamed to life throughout the Soviet Union and its satellite states.

Latvia is one example, although lesser known because the demonstrations in East Germany, Poland, and Czechoslovakia received better coverage in the West. On November 19, 1989, half a million people, almost a fifth of the country's population, took to the streets of Riga in Latvia to celebrate "Independence Day." In a way, it had grown out of what had begun as a small religious incident.

The conflict began when an energetic theological student, Maris Ludviks, was blocked from ordination by the Council for Religious Affairs. When a Lutheran bishop in Lithuania ordained him in 1985 anyway, the conflict intensified. In January 1987 a Latvian newspaper published an attack on Ludviks so damaging that a group of five clergy, led by pastor Modris Plate, went to the newspaper to demand that they withdraw the calumny.[26]

Plate was attacked next. A lecturer at the seminary with a congregation that had doubled under his leadership, Plate was already persona non grata with the Council for Religious Affairs. His support for Ludviks gave the authorities a reason to dismiss him, but they leaned on the archbishop to carry out the deed. This provoked a group of nineteen clergy to draw up a petition in Plate's defense. Plate was dismissed, but his parishioners continued to support him, and he continued serving them. This open support for him made the authorities unsure what to do. The Council for Religious Affairs offered to back down if Plate would drop his support of Ludviks.

Plate responded with deeds, not words. With fourteen other pastors, he founded Rebirth and Renewal, a group whose stated purpose was to "defend openly the right of Latvians to lead a Chris-

---

26. Bourdeaux, *Gorbachev, Glasnost and the Gospel,* pp. 152-53.

tian life." It was a moral movement more than a political one. Group members worked to implement a range of faith-based goals: an alternative to military service, religious instruction for children, legal rights for the church, the production of more religious literature and radio and TV programs, and the right of believers to work in hospitals and nursing homes.[27] In response, the archbishop banned him from the seminary. Students and lecturers there in turn staged a protest, forcing suspension of all teaching. Lutheran pressure from West Germany and the United States seems to have influenced Plate's being reinstated in January 1988. Ludviks, the young man over whom the whole affair had started, had since emigrated, but the spark of resistance had ignited something far broader and deeper.

Juris Rubenis took the stage next, holding services with Plate in Riga's Lutheran Cathedral, which had not been used for religious purposes in thirty years. Television and radio carried the message, the first such transmissions in Latvia since World War II. Later, Pastor Rubenis commented that the TV broadcast "led to a kind of seismic disturbance in people. . . . On that day a great many people reconsidered all that they had built up against faith in God."[28]

From that point on, the renewal of the country was closely identified with the struggle of the church, which served as a catalyst for change both political and spiritual. The movement's strength was powerfully illustrated by the half a million people who poured onto the streets of Latvia in November of 1989.

$$* \quad * \quad *$$

Nineteen-eighty-nine was the breakaway year in the Ukraine, too.[29] Before Gorbachev was to meet with the pope, Ukrainians turned out by the hundreds of thousands to support the Ukrainian Catholic Church. It too had proved to be a rallying point for both religious and nationalist

27. Ibid., p. 154.
28. Quoted by Bourdeaux in ibid., p. 156.
29. The historical information in this section is drawn from Chapter Eight of Bourdeaux's *Gorbachev, Glasnost and the Gospel.*

distancing from the Soviet Union. In June, 100,000 people gathered for an open-air mass in support of the church. In September, 150,000 took to the streets; in November, 200,000. By this time, demonstrators in East Germany, Czechoslovakia, and elsewhere in the Eastern bloc were pouring into the streets. Revolution was in the air.

Here the resistance to the Soviets had a long history. The Ukrainian Catholic Church is not Roman Catholic but Uniate, or "Eastern Rite," sometimes known as Greek Catholic. Initially created in the sixteenth century as a kind of buffer zone between the Orthodox Church and the advancing Catholic Church, it combined elements of both. For the next several centuries, it became the object of both political and ecclesiastical conflicts. Because it had been the focus of Ukrainian nationalism in the Austro-Hungarian empire in the nineteenth century, Stalin feared that it would undermine his authority in the twentieth. Consequently, he persuaded the Russian Orthodox patriarchs to join him as accomplices; they in turn demanded the allegiance of the Ukrainian Catholic Church to Moscow rather than to Rome. Initially many bishops endured torture rather than transfer their allegiance, but threats made on the families of married clergy broke down their resistance.[30] After the church was co-opted under Orthodox rule in 1946, those who were not persuaded were to face decades of imprisonment. Eventually the church was outlawed.

More recent resistance coalesced around a layman named Iosyp Terelya. Because of his allegiance to the Ukrainian Catholic Church, he was sent to prison on falsified criminal charges in 1962. In 1969 he was sentenced again, this time receiving seven years' hard labor for anti-Soviet agitation and propaganda. Three years later he was committed to a psychiatric hospital. When he was finally released in 1976, he was denied employment and imprisoned again, this time on charges of "parasitism." When he was released again, he continued working for the cause of the church. In 1982 he cofounded the Action Group for the Defense of the Rights of Believers and the Church to campaign for legalization of the Ukrainian Catholic Church. As a

---

30. According to the policy of this denomination, priests could marry, but bishops could not.

consequence, the authorities began to exert increasing pressure on him, and in 1984 he renounced his citizenship and went underground to escape them. But in 1985 he was arrested and sentenced once again, this time to seven years in a strict regime camp and five years in exile. He was spared serving the full length of his sentence by the amnesty of 1987, during which he was released and permitted to emigrate to the United States.

Stepan Khmara, another layman, was one of those who had joined the fight for the legalization of the Ukrainian Catholic Church. In 1980 he was arrested for editing a *samizdat* journal, and he served seven years in a labor camp before being released during the amnesty in 1987. Ivan Hel, another man who spent seventeen years in Soviet prisons, emerged as the principal spokesman for the Ukrainian Catholic Church.

Championing its cause was not an easy task. This church faced the combined resistance of the antireligious policy of the Soviets, the antinationalist policies of the local Ukrainian authorities, and the Russian Orthodox Church's attempts to co-opt or squelch its existence. A great deal was at stake. The Ukraine is the "Bible belt" of the former Soviet Union, the region with the highest concentration of believers and churches. It is also the "corn belt," as well as one of the regions richest in natural resources. Both the Soviets and the Russian Orthodox Church had their individual reasons for wanting to maintain control of it.

Other believers and human rights activists took up the cause, including Gleb Yakunin, Alexander Ogorodnikov, Georgi Edelstein, and Vladimir Poresh. When Andrei Sakharov traveled to Rome to see the pope in 1989, he pleaded the church's cause, as he did in Moscow in the last months before he died, calling the continuing repression of the Ukrainian Catholic Church "absolutely inadmissible." When Gorbachev went to London in April 1989, the Foreign Office put the issue to him. When the Helsinki congress on human rights convened in Paris shortly thereafter, it was raised again. Bishops of the Ukrainian Catholic Church petitioned Gorbachev personally.

In 1989, members of the church staged successive hunger strikes on Moscow's main shopping street, the Arbat, for nearly half a year, until the police forcibly removed them from the site. Hundreds had gathered around the group daily. In June of 1989, about 100,000 people gathered for an open-air mass in Ivano-Frankovsk in support of the church. In September, 150,000 people took to the streets to celebrate mass and march. On November 26, 1989, just before Gorbachev was to meet the pope, 200,000 demonstrators turned out in Lvov to support the beleaguered church.

After their meeting, Gorbachev and the pope announced that diplomatic relations would be established between the Vatican and the USSR. Despite shrill criticism from Russian Orthodox, the path was opened for registration of the outlawed denomination. But the conflict, like its resolution, always had been more than a religious one. There was no question that the nationalist elements in the Catholic Church here were strong, and that there was a clear political element in its resistance to Moscow.

This religious conflict served as a spark that ignited general resistance. The long-smoldering issue of the autonomy of the Ukrainian Catholic Church flamed into an increasingly fiery breakaway movement that spread quickly throughout the Soviet empire.

*   *   *

Long after the winds of *perestroika*'s change had begun to blow elsewhere, Lithuania was still waiting. Banned bishops and imprisoned priests left believers there with dampened enthusiasm, while the rest of the Soviet Union appeared to be edging toward increased freedom. Only in 1988 was a shift finally perceptible — when Fathers Alfonsas Svarinskas, Juozas Zdebskis, and Sigitas Tamkevicius, who had incurred the wrath of authorities by founding the Lithuanian Catholic Committee for the Defense of Believers' Rights, were let out of prison. But their freedom was not without a price: Svarinskas was released but forced to emigrate, and authorities tried to get Tamkevicius to sign a statement admitting his guilt. But Tamkevicius refused to sign, thus winning a small victory. He was welcomed home by a crowd of several hundred, waving the forbidden red, green, and yellow national flag.

To have the Vilnius Cathedral returned — that was the fervent wish of the 31,000 people who had signed a petition sent to Gorbachev. The authorities finally gave in and announced their decision in October 1988.

When the cathedral was reconsecrated on February 5, 1989, 30,000 witnesses filled Vilnius. Having been seized decades ago — in 1949 — and used as an art gallery since the sixties, the cathedral was finally to be used for worship again. Bishop Steponavicius presided, a man who had spent twenty-eight years under house arrest in a remote Lithuanian village for refusing to forbid the teaching of catechism to children. Now he was greeted by children in national dress carrying flowers. When he addressed the crowd, he did not complain; he simply said that the time he had been in exile had strengthened his faith. Michael Bourdeaux, who was part of that crowd, writes,

> The vast crowd on Gediminas Square welcomed him with prayer and the near-silent waving of a thousand flags. The colors of pre-Soviet Lithuania, gold, green and red, were everywhere. . . . The impact of this event, seen by the whole nation on TV, must have convinced them all that basic change was indeed well on the way.
>
> Parting the crowds as Moses did the Red Sea, the bishop strode across the square at the head of his procession, then paused at the west door for a moment of prayer before walking majestically up the nave to prostrate himself at the altar steps. Filling every square inch of the cathedral, the 3,000-strong congregation prayed with him in silence. The years spent by the bishop in quiet study and prayer in his remote place of exile now brought their reward in this most solemn act of reconsecration: a natural leader under God among his people.[31]

❧

31. Ibid., p. 146.

The Power of the Spirit

The kind of character produced in the crucible of conflict can be striking. Nijole Sadunaite is a Lithuanian nurse who was thirty-six when she was tried and sentenced to jail in 1975. She had continued the *samizdat* documentation of persecution in the *Chronicle of the Lithuanian Catholic Church* after its first founders were jailed. Letters she wrote from prison were smuggled out from the Siberian Gulag to Lithuania, where they inspired many. Her reaction to her circumstances in jail goes beyond a lack of complaint: "How good it is that the small craft of my life is being steered by the hand of the good Father. When He is at the helm I have nothing to fear. . . . We have many old women and sick people here, so I rejoice that I have been brought here in accordance with my calling — to nurse and love."*

Jadvyga Bieliauskiene of Lithuania was imprisoned in 1982 for teaching children about the Christian faith. She became so sick in prison that it was not certain that she would survive. At that time she wrote,

> I became very ill, with three relapses, but my soul was flooded with a clear light never seen before, which still accompanies me when I suffer. If I die, rejoice and praise the Lord that the humble sacrifice of this most unworthy and wayward being has been accepted for the purpose of saving our children. I have come to understand that suffering is fruitful only when we accept it humbly — only then does it open the eyes of the soul.**

Michael Bourdeaux writes of these two women, "It was the spirit of these two more than anyone else [that] convinced me that no human force could quell the indomitable spirit of these people."***

*Quoted by Michael Bourdeaux in *Risen Indeed* (Crestwood, N.Y.: St. Vladimir's Seminary Press, 1983), p. 101.

**Quoted by Bourdeaux in *Gorbachev, Glasnost and the Gospel* (London: Hodder & Stoughton, 1990), p. 141.

***Ibid.

The changes that Mikhail Gorbachev introduced, whatever their motivation, radically altered the course of history, introducing reforms far beyond those he had intended. When he introduced increased personal freedoms, he let go of the only tool that had allowed Communists to rule effectively: the tool of coercion. Each new freedom increased the people's appetite for more, while the means to control the potent changes decreased. These changes proved so powerful that they were to trigger a political and spiritual earthquake which would rumble through the entire continent. A revolution was in the making.

The resistance movement against the Communists was a deeply moral one. So it was no accident that the flash points of the gathering revolution occurred around figures of moral authority, many of whom (though certainly not all) were Christians.

Soviet leaders acknowledged the moral nature of the revolutionary change — and the need for it. In writing about the peaceful revolution that followed, former U.N. Ambassador Jeane Kirkpatrick quotes Aleksander Yakovlev, the man believed to be Mikhail Gorbachev's closest advisor in the late 1980s through 1990: "We have suffered not only a crisis in economics but a crisis of the soul. . . . I am convinced that the time has come for truth. To speak of nobility, charity, honor, and conscience even at a Congress of Communists, shaking from our feet the mud of enmity and suspicion that has built up over the decades. It is the very time for the party to take the initiative in the moral cleansing of our existence and our consciousness." Yakovlev concluded with a line that has become famous among his countrymen: "Let us remember not the empty shelves but the empty souls who have brought a change to our country which demands revolutionary change."[32]

That revolution was imminent.

---

32. Quoted by Kirkpatrick in "Exit Communism, Cold War and the Status Quo," in *Man and Marxism* (Hillsdale, Mich.: Hillsdale College Press, 1991), pp. 159-60.

CHAPTER 7

Growing Resistance in the Eastern Bloc

The two powerful men sitting in the sauna in Rome were an unlikely couple. There they sat, dripping sweat side by side, their faces and bodies flushed. Whether this was a chance encounter or part of a broader plan, they were to have a conversation that would have an impact far beyond the walls of the sauna, the city — and the country, for that matter.

Klaus Gysi was the East German Ambassador to Rome, and as such he was a lifelong Communist and emissary of a realm ruled by an ideology based on atheism. His sauna-mate was Cardinal Agostino Casaroli from the Vatican, a man of God, an emissary of the Roman Catholic Church.[1] As Gysi recalls, the two of them sat, sweating, on towels, engaged in a philosophical debate about the nature of man and of the state.

Gysi had become a Communist in his youth, distraught at having seen killing in the strike-torn streets during the economic crisis of the late twenties. As a teenager he had built his hopes on a system that he believed was committed to eradicating greed and materialism, a socialist system that was to produce an order that was peaceful and fair. That is how he had seen the promise of com-

---

1. Agostino Casaroli was Archbishop under Paul VI and became a cardinal under Pope John Paul II. Here he is referred to simply as Cardinal Casaroli. This incident is based on the author's interview with Klaus Gysi on May 6, 1990, in Berlin.

munism. He believed that the state and the socialist system it produced would perfect human nature, reshaping it according to a new ideology.

But Cardinal Casaroli was challenging the assumption of reshaping human nature. If that was to be accomplished, perhaps it would take longer than one generation, he suggested to Gysi. How would it be possible to reshape the inner convictions of an entire people so quickly? Religion was a part of their upbringing. They couldn't be forced to embrace socialism on a timetable; the two belief systems would have to coexist. Gysi protested that religion was the opium of the masses and should be rooted out. But Casaroli remained insistent that such a change, if it could be accomplished at all, would take time.

Casaroli was not new to this argument. He had often been deployed in the Ost-Politik of the Holy See by its architect, Pope Paul VI, who hoped for some rapprochement with the political powers of the Eastern bloc. The goal was to be granted what Casaroli liked to call "breathing room" for the church. He and the Vatican diplomats were talking to Communist leaders in Poland, Czechoslovakia, Bulgaria, Romania, Hungary, Yugoslavia, and the Soviet Union. Perhaps an exchange like this one could "buy" a little space for Christians in the German Democratic Republic.

Gysi the idealist had long since become Gysi the pragmatist in his Communist career. And from a pragmatic standpoint, he could see advantages in avoiding head-on conflict with the church. According to Marx, religion's sole function was to fill a need that would in time disappear, once the material needs of the people had been met. But while East Germany was materially better off than most of its neighbors in the Eastern bloc, the Christians there had not faded away. They were a minority, but a stubborn, apparently strong remnant remained. What to do with them for the interim? If the Cardinal was right, maybe the Communists should talk to the church people and see what could be worked out.

Gysi agreed to talk to the Communist leaders in Berlin and urge them to meet with the Christians.

Protest in the Church

On March 6, 1978, Communist leader Erich Honecker and members of his regime sat at a round table with leaders of the Federation of the East German Protestant Church in a meeting that was of seminal importance. Announced with great fanfare and trumpeted as a major event, it was in fact a turning point for a new era of relations between the church and the state, which had previously been antagonistic. (It was to be a full ten years before a parallel meeting between Mikhail Gorbachev and leaders of the Russian Orthodox Church was to take place.)

New freedoms were granted to the East German church, which had been far freer than its Soviet counterpart, but nevertheless limited. Rules were established governing use of church property, granting more autonomy. Policy changes included allowing pastors to receive theological literature from the West, granting Christians increased radio time and access to television broadcasting, and allowing them to hold more prison chaplaincies. While the changes were not all dramatic, some of the freedoms won in this round-table meeting were significant for a church that was to become increasingly active in the coming decade. In an interesting quirk of fate, Klaus Gysi was soon to be named the new secretary for church affairs for the East German regime.

Roughly 5 million of East Germany's population of 16.7 million belonged to the Protestant Church, the *Evangelische Kirche* (in the Lutheran tradition), while only about one million were Catholic. But only about 3 percent of the total East German population attended church every Sunday. The Catholic Church had deliberately distanced itself from the state, whereas the *Evangelische Kirche* since Bishop Albrecht Schönherr had seen its place as the "church in socialism." It had a certain amount of latitude in this role. Compared with the Soviet churches, those in East Germany were economically stronger, socially more active, and more independent. Since 1929, Soviet churches had been prohibited from performing any charitable works, but East German Christians were permitted to run hospitals and homes for the mentally handicapped and visit prisons. As a rule, pastors had not been imprisoned since the 1950s.

But while Christians were not, strictly speaking, persecuted on the basis of faith, they were clearly discriminated against, particularly in access to higher education and management positions at work. And anything construed as political opposition was very likely to land one behind bars. The dividing line between the nonpolitical and the political was very thin, and the application of law was extremely elastic. However, the clergy were protected from prison in a way laypeople were not.

Still, the church was not without a certain amount of clout. It had some success in intervening on behalf of those who wanted to study at a university, travel, emigrate, or obtain release from prison. In the 1970s, the church had also won a skirmish on the issue of compulsory military service, after which young recruits could fulfill their obligation in unarmed construction units called *Bausoldaten*. The discussions about the legitimate use of force that accompanied this development were the genesis of the peace movement that grew in the early 1980s, the proponents of which met in the churches. The deployment of Soviet SS–20s and American Pershing missiles made many concerned about the prospect of a "limited nuclear exchange" in Europe, and young Christians wore patches on their jackets with the quote "swords to plowshares." They were critical of both super-powers.

The church was the only place in East Germany where people could legally meet for discussion without overt interference. It was an oasis of freedom that various groups began to utilize. In addition to the issue of nuclear war, the issues of ecology and human rights gained attention, with "basis groups" sprouting up throughout the country and holding meetings in the churches. This development alarmed the Communist regime, which had never abandoned its conviction that the church was an element of opposition that must be controlled; indeed, it had assigned the Ministry for State Security, the Stasi, to do just that. Division XX/4 of the Stasi apparatus, which was responsible for moni-toring all politically questionable elements, routinely placed agents at all levels of the church, penetrating it from top to bottom. A report dated February 10, 1983, confirms the Stasi's commitment to block the church and the "political-negative activities of these powers." A 1982 Stasi report from Leipzig puts it clearly: "The church can never be fully integrated into socialism. The church remains the church, there is no socialist church. The church is diametrically opposed to Marxism-Leninism and propagates its own views."[2]

As the yeasty mixture of activists grew, there was dissension within the church itself. Some believers dismissed activists as *Trittbrettfahrer*, riding on the running board but not inside the car. (Some Christians, particularly the Catholics, refused to view the realm of politics as the proper place for their main concerns; politics was and would remain secondary.) Interestingly, fundamentalist Christians and Communist critics used the same line of argument: if these activist groups were not part of the mainstream church, they had no place under its roof.

Were these groups legitimate or not? Protestant Superintendent Rev. Werner Krätschell was one of many church leaders repeatedly consulted by the Communists on that issue. According to him, the root of the answer lay in past centuries, when deeply religious kings and a Christian ruling class governed the land:

> The intertwinement between faith, education and upbringing had a significant shaping influence over centuries, which forty years of communism could not eradicate. It lay deeper in the language, in the culture, in the art, in many fundamental elements which were still alive. Culture had been strongly influenced by religion. In that sense, one cannot speak of pure atheists. [The members of these groups] were not "confessing Christians," but they had been unconsciously, sub-consciously shaped by many religious impulses and truths. . . . Perhaps only 15 percent were "confessing Christians" but the others were people who had been religiously shaped.[3]

2. This quotation is displayed in the *Runde Ecke,* the former headquarters of the Stasi in Leipzig.

3. This and subsequent quotations in this chapter are taken from the author's interview with Werner Krätschell in Berlin on May 28, 1991.

In response to this debate, Pastor Christian Führer had demonstratively opened the doors of the Nikolaikirche in Leipzig, painting in bold letters on the sidewalk outside "Nikolai Church open for all."[4] Beginning in 1980, he had held *Friedensdekade*, a ten-day conference in November devoted to the issues of peace in the context of Christian thought. Beginning in 1983, the Nikolaikirche opened its doors every Monday at five p.m. for the *Friedensgebete*, or "Prayers for Peace." It became a weekly event that was to have unanticipated consequences. Some would say it was the spiritual spark that ignited East Germany's peaceful revolution of 1989.

Christian Führer and the "Prayers for Peace" quickly won the attention of the Stasi. As records unearthed later indicate, two informants — "Wilhelm" and "Erika" — were consequently planted in the Nikolaikirche, and began to file regular reports on its activities. Christian Führer was dubbed *"Igel"* — Porcupine — in the reports, the Stasi's private little joke about his burr haircut. He was put under constant surveillance.

Other Christian pastors who were activists also became the objects of Stasi attention — among them Rainer Eppelmann, pastor of the Samariter-Kirche in Berlin. As a young recruit, he had been imprisoned for refusing to carry a weapon or swear the oath of loyalty to the socialist state required of military draftees. He later founded a peace initiative called the Berliner Appell with the motto *"Frieden schaffen ohne Waffen"* — "Make peace without weapons." The Stasi considered arranging a car "accident" to silence him. In one of the more remarkable quirks of events, he became the Minister of Defense and Disarmament in the new government when Communism was toppled.

Mounting Discontent and Desperation

When Mikhail Gorbachev assumed office in the Soviet Union, he was hailed as the darling of reform, and East Germans hoped that

---

4. This and subsequent information on the Nikolaikirche is based on the author's interview with Christian Führer on February 28, 1991, in Leipzig.

the winds of change from Moscow would blow their way. But they were to be disappointed. Erich Honecker's regime was utterly resistant to *glasnost* and *perestroika*. As East German ideology chief Kurt Hager put it acidly, "If your neighbor changes his wallpaper, it doesn't mean you have to, too." Suddenly the young people who had squirmed under the Soviet yoke put more of their hope for change in Gorbachev than in their own rulers.

Given the conditions in the country, the rising political unrest was not surprising. East Germany was widely regarded as the powerhouse of the Eastern bloc, but in reality things were anything but rosy there. As East German journalist Ingrid Ebert wrote in her personal journal,

> We don't want to take off our rose-colored glasses, or we would have to look at the grey facades of the houses, the collapsing buildings in our inner-cities, the shattered windows nailed shut, the broken roof tiles, the moss in the rain gutters. We would see the trash in the parks, the filthy train stations, the malfunctioning playground equipment, the dirty sandboxes, the dying trees and vanishing breeds of animals. We would be horrified by the broken families, the alcoholics, the defeated.[5]

Ebert was right: because of years of careless industrial growth and environmental neglect, the rivers were fouled, the scraggly trees were dying, and the air was a gray, smudgy stench. Entire cities had been evacuated and resettled because they were declared ecological disaster areas impossible to inhabit. Parents with children who had developed lung disease from the pollution were advised to move to save their lives.

And daily life meant enduring perpetual scarcity. It could take three years to get a bathtub, as long as fifteen years to get a car. Standing in line was a fact of life. In fact, people slept in lines

---

5. Ebert, "In mir ist alles durcheinander," from *Die Revolution der Kerzen, Christen in den Umwälzungen der DDR*, ed. Jörg Swoboda (Wuppertal: Oncken Verlag, 1990), p. 88.

overnight when they heard that televisions could be bought at a particular location. Whenever the rumor was out that something as basic as sheets could be had at a certain store, there would be a near-riot as people rushed to get there before the sheets were sold out. People stockpiled everything imaginable, bartering an extra exhaust pipe for hams. Anybody who wanted to repair a house had to "organize" — in other words, barter for or steal — every board, nail, and bag of cement. Such materials were simply not available on the normal market. In many cities, ghostly, half-finished houses stood blankly staring, their facades peeling, seemingly abandoned, construction having been halted due to lack of materials. Every day factories would run out of parts, and they would stand idle for entire shifts. A two-tier economy was in place, one running on Western currency, the other running on what they called "vitamin B" or *Beziehungen,* the German word for "relationships." In short, what you got depended on who you knew. And this was the "economic powerhouse" of the Eastern bloc. Elsewhere it was even worse.

East Germans knew it wasn't like that in the West. When a family was visited by an uncle of relatively modest means from the other side of the Wall, they were agog at the presents he could bring. And television told the other side of the story. Nearly all of East Germany could receive West German television, and East Germans watched it avidly. It gave them an alternative source of information, something the Communists strictly controlled in every other way. Given this basis of comparison, the lies of the state were even more obvious. The discrepancy between what the people were told and what they knew was growing. Their knowledge was also fed by travel. More and more of them won the opportunity to visit relatives in the West and see the night-and-day differences for themselves, a privilege they gained by intervention of the West German government. At one time only retirees had been able to visit West Germany, but during the mid-1980s more younger people were permitted to go. Some were so intoxicated by the freedoms of the West that they decided they would rather risk fleeing than stay in East Germany.

Risking All to Escape: Matthias Melster

The jeep patrolling the Czechoslovakian border to West Germany had just pulled away, observed through binoculars by a young man and woman concealed in the woods nearby for the past two hours.* Now the countdown began. In fifteen minutes the two East Germans would make a break for the West, for freedom. After months of planning, they had all the necessary equipment — a compass, spiked track shoes to help them climb the fence in front of the border, a blanket to throw over the top loop of barbed wire on the fence, and heavy gloves to keep their hands from being cut.

At the appointed moment, they sprinted to the fence. When they clambered over it, their spikes held. They tumbled over the blankets they had thrown over the barbed wire and hit the ground running, racing through a hole in the second wire fence left by shoddy construction. Running for all they were worth, lungs bursting and sides aching, they covered the mile of no-man's-land separating the fence from the actual border. Finally in the home stretch, they were jubilant — and unaware that they had tripped an invisible electronic alarm. Suddenly they could hear the drone of approaching jeeps, and seemingly out of nowhere came a huge attack dog that lunged at the young man, Matthias Melster, grabbing his arm in its jaws and taking him down. The girl screamed as she tripped over a stone. Ten armed Czech soldiers ran toward them, shouting. As Matthias lay face-down with his forehead in a last patch of April snow, handcuffs were snapped on him. He could see the border from where he lay — twenty yards between him and freedom.

Matthias could only think, *Don't make a false move or you could be dead.* "The soldiers were only eighteen or nineteen, and as nervous as I was," he explained as he looked back on the incident. "They all had

---

*This account is based on the author's interview with Matthias Melster in 1988 for a TV broadcast on "European Journal," as well as a subsequent interview in Köln on October 27, 1990.

guns." Matthias and the girl were blindfolded and led away. Unbeknownst to them, the whole episode was being observed by Western border guards, who stood by helplessly, unable to intervene.

While he was being interrogated, Matthias was kicked in the back by a guard. Unable to break his fall because his hands were cuffed behind his back, he smashed into the Wall, breaking his nose. He was subsequently flown to East Berlin in a military transport plane and put in solitary confinement, having been declared a "dangerous enemy of the state." While confined, he was subjected to intense interrogation sessions by Stasi agents. His interrogators knew that he was an active young member of a Berlin church that had apparently supported other young people in their decision to try to leave the country.

Matthias knew he had risked his life in his attempt to escape. But it was something he felt he had to do. "If you're a Christian, then there are so many things about the Communist system you can't accept," he explained. "I tried to stay and change them, but it wasn't possible for me. I saw no chance but to go."

In 1987 Matthias was released in an amnesty arrangement in which the West German government bought his freedom.

In addition to those trying to escape, numerous people, most of them young, decided that "West was best" and applied to leave the country legally. It meant risking being demoted or fired, being ostracized by others who feared associating with them, and living out of packed suitcases, daily hoping for a permission to leave that might never be granted. Sometimes they took desperate measures: in January 1988, a number of demonstrators at the parade for Rosa Luxemburg in Berlin had been arrested in an action they hoped would provoke their expulsion from East Germany. Those trying to emigrate, the *Ausreisewilligen*, were like lepers — no one wanted to get near them for fear of political infection. But the Nikolaikirche in Leipzig opened its doors to them, and in February 1988 Christian Führer announced that a discussion would be held on the problems they faced. He thought fifty people might show up; instead, a crowd of 800 came. He pleaded with them to stay in East Germany, warning that they should not succumb to the siren song of materialism in the West.

The church was divided in its response to those who wanted to emigrate, the peace groups, and the others who were increasingly seeking shelter under church roofs. Looking for a solution, Catholics and Protestants came together in February 1988 at the first gathering of the *Konziliaren Prozess,* or conciliatory process. Just as Dietrich Bonhoeffer had felt compelled to respond to the Nazis in the 1930s, so these people felt compelled to respond to the Communists in the 1980s. They agreed upon making a plea for "peace, justice, and preservation of the creation," and they formulated papers on the issues. While the "basis groups" represented here were certainly not all Christian, many of their leaders were. On their own, most of them did not dare speak out publicly, for fear of losing their jobs — or worse. But in the *Konziliaren Prozess* they were united. And because the church enjoyed some independence, the Christians in the synod of the more politically active Protestant Church became in a sense the vox populi. Alarmed at this growing articulation of resistance, the Communists penetrated all these groups thoroughly, holding special training sessions to prepare their informants. According to Stasi reports, there were agents in every group imaginable; sometimes the number of agents matched the number of actual participants.

However, this invasion offered one advantage, according to Werner Krätschell: "In this training field the art of nonviolent confrontation was taught in action. It wasn't theoretic, or [done] with a simulator. The enemy was in the room. It was up to those in the room to learn how to deal with the 'forces of darkness' in actual practice. . . . An elite was prepared brilliantly for the confrontations during the weeks preceding November 9, 1989. This was a fire that sprang over from a trained elite to tens of thousands more." Because this core of people exercised restraint, others did too.

The "Prayers for Peace" meetings that began in Leipzig and Berlin sprang up in other places too — in Dresden, Plauen, Rostock, and Zwickau. Wanting to shut them down, the regime leaned on the church hierarchy. But Christian Führer, the instigator of these meetings, stood firm, quoting Dietrich Bonhoeffer: "The church is only the church when it is there for others."

But the church was not free of tension over this issue. Some of the political activists clashed with the Christians, claiming, "We risk everything, and all you do is pray." And Christians themselves were divided. Some claimed that the political realm was not their kingdom, while others felt obligated to influence it. Some felt that they must leave East Germany, while others claimed it was their Christian duty to stay. At one of the "Prayers for Peace" meetings in Leipzig, which had attracted many of those who wished to emigrate, a small group began to chant, "We're staying here." The violent treatment they received from police forced some to wonder why a regime had more problems accepting reform than expatriating its citizens.

Czechoslovakia Chafes

In Czechoslovakia, even the tanks that rolled to crush Prague Spring in 1968 did not succeed in the task that later years of repression accomplished. A nation of wit, whimsy, and pluck was slowly transformed into one of cynicism and resignation. Censorship was complete, and professional advancement was firmly in the hands of the Communist party. The result, according to Timothy Garton Ash, was an inverted society, with the intellectual and spiritual leaders at the bottom: bishops delivered the milk, and philosophers washed windows.[6]

Since Stalin, the repression of the church had been among the harshest in all Communist countries. According to Ash, "In the early fifties . . . some 8,000 of the country's 12,000 Catholic monks disappeared into labor camps. Bishops, priests, and theologians were im-

---

6. Timothy Garton Ash, in "Czechoslovakia under Ice," in *The Uses of Adversity: Essays on the Fate of Central Europe* (Cambridge: Granta Books, 1989), p. 58.

prisoned for up to 15 years."[7] The state had taken the church's property, dissolved its orders, and controlled the naming of bishops. Priests had to be licensed, which meant in practice that many were suspended at the whim of the regime. No new bishops were ordained; official priestly ordinations came to a virtual standstill. However, a catacomb church of banned priests thrived.[8]

Against this backdrop of repression, Charter 77 was founded. Its manifesto of January 1, 1977, attacked the regime for denying the rights guaranteed by the Helsinki Agreement, and called for freedom of religion and of expression in Czechoslovakia. The eight priests who signed the manifesto had their licenses suspended. The Chartists, as they were called, got together for late-night conversations with a group member who was to become prominent — the playwright Václav Havel. Virtually all of them were persecuted.

Because he had signed the charter, Father Václav Malý was stripped of his priestly duties. Forced to take on menial jobs to survive, he cleaned toilets, emptied bedpans, and worked as a stoker in a hotel in downtown Prague. Father Malý soon joined a Catholic layman, Václav Benda, in founding a group that was an offshoot of Charter 77: the Committee for the Defense of the Unjustly Persecuted, known by its Czech acronym VONS. This group smuggled out documentation of more than one hundred cases of persecution.[9]

Václav Benda had gone to great lengths to avoid confrontation with the regime. A philosopher by training, he had lectured at Prague's Charles University. When he was fired from his post, it was obvious that he would have to join the Communist party to get another position in the same field. So he retrained in mathematics, hoping to

7. Ibid., p. 60.

8. See Felix Corley's "The Secret Clergy in Communist Czechoslovakia," in *Religion, State and Society,* vol. 21, no. 2, 1993.

9. For personal portraits of Václav Malý and Václav Benda, see Bud Bultman's *Revolution by Candlelight: The Real Story behind the Changes in Eastern Europe,* ed. Harold Fickett (Portland, Ore.: Multnomah Press, 1991), pp. 75-90. There is more information on Malý and Benda in George Weigel's *The Final Revolution* (New York: Oxford University Press, 1992), pp. 171, 175-77. For a discussion of the pre-revolution years in Czechoslovakia, see Ash's "Czechoslovakia under Ice," pp. 55-63.

move to sufficiently neutral intellectual territory. But he discovered that in this field he was blocked from publishing or assuming higher responsibility. He made yet another career change, this time to computer programming. But eventually his convictions prompted him to join Charter 77, and subsequently to found VONS with Father Malý. Ultimately Benda worked as a stoker to survive. He felt compelled to act on what he believed, although he saw no chance of reforming the Communists. As he wrote one morning, "We are right, but we are lunatics. We don't have a chance of winning this fight between a dwarf and a troop of giants."[10] Shortly thereafter, Benda was arrested.

Along with Benda, Father Malý, Václav Havel, and seven others involved with VONS were arrested in 1979. Benda received a sentence of four years; Havel, four-and-a-half years. Havel had emerged as a spokesman for the independent Czech intellectuals. Since 1967, when he had called for an end to censorship, he had been banned from publishing his plays. Still determined to speak out, he had collected a number of essays reflecting the diversity of Czech intellectuals' thinking and put them, together with his own, in a collection he titled *The Power of the Powerless*. Havel and like-minded intellectuals articulated the need to live with integrity, to risk confrontation with the Communists, and to give personal witness to their convictions through the way they lived their lives. The moral power that emanated from this stance was striking.

Augustin Navrátil, a sixty-year-old Moravian railway signalman who had been locked up in the psychiatric ward of a hospital for his convictions, was to spark the next major event in the growing resistance. Navrátil had been "hospitalized" because he had written a thirty-one-point petition for religious freedom in Czechoslovakia. This wasn't the first time that Navrátil was subjected to psychiatric examination. He had already been locked up in a psychiatric institution in 1977 for circulating petitions for civil rights.[11] He had been

10. Benda, "From My Personal File," quoted by Bultman in *Revolution by Candlelight*, p. 78.

11. See Bultman's portrait of Navrátil in *Revolution by Candlelight*, pp. 86-88. See also Timothy Garton Ash's encounter with Navrátil, which he describes in "Pre-Spring" in *The Uses of Adversity*, pp. 192-95.

pronounced mentally unfit to stand trial; the medical examiners said he suffered from "hysterical self-stylization toward the ideal of a strong leading personality and . . . a strong moral responsibility which the subject understands as 'fidelity to his principles' and an inability to adapt to an adequate view of social reality. The subject thinks that for the truth, one must logically suffer."[12] That was, by the examiners' definition, insane.

When he was released, Navrátil took his petition for religious freedom all the way to Cardinal František Tomášek, archbishop of Prague, asking him personally for his endorsement. Tomášek gave it, and in so doing he took a public stance identifying himself and the Catholic Church with the resistance movement. Within less than a year, more than 600,000 people had signed the petition, a major indication of the burgeoning resistance in Czechoslovakia. As George Weigel concludes in *The Final Revolution*,

> The 1988-1989 Navrátil petition, whose thirty-one points spelled out the implications for Czechoslovakia of the fundamental democratic principle of the separation of Church and state, was a watershed event in the "pre-revolution" — the events and the moral reawakening that finally gave birth, in November and December 1989, to the Velvet Revolution.[13]

One more event in 1988 was to draw clearly the lines of pre-revolutionary confrontation. Catholic activists organized a demonstration in Bratislava's public square to express support for Navrátil's petition for religious freedom and for the ordination of new bishops. Concerned, the regime intervened. Police blocked traffic for 100 kilometers around Bratislava, and leading activists were detained for interrogation. Despite this, as many as 15,000 came on March 25, 1988, carrying candles in the rain. Police attacked them with ferocity, unleashing attack dogs and wielding water cannons and tear gas; even foreign television crews were

12. Quoted by Bultman in *Revolution by Candlelight*, p. 86.
13. Weigel, *The Final Revolution*, pp. 180-81.

beaten. The confrontation became known as "the Good Friday of Bratislava."[14]

Dynamiting the Wall

Meanwhile, the Wall in East Germany still stood. In 1987, when he had faced the Brandenburg Gate in Berlin, President Reagan had proclaimed, "Mr. Gorbachev, tear down this wall!" As impossible as it had sounded then, Gorbachev now seemed a more likely candidate for the task than Erich Honecker, who announced in January 1989 that "the Wall will still remain in fifty, even a hundred years if the reasons for its existence have not been resolved."

The election in May 1989 was the spark which lit the long fuse that dynamited the Wall. Ironically, the fuse was lit by the East German Communists themselves when they blatantly falsified the election results.

$\sim$

Determined to Vote: Gabriele Anger

Gabriele Anger was nervous.* It was May 7, 1989, the first time she had voted in East Germany, and the men standing around in the room looked irritated that she had interrupted their cigarette break. One shoved a ballot at her.

"Excuse me," she ventured timidly, "but isn't there supposed to be a booth somewhere so you can mark the ballot in privacy?"

With grunts and unwilling shoves, the men improvised a makeshift booth. The new voters had been sent in ahead of others, and obviously

---

14. Ibid., pp. 182-83.

*This account and the subsequent one titled "Candles and Courage" are based on the author's interview with Gabriele Anger in Köln on January 4, 1991.

officials weren't prepared for a 21-year-old first-time voter to insist on the right to a secret ballot. As Gabriele entered the booth, the official who seemed to be in charge offered her a pencil.

"No, thanks," she answered cheerfully. "I have my own pen." *I'm not going to make it that easy for you to erase my vote,* she thought to herself.

When she came out of the booth and handed the official her folded ballot, she glanced down. She noticed that a clear black mark had been made next to her name in his register. Was it because she had insisted on casting a secret ballot and on using a pen?

After the polls closed, many citizens all over East Germany stayed in the polling places to watch the counting of the votes. Gabriele's brother and others who stayed as observers were shocked to see that the results were brazenly falsified. "Official" tallies for voting districts didn't match what the observers saw. What was trumpeted in the official party press the following day as a huge victory for the socialists was met with cries of outrage. Like a drumbeat that began to roll across the land, the accusation of election fraud was heard everywhere, first in sporadic bursts, then in a steady beat rising to a crescendo. It reached even the ears of the politburo members, who reportedly wondered if they had overdone it this time.

~

Flying Sparks of Resistance

Politically, the summer of 1989 was a hot one. The churches were full of protesters who were angry about the manipulation of the election results. As the "Prayers for Peace" meetings continued, the police arrested people coming out of the churches afterward. Those carrying candles had them clubbed out of their hands. If the swelling resistance thought it might be able to reform socialism and give it a more human face, it was in for a shock. In June, the Chinese police opened fire on those demonstrating for democracy in Peking's Tiananmen Square. Stunned, those in other Communist countries wondered out loud, *My God, can that happen here?*

Stasi informants planted in every single resistance group in East Germany kept the Stasi meticulously informed about the increasingly unstable political situation. Although the Stasi had successfully hindered some demonstrations by putting some instigators under house arrest and nabbing others on their way to the planned events, this kind of intervention was getting harder as the number of resisters increased. They were also challenged by the independent (and illegal) political parties that were springing up. *Demokratische Aufbruch, Neues Forum,* and *Demokratie Jetzt,* among others, joined the landscape previously ruled by the Communist SED (Social Unity Party of Germany) and its controlled junior parties. Key Christians were prime movers in these new parties, and they played a significant role in setting the tenor of the group's discussions. They were committed to peaceful change.

Many East Germans had concluded that there was no hope for change, and more and more of them began to leave the country. Those lucky enough to get permission to visit relatives in the West simply didn't return. Thousands headed into Hungary and Czechoslovakia, hiding out in the forests, hoping to cross the "green border." If their gerontocracy was too old and brittle to change, then they would risk leaving it, even if that meant crawling through the woods on their bellies or fording a river with children on their shoulders to elude the border guards.

Over the summer a flood of East Germans crossed the border into Hungary, perhaps as many as 300,000. The steady hemorrhage was creating a crisis for the East German regime. Factories and whole sections of cities were deserted, ghostly places from which people had suddenly vanished. Then-classified reports from Erich Mielke, the head of the Stasi, document the Communists' growing alarm at the mass exodus. There were clear signs that events were starting to spin out of their control.

"What's the mood in the factories?" demanded Mielke of one of his Stasi majors.

"That is of course a very complicated question at the moment, Comrade Minister," the major replied.

"That's a very simple question. It's a question of power, nothing more," Mielke barked back.

The situation grew increasingly critical. Those who stayed were furious, and those who left created gaping holes in the workforce. Mielke made this pragmatic assessment: "A lot of them who are leaving are filthy swine. . . . [But] the total that's leaving, that is sensitive. Even if they're swine, the fact is that it's the labor force that's leaving." A Stasi lieutenant summed up the volatility of the situation: "The mood is miserable. There are discussions going on everywhere. . . . One spark is enough to ignite things."[5]

And ignite they did. But not only for the reasons the Stasi could anticipate.

Hungary under Pressure

In July 1989, at the Warsaw Pact meeting in Bucharest, Miklós Németh, the new prime minister of Hungary, and Gyula Horn, the foreign minister, spelled out the reforms their country was undertaking. They were clearly moving toward democratization and national sovereignty. East Germany's Erich Honecker, Romania's Nicolae Ceauşescu, and Czechoslovakia's Miloš Jakeš were furious, saying this threatened "socialist achievements." According to Németh, shortly thereafter Ceauşescu attempted to link up with the other two hard-liners to lobby the Soviet Union to put down this insurrection with a Warsaw Pact invasion into Hungary. Catching wind of their plan, and not wanting a repeat of 1956, the Hungarians scrambled for maneuvering room. "It was a dangerous situation because the hard-liners [Ceauşescu, Honecker, and Jakeš] were ready to interfere," says

5. For the transcription of the entire crisis meeting, see MfS, ZAIG B/215, Berlin, August 31, 1989, in *Ich liebe euch doch alle!: Befehle und Lageberichte des MfS* (Berlin: Basis Druck, 1990), pp. 113-38.

György Jenei, who was an advisor to Németh. "They wanted the Soviets to attack."[6]

Németh had cautiously tested the winds of reform blowing from Moscow during his first visit with President Gorbachev in March 1989. In a meeting scheduled to last half an hour that turned into an intense, three-hour-long discussion, Németh put the question to Gorbachev bluntly: would he intervene? Gorbachev's answer was unambiguous, according to Németh: "1956 was a mistake, and we will not repeat it. The Brezhnev doctrine is dead." Gorbachev said he wouldn't introduce a multiparty system in the Soviet Union. "But," he told Németh, "if you believe it is right, go ahead. I doubt it, but you must decide."

Németh had returned from his visit with the assurance that Soviet tanks would not roll to halt Hungarian reforms. But the wild card was the hard-liners in Moscow, who were already then a clear threat to Gorbachev's power. If there were to be a Soviet coup, there was no guarantee that his assurance would prevail. Accordingly, Németh asked Gorbachev for the names of the Russian military commanders in Hungary so that he could contact them directly in the event that military circumstances might change. Two weeks later, Németh received the names in a sealed envelope from the Soviet ambassador. The fact that the contents were withheld even from the ambassador sent Németh a signal he did not overlook.

The Hungarians were understandably nervous, according to Jenei, because in February they had discovered that Soviet nuclear warheads had been stationed in their country without their accord. In March, Németh arranged to meet with Soviet Prime Minister Ryshkov alone, with only a Hungarian interpreter present. At that meeting, Németh reportedly stated that he had irrefutable evidence on the warheads, and that they put his country in an untenable position. In response, the Soviets did in fact remove the weapons in August of that year.

The Hungarians were also struggling with the influx of a third

6. This recounting is based on the author's interviews with Miklós Németh in New York on January 29, 1991, and in Bonn on October 29, 1992; and with György Jenei in Rome on May 25, 1991. It also draws on the memoirs of Gyula Horn, excerpted in *Der Spiegel*, 36/1991, from *Freiheit, die ich meine* (Hamburg: Hoffman & Campe, 1991).

of a million East Germans. Desperate East Germans were also storm-ing the embassies in Prague and Warsaw. In late August, 700 of them were already occupying West Germany's Embassy in Budapest. A Hungarian border guard had shot two East Germans who had at-tempted to take his weapon and escape. In addition to the deluge of East Germans, 20,000 refugees from Romania had fled into Hungary. The situation was tense and growing more so.

In May, Foreign Minister Gyula Horn had demonstratively cut through the barbed wire at the Austrian border, in effect tearing the Iron Curtain. The legal framework for this symbolic action had been laid in the preceding months, when Hungary signed the Geneva Accords. According to the new terms of this agreement, refugees from other countries would be released and allowed to travel freely. But the old treaties of the Warsaw Pact obligated Hungary to round up the refugees and send them back home. Which agreement would govern Hungary's response?

There were clearly growing movements supporting democratiza-tion in East Germany and Czechoslovakia. If Hungary made a move to free the refugees, it would strengthen that process, which was akin to Hungary's own. But how would Honecker, Jakeš, and Ceauşescu react if their refugees were given passage to freedom in the West? Would they be able to persuade the Soviets to stage a Warsaw Pact invasion, despite Gorbachev's promise? How would the hard-liners in the Soviet Union react, even if Gorbachev tolerated Hungary's freeing the refugees? Could they send tanks and soldiers independently?

The debate among Hungary's top ministers was both spirited and marked by fear — a fear that wasn't paranoid, as events that occurred in the Baltic States in 1991 have since validated. There were Soviet generals who were willing to send tanks and give orders to fire. "We knew the KGB, and we knew all our enemies," Jenei ex-plained later. "My luggage was under the bed."

If Hungary decided to let the East German refugees go, that could give Honecker such domestic headaches that he would be forced to back off. And it would be a humanitarian solution to the problem. But at what risk? No one knew. Ceauşescu had written a letter to all the Warsaw Pact leaders except those from Hungary and Poland, two countries that he saw as politically unreliable. He wanted to hold an emergency meeting of the Warsaw Pact countries to "save the future of the socialist world," as he put it. He urged the invasion of Hungary. "The devils are working against the socialists," he claimed.

On a Tuesday afternoon in August 1989, six men sat in a secret meeting to decide what the country should do. Németh had gotten a copy of Ceaușescu's letter from Gorbachev, with a note indicating that he did not support the plot for intervention. "We were fully convinced," Németh says now, "that the others alone could not undertake hostile reactions against us." Still, there were many other things to consider. Ministers from the interior and justice departments laid out the legal and political ramifications of the various options. Foreign Minister Horn summarized the arguments for each of the options, concluding that he was in favor of releasing the refugees and opening the border.

"In that case, we're on the side of the West Germans," Istan Horvath, minister of the interior, reportedly said.

"Yes, you're right," Németh replied. "From this moment on, we're on the side of West Germany." The six men agreed.

That decision proved to be the knockout punch for Erich Honecker's regime. And its fall set off a chain reaction of shock waves that rocked the entire Eastern bloc, bringing one government after another crashing to rubble. The Hungarians may not have fully anticipated the far-reaching ramifications of their decision — nor did anyone else at that moment.

Németh and Horn had to talk to the West Germans about their decision. But they wanted to keep the content of that talk under wraps — and they were justifiably anxious about a leak. A 1988 meeting between the Hungarians and the West Germans had been perfectly detailed in Communist intelligence reports that had later crossed Horn's desk. Moscow had apparently also gotten the report. Obviously the Stasi had a spy in the chancellor's office in West Germany.[7] But where?

In a hastily arranged meeting, Németh and Horn flew to West Germany on August 25 to talk to Chancellor Helmut Kohl and

7. Horn, *Der Spiegel*, 36/1991, p. 119.

Foreign Minister Hans-Dietrich Genscher. To maintain secrecy, Németh and Horn landed at a military facility, then took a helicopter to Gymnich Castle. Németh and Horn had to repeat their message three times before the Germans believed that they were serious. Kohl was startled and visibly moved when he heard what they had decided. With tears in his eyes, he said, "The German people will never forget what you have done by making this decision." When asked what the Hungarians wanted in return, Németh said that their decision had no strings attached. In fact, he even asked that Germany postpone the loan package it was readying for Hungary. He wanted to make it perfectly clear that this decision had not been bought.

Horn had the unsavory task of informing the East Germans about the decision. Since Honecker was by now too ill to hold political meetings, Horn met with his counterpart, Oskar Fischer, on August 31. In a full hour's diatribe, Fischer demanded that the refugees be returned.

"Are you finished?" Horn finally asked. "Is that everything?"

Fischer nodded in surprise. Then Horn fired back, "You haven't proposed anything — only repeated your old position. That only strengthens my conviction that we've made the right decision." He explained what Hungary intended to do.

Horn recalls that Fischer's astonishment changed to consternation. His eyes narrowed to thin slits. "That is your proposal!"

"No," replied Horn. "That is simply information about our decision."

At that point Fischer exploded. "That is blackmail! Even treason! Do you know that with that you betray the GDR and change sides? That will have serious consequences for you."[8]

On September 8, Fischer fired off a strongly worded dispatch to the Hungarians saying that they must change their decision. The next day Honecker sent a "message studded with threats," Horn recalls. The Hungarian response was "a polite but firm decline." They were hanging tough and praying there would be no retaliation.

Certain grim precautions were taken. "Don't ask why," Hungar-

---

8. Quoted by Horn in ibid., p. 124.

ian intelligence officers told Németh, "but even your children will be escorted by security agents now." The entire family was put under increased protection. A report later confirmed that the Stasi had made Németh a target for violence.

The Soviets were informed one day before Hungary made its official announcement that it would open its border for refugees. Their response was measured and studiously neutral, indicating only that they were "surprised." In Horn's opinion, Gorbachev and his foreign minister, Eduard Shevardnadze, approved of the action.

On September 10, Horn announced the Hungarian decision on television. Beginning at midnight, the liberated poured across the border into the outstretched arms of Westerners who showered them with flowers, champagne, and uncharacteristic hugs. The refugees were seizing a political opportunity that would grow into a revolution.

Tense Confrontation in East Germany

By mid-September, thousands more East Germans were storming the fences outside the embassies in Prague and Warsaw in the hope of being granted permission to emigrate to West Germany. Lines of abandoned *Trabis,* the rattletrap cars so cherished because there were so few of them to go around, littered the streets of the capitals. Pursued by police, parents with small children on their shoulders tried to scale the fences; these heart-wrenching scenes were filmed by Western journalists and beamed into living rooms around the world. In Prague, 6,000 East Germans filled the embassy grounds, living in unspeakably unsanitary conditions, having abandoned everything they owned.

The West German government pleaded for a settlement on humanitarian grounds and won an agreement to evacuate them. Accordingly, on October 4 these individuals were sent from Prague to West Germany in sealed trains. As the trains sped through East Germany, people desperate to flee mobbed the train stations, tried to climb into the cars, laid across the tracks to block them, and wept.

Erich Mielke, the Stasi general, decided force was needed to get the explosive situation under control. In orders he issued on October 5, he wrote, "Hostile enemy activities are to be firmly put down with all means."[9] He ordered a marshaling of the troops and mobilization of the reserves. Young recruits were given orders to be prepared to use force on those blocking the train station in Dresden. The night ended in violent clashes.

One young soldier wrote to his pastor describing his conflict of conscience. He said there were only two choices, to "obey orders, or go to military prison for a long time." He describes the horror of what happened when he and other soldiers were sent to police the train station:

> People were standing opposite us who threw stones and Molotov cocktails. . . . We were afraid. They were hitting the asphalt in front of us. Two of our men fell; stones got them through their visors. . . . For the first time, I feared for my life. In front of us was an angry mob and behind us officers, Stasi and the military court back in the barracks. What we did in the crowd was out of fear, just for sheer survival. . . . I just ask one thing of you: pray for me and forgive me if you can. Read this letter to the youth of the parish and show it to everyone who wants to know what it's like as a draftee to be forced into compromising actions by a socialist state.[10]

The "Prayers for Peace" had resumed in September after the summer break, and the numbers of participants were swelling. By October 2, 15,000 people were gathering on Mondays for the *Friedensgebete* in Leipzig alone, much to the consternation of the regime. Now similar *Friedensgebete* were being held in other cities, including Berlin, Zwickau, Dresden, Halle, Weimar, Erfurt, and Rostock. All attempts to persuade the churches to call them off and disband the groups meeting in the churches had failed.

9. MfS Dokumentverwaltung, Nr. 103625, VVS-Nr. 0008, MfS-Nr. 69/89, October 5, 1989, from *Ich liebe euch doch alle!: Befehle und Lageberichte des MfS*, p. 199.

10. Quoted in "Dieser Herbst nach vierzig Jahren" by Günter and Hartmut Lorenz in *Die Revolution der Kerzen*, pp. 49-50.

Candles and Courage

"The church grounds were like the Forbidden City," says Gabriele Anger, who was a regular participant in the *Friedensgebete*. The churches became centers for political communications, with bulletin boards listing missing persons, most arrested on political grounds. Any information about them would be routed to their families. Candles were lit in churches for dissidents in prison. Telephone numbers were posted for people seeking legal or spiritual help. Instructions were given in case of arrest: "Call out your name loudly. One of us is certainly somewhere nearby" — "us" meaning "the people."

Most often when people came to the *Friedensgebete* for the first time, they were angry, frustrated, and afraid. But what they experienced was liberating. Individuals got up and went to the front of the church to take the microphone and tell others of their despair and shattered hopes. There they could speak without fear of arrest. "It had an incredible effect on people who came for the first time, who had never heard others speak so openly," recalls Gabi. "Then they would go home and bring a friend the next week. It set off a chain reaction." Like one candle lighting another, the light of courage to speak out spread from one person to another. Week after week, these people prayed for the country, for peace, for justice, and for peaceful change. Candle-lit processions streamed out of the churches onto the streets. The message repeated again and again by Christians was "no violence." They knew that the future of the country might depend on how they reacted.

"Inside the church, we had the most incredible feeling of security and warmth," Gabi explains. "People were changed somehow. You would notice it in a squeeze of the hand, or somebody giving you an unexpected hug and saying, 'We have to stick together.' They would look deep into your eyes just for a second longer than normally. It had a fascinating effect on all of us. We would go outside through the lines of police that had surrounded the church, and it was impossible to think *You pig*. Instead I would think, *If you only know how rich we are*. And we would smile and go through the narrow path between the soldiers in a human wall to the left and the right of us, and look them in the eyes." Most were young draftees who were not at all happy about having to point guns at people their own age. "We could often tell who was with us just by looking," said Gabi. "They would avert their glance."

Some Stasi agents were planted as provocateurs. In the midst of a crowd, one would begin to shout insults about the Stasi and wait for the crowd to take up the chant. Those who did could be beaten and arrested — demonstrators in Leipzig fell into that trap. In response to this tactic, Gabi and her friends developed a tactic of their own. They would join hands to form a circle around the person shouting, isolating him. Then, still surrounding him, the group would walk to the nearest policeman and turn him over, saying he was causing trouble. The police then had no choice but to take the undercover agent and lead him away.

"Over My Dead Body"

Not surprisingly, Protestant Superintendent Werner Krätschell of Berlin-Pankow was repeatedly called in to the authorities to deal with complaints about the *Friedensgebete*. As he explained, "They protested that the groups were made up of 80 percent non-church members, and for that reason should not be permitted to meet there."

The local official he had to deal with, Herr Milcke, a man Krätschell describes as "a weak figure," habitually read a statement prepared for him by the higher-ups of his department, who in turn were acting on orders from the Stasi. In one of these exchanges, Krätschell said, "Herr Milcke, I'm going to tell you things you should please tell those behind the curtains. I am not just talking to you; you are here talking to me because you are under orders. You are a functionary. Tell the people behind you that if they are trying to destroy my work, then I am telling you, only over my dead body. I will defend this work to the end." Because there were a number of church leaders in the country who said, in effect, "over my dead body," the *Friedensgebete* movement was protected. But this allegiance was dangerous. Krätschell was warned that the churches would see a "Chinese-style solution" if they were not careful.

On October 7, 1989, the GDR celebrated its fortieth anniversary with a state visit by Mikhail Gorbachev. Stasi reports indicate that Stasi officials feared that demonstrations might mar the occasion — and they had reason to worry. In Berlin, 7,000 people took to the streets, and the authorities arrested 700 of them. Demonstrators also flooded the streets in Leipzig. They were clubbed with riot sticks and attacked by dogs; even pregnant women were beaten. At the end of the evening, more than a thousand people, many of them bloodied, were put behind bars. Information about these conflicts was discreetly withheld from Gorbachev. But in an unmistakable signal to the unyielding Erich Honecker during the anniversary ceremony, Gorbachev announced, "He who comes too late is punished by life!" ("Wer zu spät kommt, den bestraft das Leben!"). His words were prophetic.

On October 7, the Stasi had mobilized 10,000 additional paramilitary men to bolster their police and army forces. But they discovered that there were some who refused to obey orders. These men had wives, mothers, and sisters in the crowds, and they had no intention of manhandling them. So military discipline was not a certain thing.

Erich Mielke, the head of the Stasi, knew that the regime was up against the wall. On October 8 he issued orders from Stasi headquarters that all informants, military units, police, paramilitary troops, and reserve troops should be fully mobilized on highest alert, that they should carry weapons at all times, that all private weapons should be confiscated, that journalists should be prevented from covering any disturbances, and that Stasi agents should be prepared to use "all means available against terror and every act of violence."[11] Plans were made to arrest between 1,200 and 1,500 "activist" clergy, who were to be incarcerated in remote castles in Thuringia.[12] The nation stood poised on the brink of civil war.

---

11. MfS Dokumentenverwaltung, Nr. 103625, VVS-Nr. 0008, October 8, 1989, Berlin, from *Ich liebe euch doch alle!: Befehle und Lageberichte des MfS,* pp. 201-3.

12. Willmar Thorkelson, "East Germans Said to Have Had Plans to Arrest Activist Clergy," *Religious News Service (RNS),* October 2, 1990, p. 3.

CHAPTER 8

Political Earthquake
Rocks the Eastern Bloc

East Germany

Many people in Leipzig were afraid. It was October 9, 1989, and no one had forgotten the blood-spattered deaths of the demonstrators in Tiananmen Square only four months earlier. Now tens of thousands of people were expected to come to the Nikolaikirche for the weekly *Friedensgebete*, or "Prayers for Peace." Only three days earlier, a Leipzig newspaper had conveyed the threat: "We are ready and willing to . . . conclusively and effectively put an end to these counter-revolutionary actions. *If need be with a weapon in hand!*"[1] Live ammunition was distributed to the military.

A week earlier, 2,000 people had pressed into the overflowing Nikolaikirche for the Monday night *Friedensgebete*, with another 3,000 massing in the square outside the church. Leipzig resident Petra Seela witnessed the assault at the end of the evening: "It was [done with] brute force, with riot sticks, attack dogs, and walkie talkies, and we were shocked. . . . We knew some of the people fleeing, and we saw the fear and terror in their eyes."[2]

---

1. Commander Günter Lutz, from the Kampfgruppenhundertschaft "Hans Geiffert," *Leipziger Volkszeitung*, October 6, 1989, p. 2.

2. Seela, "2. Oktober bis 8. Oktober," in *Jetzt oder nie — Demokratie: Leipziger Herbst '89* (Leipzig: Forum Verlag, 1989), p. 51.

Now, a week later, the city of Leipzig looked as if it were preparing for a civil war, an image that was not far from the truth. Army
units, helmeted police in riot squads, reservists, and paramilitary
squadrons were being trucked in, all having been put on alert. Armored vehicles, military transport vehicles, and water cannons lined
the streets near the Nikolaikirche.

Other warlike preparations were being made. Thousands of
pints of blood for transfusions were rushed to the hospitals, where
staffs were rescheduled to treat the anticipated victims. Heart surgeons at the Karl-Marx University were on emergency call; surgeons
and doctors working in intensive-care units throughout the city were
told to be prepared to treat shooting victims. The Thomaskirche, one
of the three churches in Leipzig that had agreed to hold *Friedensgebete* along with the Nikolaikirche in order to accommodate the expected overflow crowds, had been designated as an emergency first-
aid center to treat wounded. When he heard that news, one doctor
blurted to another, "My God, they're going to shoot us all!" Children
in school were warned not to go into the center of town because
there could be shooting. Parents were told to collect their children
from kindergarten earlier than usual, so they would be safely home
before the danger was acute.

Although the Prayers for Peace weren't scheduled to begin
until five p.m., the troops were briefed in the morning before being
posted. Some military personnel were asked to sign statements
that they would obey orders to fire, even if members of their
family were in the crowd. *Bereitschaftspolizisten,* the reserve police
commonly called *Bepos,* had a chilling exchange with their chief
officer:

> "Comrades, from today on it is class war. The situation is like June
> 17, [19]53. Today it will be decided, either for us or for them. . . .
> If the truncheons aren't enough, then guns will be used." The *Bepos*
> asked: "People will be coming to the demonstration with children.
> What will happen to the children?" The officer's answer: "They
> have bad luck. We have guns, and we don't have them for nothing!"
> As indignation swelled in the room, the *Bepos* pressed the question:

"Who will take the responsibility for that?" The prompt answer: "We take the responsibility!"[3]

After the briefing, the atmosphere in the barracks was as edgy as it was on the streets. Some of the reservists argued with each other about obeying an order to fire on the crowds in Leipzig's streets. "Many lay on their beds and cried. They knew that their own wife could be among the demonstrators."[4] Their brother or mother could be opposite them, their nearest friend. And yet they knew that if they refused to fire, they could end up in jail or be shot from behind.

However reluctantly, the *Bepos* took their place along with the paramilitary groups, special riot units, army soldiers, and members of the Stasi secret security forces. Armored vehicles rumbled through the streets, taking positions at critical intersections throughout downtown Leipzig. Stasi cameras mounted on tall buildings at six strategic points throughout the city recorded every movement on film. Thousands of military and security personnel flooded into the city in convoys. At the intersection of the *Runde Ecke* alone, where the Stasi building was located, there were thirteen military vehicles, six of which were manned by military police with machine guns. Some of these guns were filled with tear gas cartridges, others with bullets. Ten armored vehicles stood nearby with motors running. All of them carried live ammunition.[5]

Friedensgebete *in the Face of Threatened Violence*

Inside the offices of the Nikolaikirche, the phone was ringing off the hook. Numerous people, some choking back tears, were calling to

---

3. The comparison of the situation to that of June 17 is a reference to the East German uprising against the Communists on June 17, 1953, which was put down with the help of Soviet tanks and bullets. The quotation is from Neues Forum Leipzig, *Jetzt oder nie — Demokratie*, pp. 92-93.

4. Ibid., p. 93.

5. Ibid.

warn Pastor Christian Führer not to hold the *Friedensgebete*. These indiviuals had reason to fear. State officials had already confronted Führer repeatedly and ordered him to cancel the service. But he remained unwavering.

All over the city, families were having earnest discussions about who should go to the Nikolaikirche and who should stay at home. Those who would dare to go would risk arrest — and possibly their lives. Christoph and Maria Bormann were having just such a discussion. Both of them had been regular participants in the *Friedensgebete* for several years, and Maria was a long-standing member of the Nikolaikirche's vestry. Understandably, both of them wanted to attend — but when Maria looked at their small daughters, she said, "One of us has to be here for the children." So she decided to stay home. Did she think that her husband might be risking his life to go? "That was certainly a possibility," she admitted later.[6]

Christoph headed for downtown Leipzig without Maria, joining the sea of humanity streaming toward the church. Traffic was blocked everywhere, and people abandoned their cars to continue on foot. All public transportation was jammed to overflowing, and ultimately stopped running altogether. Nearly every face was ashen, and there was no idle chatter. The fear in the air was palpable. Those on foot were shocked to see the armored vehicles as they neared the church. The rows upon rows of helmeted and masked riot police armed with truncheons were a sobering sight, almost surrealistic figures with hidden faces.

Across town, Helga Wagner, a member of the Communist party and professor at Karl-Marx University in Leipzig, was in a meeting when the call came: "Five comrades should go to the Nikolaikirche!" Sensing something important was happening there, she answered spontaneously, "I'll go along." As a member of the party, she was supposed to shun the church, but now she was responding to an official request. At two p.m. she entered the Nikolaikirche, one of 500 members of the Communist party there under orders to take

6. Drawn from the author's interview with Christoph and Maria Bormann in Leipzig on February 26, 1991.

seats in the church.[7] Although the service wasn't supposed to begin until five p.m., the nave was already packed, and the rest of the church was filling rapidly. At 3:30 the doors had to be closed on the bursting crowd.

Lutz Ramson had worked his way through the crowds with the greatest difficulty. When he finally made it to the Nikolaikirche at 2:30 p.m., he was startled to see that the church was already almost full. Since he was a member of the vestry, he went to the front of the church and began to set up the microphone. When he took a second look at the crowd, it confirmed his gut feeling that something was very different. Because of his association with the *Friedensgebete* over the past six years, he recognized many of the people there. But the Communists in the church changed the composition. What Lutz saw everywhere was naked fear. "We were afraid — that was visible, but they were afraid too."[8] Catcalls, shouts, and boos floated inside the church. "We thought it was for us," Helga Wagner recalls, "because they knew who was sitting . . . inside." The party members wondered fearfully if word had spread that the Communists had infiltrated the church.

Meanwhile, the pilgrimage to the churches continued. Seventy thousand people were on foot and moving through the city. "It was unbelievable," Christoph Bormann recalls. "Everywhere you looked there were people." The forces that were supposed to put down this demonstration were every bit as nervous as the participants. Riot police held their shields with sweaty palms. The hour of the prayers drew nearer, and six thousand people pressed against one another in the Nikolaikirche and the three other churches participating in the *Friedensgebete* — the Reformierte Kirche, the Thomaskirche, and the Michaeliskirche. As the clock ticked toward five p.m., Leipzig was strung taut.

Even as Christian Führer began the *Friedensgebete* in the Nikolaikirche, his wife continued to take frantic phone calls from

7. Neues Forum Leipzig, *Jetzt oder nie — Demokratie,* p. 88.

8. Drawn from the author's interview with Lutz and Marianne Ramson in Leipzig on February 27, 1991.

people begging him to cancel the service to avoid civil war. But the service was held in the usual way, as it had been every Monday. To open the service, he read from Isaiah 45; then the participants read the Beatitudes, as they did each week, letting the words ring out:

> Blessed are those who hunger and thirst
>   for righteousness,
> for they will be filled. . . .
> Blessed are the peacemakers,
> for they will be called sons of God.
> Blessed are those who are persecuted because
>   of righteousness,
> for theirs is the kingdom of heaven.
>
> (Matt. 5:6-10)

The liturgy was kept deliberately simple. To create a feeling of familiarity, the same hymns and passages from the Bible had been read and sung again and again in the *Friedensgebete*. In the course of the service at the Nikolaikirche, two men from Dresden reported that first steps were taken toward a dialogue between their mayor and demonstrators. *Neues Forum* had issued a written appeal to those in Leipzig, urging them to remain peaceful.

Shortly after the service began, a very pale and bedraggled Peter Zimmermann, a theologian at Leipzig University, handed Christian Führer a message that he begged him to read over the microphone so that those in the church as well as those outside listening to the service via loudspeaker could hear. Zimmermann had spent the day frantically brokering a joint appeal from six well-known Leipzig personalities to the people of the city in an attempt to avoid brutal confrontation and seek peaceful change and dialogue. The document that he had brought with him was the result of harried negotiations with three secretaries of the Communist party and the unlikely coalition of the conductor Kurt Masur, the cabaret artist Bernd-Lutz Lange, and Zimmermann himself. Christian Führer took the paper from Zimmermann's shaking hand and read it to those assembled.

The effect was electrifying. Was there a way out of the seemingly certain shooting waiting in the streets outside? Susanne Rummel, a participant in the *Friedensgebete,* recalls that the entire church breathed a communal sigh of relief, and when the news went out over the loudspeakers, those outside experienced a brief flicker of joy. "But it didn't last," Susanne notes. From outside there came waves of chants, accompanied by whistles and boos and clapping: "Stasi out!" "Gorby, Gorby," and "We're staying here!" The atmosphere in the church was bursting with tension. "Somehow," Susanne recalls, "we all seemed to be ducking in expectation of a terrible blow. . . . No one wanted to say the words 'civil war' or 'spilled blood,' but it was all tangibly near to each of us. The pastor offered to keep the church open for all who didn't want to go out."9

Bishop Werner Leich made a compelling appeal for nonviolence, which he personally delivered at each of the four churches holding the *Friedensgebete.* He hurried from one church to the next with his message. This was a familiar and recurrent theme. Nonviolence had been preached week after week at all the *Friedensgebete* gatherings. The Christians were determined not to return evil for evil. Tonight more than ever, the course of events might depend on whether they could act on that belief.

And then something remarkable happened. In the words of Protestant Superintendent Friedrich Magirius, "The spirit of peace and non-violence spread over those assembled. Everyone held his neighbor tightly, and this spirit went out with the people onto the square." Those who had been inside the church mingled among those assembled outside, bringing the spirit of peace with them. "The power was contagious," Magirius recalls.10

Pastor Christian Führer remembers the moment this way: "The spirit of Christ, the spirit of non-violence and renewal fell on the masses, moved the people deeply and became a tangible force of peace. . . . It was like the Book of Acts when the Holy Spirit fell on Cornelius and his household. This is something quite remarkable

---

9. Neues Forum Leipzig, *Jetzt oder nie — Demokratie,* pp. 83-84.
10. Magirius, "Wiege der Wende," *Leipziger Demontagebuch* (Leipzig: Gustav Kiepenheuer Verlag, 1990), p. 13.

because these people were mostly not Christians. And yet these people behaved then as if they had grown up with the Sermon on the Mount."[11]

Nineteen-year-old Raphaela Russ recalls, "With an amazing composure the mass began to move, past the curious onlookers who hemmed the edges of the streets, past the mobilized security forces, past the barking dogs in the narrow streets and alleyways, past the heavily guarded Stasi building."[12]

An amorphous mass of 70,000 people assumed purpose and form, moving slowly through the city of Leipzig on the streets that ring the center of the city. Some people carried candles, each shielding the tiny flame with one hand. Others linked arms with each other in encouragement. Demonstrators saw the light glinting off the weapons, looked at the walls of shields and helmets and armed vehicles, and walked peacefully between them.

As the crowd moved through the streets of Leipzig, voices rang out. "We are the people!" and "No violence!" they repeated in chorus. As the procession neared the *Runde Ecke* where the Stasi headquarters were, the mood grew ugly, with some among the crowd hissing boos and catcalls. But others shouted even louder, "No violence! No violence!" When the word came that they must turn back, some went scrambling in wide-eyed panic onto the side streets, clambering over fences, fearing that the order to shoot had been given. But it was a false alarm; the attack had not come.

The soldiers, reservists, and paramilitary troops all stood tensely on guard, watching in near disbelief at the human flood flowing past them, people as far as the eye could see, and more coming. Those driving the military vehicles kept the motors running in readiness for the anticipated order to move in on the crowd. The young men on the front lines fixed their gaze on their feet when demonstrators tried to look them in the eye. They shifted their weapons uneasily.

---

11. This and subsequent quotations are drawn from the author's interview with Christian Führer in Leipzig on February 28, 1991.

12. Russ, ". . . wenn es sein muss, mit der Waffe in der Hand!" *Die Revolution der Kerzen: Christen in den Umwälzungen der DDR*, ed. Jörg Swoboda (Wuppertal: Oncken Verlag, 1990), p. 144.

In a tone both desperate and courageous, one among the crowd blurted out the question that thousands more wished they could articulate: "We are the people and you are the people. Are you really going to shoot us?" He aimed his question at a perplexed reservist.

Susanne Rummel and those with her did the same. "We walked together, hesitatingly at first, until we came to Karl-Marx-Square and then we saw them — the wagons where the troops sat with their helmets and shields. . . . We talked with them, asked them whether we looked like enemies of the state or anarchists and whether they really would beat us."[13]

Seventy thousand demonstrators moved through Leipzig's streets without offering a single provocation to the armed guards who were waiting for the order to shoot at them. No one hurled a stone through a window in frustration at the mute and fearful years. No one shouted defiantly at the massive display of police and military power. No one so much as knocked off a policeman's cap. The only fires that were lit were candles. Forty years of frustration, repression, and pent-up resentment were not expressed in any way that gave the armed forces reason to shoot. The order to open fire on the demonstrators never came.

Eventually the crowd dispersed in an orderly way. As they made their way home, the tension slowly left the city. Some uncorked a bottle of wine in celebration. By the next morning, the country had turned a corner. *Die Wende.* It was the showdown.

Reflecting on that night she experienced on Leipzig's streets, Raphaela Russ wrote, "With the bloodless end of the 9th of October a new era began. Who would have believed it before? The question still remains, who prevented the security forces from attacking? It's clear to me that God wrote history here."[14] The battle was fought not with the weapons of this world, but with the weapons of prayer and peaceful restraint.

Pastor Christian Führer sees the event as a powerful testament to God's spirit at work on earth: "Non-violence is clearly the spirit

13. Quoted in Neues Forum Leipzig, *Jetzt oder nie — Demokratie,* pp. 83-84.
14. Russ, ". . .wenn es sein muss. . . ," p. 145.

of Jesus. With these people who grew up with pictures of class enemies, and whose parents grew up with the Nazis and violence and
racial hatred, you can prove that it didn't come from here. It's not a
question of one's upbringing. And the few Christians that there are
in this unchristian country — they didn't do it either. . . . That was
the spirit of God at work. We few people couldn't have done it. . . .
God honored us by letting us play this part in His plan."

An Echo of Jericho: The Berlin Wall Falls

It is clear that during this critical time, Gorbachev withheld explicit
approval for a bloodbath to put down the demonstration, and the
East German regime may not have dared to give the order to fire on
its own. But this was a radical change for the Soviets, in light of the
Soviet response in 1953 in East Germany, in 1957 in Hungary, and
in 1968 in Czechoslovakia. And the Soviets had threatened Poland
with invasion as recently as 1981. There was nothing inevitable about
a peaceful end, as Chinese demonstrators had found out in Tiananmen Square only months before. Had the Soviets themselves
changed? Recent behavior gives no consistent answer: they used violence again in Lithuania in January 1991. But for some reason, the
situation in East Germany turned out differently.

The East German regime was now in disarray. In a tense
politburo session on October 18, Erich Honecker was unceremoniously dumped and replaced by Egon Krenz. The number of
demonstrators swelled to 200,000 in Leipzig, then 300,000. City after
city followed Leipzig's example, with millions filling the streets. A
nation was on its feet because the people had found their voice. The
regime was scrambling to meet their pent-up demands to be able to
speak freely, to travel, to organize, to reform. So many things were
different, including the fresh creativity, wit, courage, and humor that
people used to illustrate the banners they carried. It was as if they
were negotiating by poster board, as their appetite for change was
whetted by new victories.

The turning point in Berlin came on November 4, 1989. One

million people assembled in the Alexanderplatz, with the "best and brightest" of the country addressing the huge crowd. The mass of people moved in procession to Unter den Linden, then to the Palace of the Republic, then back to the Alexanderplatz. The critical point came at the Palace of the Republic, where the street continues straight on to the Brandenburg Gate, the huge, well-known archway that is the gateway between East and West Berlin, and symbolically between the two parts of the divided country.

Anyone who could think militarily knew that if a million people continued marching straight ahead, the tanks would have to roll and the soldiers would have to intervene to stop them. But those in the procession also knew the Stasi and their methods. If the Stasi put a few hundred provocateurs into the crowd to keep marching ahead, to draw the crowd toward the Brandenburg Gate, that would provide the needed reason to attack. It was not discussed, but all the genuine participants knew that even if hundreds broke away, they must not.

As the crowd neared the curve, Werner Krätschell stood at that spot near the Brandenburg Gate with his wife. "We have to stand here and watch this," he told her. "It is unforgettable." What he remembers most is the silence: "Hundreds and thousands of people walked around this curve without saying a word. It was a silent march at this point. One heard only the soft sound of the feet of these people. Everyone knew this was the critical point."[15] There was no provocation, there was no attack. A million people silently signaled with their feet that they wanted change, but peaceful change.

Five days later, the Berlin Wall fell. Ironically, the regime hadn't intended that at all. In fact, they kicked it over by accident in a pratfall.

When the entire politburo resigned on November 8, a committee was charged with drafting a new law on travel. The draft they produced was given to staffers, who concluded that by logic it had to include anyone who wanted to travel to the West, and they amended it accordingly. Without further checks, the draft was given to the regime's spokesman, Günter Schabowski, in the middle of a

---

15. Drawn from the author's interview with Werner Krätschell in Berlin on May 28, 1991.

press conference, who simply read it. As the message sunk in, an incredulous question came from a journalist: Did that mean that any East German could cross the border to the West? Schabowski admitted that it looked that way, judging by the text. The government had intended to control travel by issuing visas, but that went unnoticed in the hubbub that boiled over immediately.

The news reached the airwaves with lightning speed, and people swarmed to the cross-points in Berlin, some still in pajamas, mobbing the surprised border guards, who knew nothing about what had happened. When the people told them what they'd heard on the radio, the guards were unsure what to do. After trying to hold back the growing, jostling crowd, some guards in exasperation and confusion simply shoved back their caps and let the people charge through. The crowd became jubilant, and the people of a nation that had been divided fell into each other's arms. There were tears, flowers, and streams of uncorked champagne.

Shortly thereafter, on New Year's Day, young people danced on the Wall in exhilaration, and the nation wept in disbelief and joy. Reunification, which occurred on October 3, 1990, took place less than a year from the moment the Wall fell.

On the night that the Wall fell, people leaving the Nikolaikirche marched through the center of the city. Week after week during the fall of 1989, they had marched in a circle around Leipzig after the *Friedensgebete.* On November 9, they marched for the seventh time, this time straight through the city. It was a silent march commemorating the fifty-first anniversary of *Kristallnacht,* the beginning of violence against the Jews leading up to World War II. And on that night, people left the Nikolaikirche praying for their country. As they walked through Leipzig for the seventh time, they heard a crash as resounding as that once heard in Jericho: it was the sound of the Berlin Wall falling. The German Democratic Republic had been in existence for exactly forty years.

The biblical allusions are startling.

*　　*　　*

In retrospect, many would say that this was not a religious revolution — and considerable evidence can be gathered to support this opinion. Only months later, the East German churches were as empty as before. While the *Evangelische Kirche* had provided the roof over the protesters' heads and defended the legitimacy of the movement, not many people bothered to say Thank You. Disappointed pastors noted that their church membership fell even lower once the church tax of the West was introduced in the East.[16] One activist spoke bluntly about the protesters' going to church: "We didn't go because we were religious; we went to express ourselves." And leaders like Bärbel Bohley, the "Mother Courage" of the revolution, admitted, "We used the church."[17]

And the involvement of the Stasi certainly tarred the church. Subsequent revelations of the massive extent of Stasi collaboration in the church are sobering, even sickening. Informants penetrated every level, with clerics reporting confidential confessions, staffers snooping on their pastors, "brothers and sisters" betraying each other in the parish, and priests spying on their own or the neighboring congregation. As an institution, the church was anything but holy.

But neither can the contribution of the religious element be easily discounted. Individual believers who remained morally intact had a tangible effect on the people around them. Their courage was contagious. And the fact that the revolution remained peaceful is largely the result of their influence: in the clinch, they intervened to keep demonstrators from hurling stones, and later also kept members of the Stasi from being lynched. They also played a prominent part in the new order: key leaders in the "basis groups" as well as members of fledgling political parties, transitional roundtables, and the new government were Christians. It would be overstating the case to say that Christians won the revolution. But as individuals they signifi-

16. In Germany, members of the *Evangelische Landeskirchen* and the Catholic Church don't make voluntary contributions; instead, their contributions are collected through the national tax system. The amount is a fixed percentage of 9 percent of the total amount of income tax they pay.

17. Drawn from the author's interview with Bärbel Bohley in Berlin on May 28, 1991.

cantly influenced its tone. (In addition, those who were not politically engaged but who consistently led a Christian life had an effect on the spiritual landscape around them.) Their revolution of the spirit preceded the political one. They prayed for their country and lived righteously, as Dietrich Bonhoeffer advocated in words and by example a generation earlier.

Two banners that demonstrators carried on the streets gave credit where it was due. One said, "We thank you, church!" The other said, "Peace! Justice! Democracy! But how? Jesus speaks: Without me, you can do nothing."

There's no question that the reunification of Germany which followed these critical events was to a very great extent due to the will and political strategy of West German Chancellor Helmut Kohl, who capitalized on the opportunity presented him. But he too saw the unfolding events as something larger. He expressed it well by quoting Bismarck when he met with Mikhail Gorbachev in July 1990: "One can only wait and listen for the steps of God resounding through events, then leap forward to grasp a corner of His mantle."[18]

The Earthquake's Epicenter Widens

Czechoslovakia

The dust of the fallen Berlin Wall had scarcely settled before the next shudder of the earthquake was to take another Communist regime down. Czechoslovakia's flash point was a confrontation similar to the one that had occurred in East Germany on October 7, when police forces had brutally clubbed demonstrators on the fortieth anniversary of the founding of the GDR. The Czechoslovakian demonstration on November 17 had begun as a peaceful commemoration of the death of a Nazi victim during World War II. But by the end of the evening, the demonstrators who had peacefully marched

18. Quoted in the *Wall Street Journal (Europe)*, November 30/December 1, 1990, p. 1.

down Národní Avenue to Wenceslas Square with bare, outstretched hands were met by white-helmeted riot police and anti-terrorist squads in red berets, who charged violently into the crowds. Reportedly hundreds were injured; one person was rumored to have died. This incident, which was dubbed "the massacre," was the spark that ignited Czechoslovakia's resistance.[19]

The Magic Lantern Theater became the unofficial headquarters, filled in the next days with a buzz of comings and goings. Students and actors, furnace stokers and philosophers, banished writers and priests sat in intense clusters amid a litter of empty glasses and overflowing ashtrays, debating the future of the nation. The leaders of Charter 77 and VONS were major players in the newly galvanized resistance movement, joining forces in a new group called Civic Forum. They drafted a document calling for the resignation of the president, Gustav Husák, Communist party leader Miloš Jakeš, and others, as well as an investigation of police actions in "the massacre," and the release of prisoners of conscience. They also declared their support for a general strike on November 27.[20]

In the following turbulent days, Václav Havel, Václav Benda, and the banished priest Václav Malý figured prominently in the revolution, both in articulating the positions of the resistance and in leading the demonstrations that swelled mightily. On November 21, four days after the demonstration that had ended in violence, 200,000 people turned out in Wenceslas Square, where they heard Father Malý read a letter from Cardinal Tomášek supporting the cause of freedom and democracy, while urging peaceful and restrained resistance.[21] At this, the crowd erupted into cheers. Tomášek had

---

19. For a fuller rendition of the events of the Velvet Revolution, see Timothy Garton Ash's *We the People: The Revolution of '89, Witnessed in Warsaw, Budapest, Berlin and Prague* (Cambridge: Granta Books, 1990), pp. 78-130; Bud Bultman's *Revolution by Candlelight: The Real Story behind the Changes in Eastern Europe*, ed. Harold Fickett (Portland, Ore.: Multnomah Press, 1991), pp. 194-216; and George Weigel's *The Final Revolution* (New York: Oxford University Press, 1992), pp. 159-90.

20. Bultman, *Revolution by Candlelight*, p. 201.

21. For the text of Cardinal Tomášek's letter, see Weigel's *The Final Revolution*, p. 160. Bud Bultman renders the scene of the rally in *Revolution by Candlelight*, pp. 201-3.

turned down an offer to serve as a mediator, instead taking his stand with the resistance.[22]

Three days later, on November 24, the crowd was again gathered in Wenceslas Square. Who would they see today? They gasped in disbelief as Alexander Dubček, the father of the reforms of "Prague Spring" in 1968 who had subsequently been living in virtual exile, appeared before them as if resurrected. Moved by what he saw, he said, "I am standing before a people who have again raised their heads."[23] After the rally, Dubček stood with Václav Havel on the stage of the Magic Lantern Theater, before the improbably appropriate set for the play *Minotaur:* a tunnel with a maze guarded by a monster. This time it was Dubček's turn to gasp when Havel whispered in Dubček's ear the news he had just gotten: Miloš Jakeš and the entire politburo had resigned. When Havel announced this news, the theater resounded with applause, and Havel toasted to a free Czechoslovakia.[24]

Over the next days, Civic Forum continued to apply pressure, demanding that a new, representative government be formed. On December 3, when they were disappointed by Prime Minister Adamec's first proposal for a revamped government, they did not buckle, but held fast to their demands. The next day they called for another strike if their demands weren't met within a week. At this point, the Czechoslovakian government promptly complied with Civic Forum's terms, and a new government was sworn in on December 10. On December 28, Alexander Dubček was elected chairman of the Parliament. The next day, Václav Havel was sworn in as president of his country. Only six months earlier he had been in prison.

The entire revolution succeeded in effecting a transfer of power so swift, so smooth, and so free of violence that it deserved the name it has borne since: the Velvet Revolution.

22. For a profile on Cardinal Tomášek and his increasingly courageous stance, see Weigel's *The Final Revolution,* pp. 176-78, 184-85.

23. Quoted by Bultman in *Revolution by Candlelight,* p. 206.

24. See Ash's *We the People,* p. 96; and Bultman's *Revolution by Candlelight,* pp. 206-7.

Romania

The shudders of the quake spread further, reaching Romania in December, where the repression was particularly harsh, and the showdown with the regime more swift but more brutal. Just as in Czechoslovakia, where resistance had coalesced around individuals who had been persecuted by the Communists, a popular uprising in Romania emerged around one resister: Laszlo Tökes.[25]

A pastor of the Hungarian Reformed Church who was committed to the preservation of the uniqueness of the Hungarian minority in Romania's Transylvania, Tökes had incurred the wrath of the Romanian regime. After a television interview he gave in March of 1989, in which he outspokenly criticized the regime's attempts to undermine Hungarian faith and culture, the regime went after him with a vengeance. He was officially suspended as pastor of his congregation in Timisoara (though he kept preaching anyway), he and his family were virtually held hostage in the parsonage, and members of his congregation were harassed.

After several months of escalating persecution, the regime threatened to evict Tökes and his family from the parsonage. The Sunday before the eviction was scheduled, Tökes asked his congregation to come witness this injustice.

On December 15, what began as a protest by Tökes's congregation became a protest that brought together the townspeople: the Reformed congregation was joined by Baptists, Catholics, and Orthodox; ethnic Romanians stood together with ethnic Hungarians. They formed a circle around the parsonage, and resistance to what was happening to Tökes grew into shouted resistance against Nikolai Ceausescu. The group surged over to the Communist party building to continue its protest. Some mobbed the building, and others tore

---

25. For a full account of Laszlo Tökes and the Romanian revolution, see David Porter's *Laszlo Tökes: Im Sturm der rumänischen Revolution* (Wuppertal: Oncken Verlag, 1991). The English version of the book is titled *With God — for the People*, published by Hodder & Stoughton. The Romanian revolution is also dramatically described by Bultman in *Revolution by Candlelight*.

through the town, destroying Communist symbols. In response, militia squads, army troops, and police arrived with a battery of weapons — and the violence began. Over the next two days, Tökes and his wife were arrested, and the demonstrators were brutally assaulted at Ceauşescu's orders: men and women, even children, were mowed down with bullets. The chaos bordered on anarchy.

In an attempt to recover public support for his government, which had been savagely criticized after this episode of violence, Ceauşescu staged a rally in Bucharest on December 21. But instead of engendering support, the rally turned on Ceauşescu. A chant of "Timisoara" came from the crowd, and that swelled into angry shouts against Ceauşescu that drowned him out. The televised confrontation documented Ceauşescu's faltering speech and abrupt ending of the rally. When he realized that he was no longer in control, he attempted to flee the country. But by Christmas Day, after the condemnation of a self-styled tribunal, Ceauşescu and his wife had been publicly executed.

While the revolution had been sparked by the spontaneous support of one Christian, another emerged during the conflict to guide and inspire: Peter Dugulescu.[26] On December 22, several days after the bloodbath at Timisoara, Dugulescu was one of a number of people invited to address the crowds that gathered in Opera Square for pro-democracy rallies. He was a Baptist pastor from Timisoara whom the Communists had harassed, even tried to kill. But, he assured the crowd, he believed that God had protected him — and that the Communists had not succeeded in killing God for the people of Romania. "God exists!" he cried. "God exists!" The crowd, galvanized by his impassioned speech, took up the chant: "God exists!" Moments later, when Dugulescu asked them to kneel and pray, they did so, offering the Lord's Prayer with him. Dugulescu has since been elected to the Romanian Parliament.

This revolution, volatile and bloody, was the exception: all the other Eastern bloc countries accomplished the transition from Com-

---

26. The portrait is based on the author's interview with Peter Dugulescu on June 5, 1993, in Budapest and on pp. 240-41 in Bultman's *Revolution by Candlelight.*

munist domination to fledgling democracy with astonishing tranquility and the near-absence of violence. And it seems that Romanians may have gained the least of all in the years since.

Poland

Poland was already well on its way to a transition as the political earthquake rocked the rest of Eastern Europe in the fall of 1989. In January of that year, the Polish regime had agreed to relegalize Solidarity. In addition, major ground had been won piecemeal during the late 1980s in roundtable negotiations for which the church had served as an observer. Major victories included the end of censorship, the release of all political prisoners, and the promise of free elections on June 4. (To his credit, it was General Jaruzelski who authorized Solidarity's return to legal status, and who implemented the orderly transfer of power from a dictatorship to a democracy.) An agreement had been made that would limit the number of seats that could be wrested from the Communists in the lower house, the *Sejm*. Solidarity was nervous when election day came, but the eventual results were staggeringly good news. Solidarity swept everything it was allowed to, winning 99 of the 100 Senate seats, and 35 percent of the lower house, the maximum percentage agreed upon.

When the dust settled on the Polish political landscape after Solidarity's volcanic triumph, Tadeusz Mazowiecki was named prime minister. Lech Wałęsa, who had won the Nobel Peace Prize, had declined the role, preferring to press into office Mazowiecki, his trusted advisor and negotiator, the respected Catholic intellectual. Solidarity's Jacek Kuroń became the minister of labor, and Bronisław Geremek the leader of Solidarity's parliamentary faction. On September 12, 1989, when Mazowiecki addressed the Parliament for the first time, he concluded his remarks with, "I believe that God will help us to make a giant step forward in the road that opens before us."[27]

27. Quoted by Bultman in *Revolution by Candlelight*, p. 258.

A little over a year later, on December 9, 1990, Lech Wałęsa was elected president of the republic of Poland. With this appointment, the feisty former electrician with the Black Madonna on his lapel completed a climb from the fence outside Gdańsk's shipping yards to Poland's White House. All this had begun with Solidarity, according to theologian Józef Tischner, who described it as a "huge forest of awakened consciences." This "forest" had changed the face of the nation — and for that matter, the continent, as the coming years were to show.

The Collapsing of an Empire

In a moral, political, and spiritual earthquake, the Communist empire in Eastern Europe came crashing down after the fall of 1989. By the time the quake's tremors had subsided, the entire Eastern bloc had been freed, including Bulgaria and (later) Albania. Hungary had early on begun a transfer of power from the Communists to an independent government, a change personified in Miklós Németh, the man who was the last prime minister under the Communist regime but who was himself not a member of the party. Certainly each country's journey was different, shaped by diverse circumstances, national interests, and unique histories. But in the end, some 400 million people were freed from what had been a monolithic structure that had ruled them with force for forty years. That this was accomplished without major bloodshed is truly remarkable. For an event of such magnitude, this phenomenon is unique in all of history.

While it may have been inevitable that the Communist reign would end, there was nothing inevitable about the timing or the way it was accomplished. On June 4, 1989, the same day that Poland held its first free elections, Chinese soldiers fired on student demonstrators in Tiananmen Square, putting down the fledgling democratic movement there with a shocking bloodbath. That massacre made it clear that there was nothing inevitable about democratic process, not even in the *annus mirabilis* 1989.

What accounted for the revolution? Was it a failure of will on the Communists' part, or had something else occurred? Many of those who rebelled claim that the people were no longer the same. The citizens who had been coerced into timid conformity suddenly stood up. They were no longer afraid. In each of these countries there was a "remnant," a minority of people who spoke about, wrote about, and lived their nonconformist convictions. Thousands of individuals who made courageous personal decisions contributed to the process of becoming free: young people who refused to join the Communist youth groups, those who forfeited careers by not joining the Communist party, young men who refused to bear arms for the regime. A generation of writers who dared to publish *samizdat* literature, even if it meant being jailed, provided intellectual nourishment for the movement. Likewise, Christians who were banned from their activities but who persisted despite harassment and the threat (or reality) of imprisonment tended the spiritual roots of the revolution. These few stood like bright candles in an otherwise dark landscape, providing light for others who later dared to stand with them when the moment of truth came for each individual and each country.

Every person who dared to say "no" and willingly accepted the consequences cast off the shackles of Communism. A critical mass of people later overcame their fear and rose up to say "no" by their presence on the streets, a witness that resounded. The moral leaders of the revolution, who were committed to transcendent truth, galvanized that witness. And while undoubtedly people demonstrated for a variety of reasons — whether economic discontent, the desire to travel, or the simple conclusion that things could not go on as they were — the seismic disturbance that they created together as they took to the streets of Eastern Europe accomplished the seemingly impossible.

The hallmark of the revolution of 1989 was its extraordinary restraint. The moral leaders of the revolution were passionately committed to change, but change brought about by peaceful means. This was a conscious decision made at the beginning of the movement's birth that was honored even in the most trying circumstances. Only days after Solidarity advisor Father Jerzy Popiełuszko was murdered by the Polish security service, writer Adam Michnik said, "Let these methods remain theirs alone." Alexander Solzhenitsyn put it this way: "Those who choose error as their principle must use violence as their method. Those who choose truth as their principle must use peace as their method." And Solzhenitsyn had spoken prophetically about the events of 1989 in the speech he had made upon receiving the Nobel prize in 1970: "Once the lie has been dispersed, the nakedness of violence will be revealed in all its repulsiveness, and then violence, become decrepit, will come crashing down."[28] Indeed it did, with a rapidity even he most certainly could not have imagined. John 8:32 had been revalidated: "And you shall know the truth, and the truth shall make you free."

28. Solzhenitsyn, *"One Word of Truth. . ."* (London: Bodley Head, 1972), p. 27.

CHAPTER 9

The Coup: The Moment of Decision

August 19, 1991
Reuters News Agency

Tass says Vice-President Gennady Yanayev has taken over as Soviet head of state because Gorbachev, holidaying in the Crimea, is ill. A "State Committee on the State of Emergency" made up of eight communist hardliners takes over, clamps down on the press, bans demonstrations and pledges to introduce curfews. Russian President Boris Yeltsin denounces Gorbachev's removal as leader and calls for a general strike. Some 5,000 people gather outside the Russian Parliament and build barricades. Yeltsin orders Army and KGB units involved in the coup to stand down and takes control of Russian territory. State of emergency declared in Moscow and Leningrad.

As the people in Moscow heard the news of the coup, they faced a crisis, a turning point. It was the moment of decision both for their country and for each of them personally. How should they respond? While news summaries give us the overall picture, what follows are the individual stories of seven people who responded to this moment by deciding to resist the takeover. These are not intended to provide an overview; they are personal histories, recountings of the moments these individuals chose to live their convictions. And they had no way of gauging the risk or the result of what they chose to do.

The Coup: The Moment of Decision

Portraits of Courage

"Thou Shalt Not Kill": Father Alexander Borisov

The morning of the coup, Father Alexander Borisov was in the Russian Orthodox Church celebrating a service commemorating St. Seraphim of Sarov, a Russian monk and mystic who lived from 1759 to 1833. Seraphim had prophesied that in the twentieth century, Russia would experience more than seventy years of darkness, but that when his bones were returned to their proper resting place in Sarov, a new period of Russian history would begin. As it turned out, Seraphim's remains were discovered in a museum of atheism in St. Petersburg in the spring of 1991, and were returned to Sarov one week before the coup in August. For more than a century, Russians had believed Seraphim's prophecy. But it certainly didn't appear that great things were happening on the morning of August 19, 1991. In his sermon, Father Alexander urged his parishioners to persevere: he said that despite the recent political changes, the people of God were called to be patient. Still, as he left the church, the gravity of the events weighed heavily on him. He feared that the worst elements of Communism were returning.

Father Alexander was a Russian Orthodox priest who had refused to collaborate with the KGB, and as a result he had been blocked from ordination for sixteen years.[1] As a man of proven integrity, he had been elected to the Moscow City Council in the first open elections held in 1990. When the council convened later that day, the members wrangled over the appropriate response to the crisis. The resolution that the council drafted was so tepid that Father Alexander felt compelled to oppose it. He stood up and protested, telling the other members that what was taking place was clearly a Communist coup and that they must oppose it unambiguously.

Father Alexander quickly drafted a declaration himself, appeal-

---

1. This story is based on the author's interviews with Father Alexander Borisov in Moscow on March 10 and November 10, 1992. For the full story of his refusal to collaborate with the KGB, see Chapter Three.

ing to the troops occupying Moscow and urging them not to attack the civilian populace. Persuaded by his forthright courage to condemn what had happened, the city council approved the declaration. "They want to deceive you once again," Father Alexander told the soldiers. "The communist party made you fight in Afghanistan. Now it wants you to fight your own people. You must answer not only to your own conscience . . . you are [also] accountable to God. 'Thou shalt not kill.'" He used the language of the Ten Commandments deliberately.

The soldiers who had been brought into Moscow, most of whom were young recruits, had been told that they were there to put down riots of young people refusing to perform military service. They had no idea that their military leaders were involved in a plot to take control of the government.

Risking Her Life to Serve: Vera Boiko

Vera Boiko first heard the news of the coup on television at 6:30 in the morning.[2] She understood immediately how grave the situation was. She remembered the coup in which Khrushchev had been overthrown, and how irrelevant public opinion had been in those events. She knew that her country was in great danger now.

Vera's husband was still sleeping. Fearing that he would react intensely to the news, Vera switched off the television and woke him gently to tell him herself. "Valodov, wake up." But there was no way to break the news gently. "We've had a coup here," she said simply. He was as shocked as she had been.

A musician, conductor, and director of a school of the arts, Vera had been elected to the Russian parliament in the first open elections held in 1990. Surprised to find herself nominated as a write-in candidate, she had accepted the call to this new and strange world of politics in Russia's fledgling democratic movement. The responsi-

2. Based on the author's interview with Vera Boiko in Moscow on March 18, 1992.

202

bility that came with the position was something she sensed keenly that morning.

As she and her husband dressed and prepared to leave the house, Vera felt they needed to say good-bye to each other in something other than the usual way. She was headed for her office in the parliament building, which was the center of the maelstrom for the coup. It was altogether uncertain what would happen in the course of the day, both to her and to her country. Although neither she nor her husband said it, it was obvious that she would be entering a dangerous situation by going to the parliament building that morning. It was also obvious that she felt it was something she must do.

In a way, the two of them settled accounts. They talked about what they had shared in their life together, and they asked each other's forgiveness for their failures. They had some money put away, and they divided it. Then it was time to go. Neither of them knew if this might be their final farewell. Vera looked at her husband and said, "Valodov, you are a strong man, and you should remain strong. You have upheld me. You helped me during my election campaign. Anything can happen to us now. You must know that I am honest, that all I have wanted was to do good." Valodov was warm and gentle in his response. "Don't be worried," he said, drawing her near to kiss her and say good-bye. Then he left for his office, and Vera crossed town to the embattled parliament building.

When she entered the building, crowds of civilians were gathering outside. Gradually the members of parliament assembled, and by noon the presidium was in place, joined by foreign reporters. Boris Yeltsin addressed the group, telling them that the parliament building had been cut off from the rest of the country, and urging the reporters to use their own channels to tell the world what was happening. He trusted that if they could get the word out, the free countries in the West would support him and the parliament.

Vera remained at the parliament building for the next four days, a willing hostage defending the country's leader and the fledgling democratic reforms against the military leaders who staged the coup. Her twin sister, Nadya Derznovenko, a senior staff member of the Committee on the Freedom of Conscience, had taken the same stand,

and she stayed with Vera in the building. "There are times you are not afraid," Nadya says, recollecting her decision. "It is simply clear what must be done."

Scores of soldiers had been moved into Moscow, and they began lining up in formation in the streets; columns of tanks also rolled into the city. The defenders of Yeltsin's government went out to talk with the soldiers, urging them not to obey the orders of the coup-makers. Vera spied one column of tanks displaying Russian flags that was headed away from the building. When she saw this column of vehicles, she exclaimed joyfully, "These are our boys!"; she knew that the young soldiers had said flatly that they would not obey the orders of their superiors. She and other parliament members tried to cross the grounds to these soldiers to give them copies of Yeltsin's appeal, but the officers in charge told them to halt. Vera took several steps in their direction anyway. The officers warned that she should stay where she was, "or we will carry you out." It was clear that they stood ready to kill her.

A Link to the West: Anatoly Rudenko

Anatoly Rudenko was wandering groggily around the headquarters of the Bible Society, having slept in his office there, when the book-keeper told him there had been a coup.[3] He picked up the phone to call his good friend Iven Kharlanov, who had studied economics with him at the university and had since become a consultant to Boris Yeltsin. When Anatoly asked how he and his coworkers could help, Iven did not mince words. He said that Anatoly could provide crucial help in the event that communications would be cut off in the parliament building. The Bible Society in Moscow had an inter-national telephone line. Would they agree to be a liaison to the West and keep the outside world informed about what was going on? Anatoly agreed immediately.

3. Based on the author's interview with Anatoly Rudenko in Moscow on March 12, 1992. For his personal story, see Chapter Five.

The two of them discussed how to sway the troops surrounding the parliament building. How could they persuade the troops not to attack? They hit upon the idea of handing out Bibles to the soldiers and urging them not to kill. The two of them agreed that such an action could have a tangible effect, since the Bibles could function as both spiritual and psychological weapons. They hoped that implementing this plan would prevent bloodshed. When the plan was completed and Anatoly hung up the phone, he prayed.

Anatoly Rudenko had good reason to resist a return to the old Communism. As a student, he had been expelled from universities three times because he had given witness to his Christian faith. When that failed to silence him, Anatoly had been incarcerated in a psychiatric prison until the church intervened and arranged for his release.

After his conversation with Iven, Anatoly promptly called the Bible Society in Germany, while some of his colleagues from the Russian Bible Society — Michael Seleznev, Valentina Kuznetsova, and Igor Kozyrev — left for the parliament building to help build barricades around it. His friend Iven called again to say that ten tanks had gone over to Yeltsin's side.

Anatoly continued calling other countries — next Norway and Scotland — to tell the Bible Societies there what was happening and to implore them to pass the word along. He was heartened by Iven's news. "This is the beginning of the end of the coup," he told his colleague in Norway. "It will end in three days, at the most four." His words proved to be prophetic. Meanwhile, Anatoly continued his calls, this time contacting *Licht im Osten* (Light in the East) in Germany. The word was spreading internationally. Throughout the world, people were clustering around radios and television sets to follow the unfolding drama.

Later on, police from the nearby station appeared at the society's door. They regularly bought Bibles from the group. They spoke openly about the recent events, calling the coup-plotters "criminals" and saying that they should be hauled into court. "We don't support them," they stated flatly. Anatoly phoned his friend Iven again. This time Iven said that society members could be a real help by taking Yeltsin's decree, keying it into their computers, and printing copies to distribute throughout the city. Anatoly agreed.

Meanwhile, Father Alexander Borisov had returned from his council meeting to the offices of the Bible Society. He was the president of the Bible Society, heading it along with Anatoly. Together the two of them went into action. The Bible Society had a Xerox machine, a rarity in Moscow, and they quickly used it to make several hundred copies of the appeal that Father Alexander had drafted during the council meeting. They also put their computers and printers to work around the clock for the next three days, producing more than 2,000 copies of Yeltsin's declaration. Teams took stacks of the appeal and the declaration directly to the troops occupying the city and pressed copies into the hands of the perplexed young soldiers, who didn't have a clue about the real reason they had been dispatched to Moscow. They read the appeal and the declaration with wide eyes.

Building a Human Chain: Alexander Ogorodnikov

When Alexander Ogorodnikov heard the news on the morning of August 19, he knew the situation was dangerous.[4] He had spent nearly nine years in prison as a Christian dissident, and he thought the coup could mean that he would be arrested again. As the founder of the Christian Democratic Union, a political party, he was an obvious target for the hard-liners who wanted to squelch democracy. Inwardly he made peace with the prospect. "I prepared myself for prison," he says simply. When he left his apartment that morning, he took a Bible with him.

As soon as Alexander arrived in his office, he quickly gathered other activists together to discuss the situation. The first thing they decided to do was write an appeal to the soldiers. They prepared leaflets for widespread distribution, urging the soldiers not to obey orders to shoot. The group's telephone line had been cut the morning

---

4. This story is based on the author's interviews with Alexander Ogorodnikov in Moscow on March 17, 1992, and in Chicago on April 24, 1992. For the personal story of Alexander Ogorodnikov, see Chapter Two.

of the coup, but one of their FAX lines was still open, and on it they received a copy of Yeltsin's appeal. They quickly made more copies, which they took along with them when they headed toward the center of the city at noon. People who had gathered near the parliament building were willing to help the resisters inside, but they didn't know what to do. The leaflets gave them a task to perform. They eagerly took handfuls of them to pass out. Some of them walked straight up to the soldiers and asked them point blank, "Are you going to shoot us?"

Alexander recalls how the crowd grew — and grew together. "Initially about thirty people gathered around the Russian parliament building. But as the news spread, more arrived. It was amazing. . . . Old women stood beside punks and rockers, young people without any political agenda. A rock bank played music. Even criminals turned up because everyone understood that our freedom was in peril. There was such an electric atmosphere among the people."[5] Some of them began to take stones and pieces of wood and slowly built the first fragments of a barricade. As more and more of them brought various scraps of building materials, the barricade grew larger.

Using this crowd, Alexander and others helped to organize a human chain around the parliament building. They formed a live barrier between the tanks and the building, with the beleaguered Yeltsin and his government inside. Tanks can obviously plunge through a crowd, but the tank drivers' will to do that may have wavered when they were confronted with a living wall of human beings. Priests were giving Holy Communion to people in the chain; some were baptized there. One person had brought an icon and made an improvised shrine with it. "I sometimes cried like a child, because I saw such elevation of feelings, such enthusiasm," says Alexander. "The people stood with their bodies against tanks, against modern weapons. It was very moving."

"I saw a woman with children in her arms block a tank with her body," Alexander recalls. "We stopped several soldiers and

5. Quoted in the Jubilee Campaign's "Moscow Special."

[pleaded] with them to turn back. . . . I talked with the chief of a military unit. 'Don't shoot the people,' I pleaded. 'Don't shed the blood of our Russian people.'"[6]

Nearly all of the people who gathered around the parliament building had come spontaneously. Although they had not brought food or supplies of any sort, they were settling in to defend the building for as long as would be necessary. As it turned out, Alexander headed a charity canteen that fed five hundred of Moscow's poor every day, so his organization was in a position to look after the practical needs of these thousands of impromptu freedom fighters. His people moved quickly to gather supplies.

A spontaneous order governed the defenders who were assembling around the parliament building. By the time Alexander and his friends had returned several hours later with food and supplies, new people were at the periphery of the growing crowd, which had closed ranks and was effectively blocking anyone outside from getting near the building. "Who are you and what do you want?" they demanded. "We helped organize the defense at the center, and we're bringing food!" Alexander answered. The van full of sandwiches was convincing enough to get them through. There was sporadic gunfire, and bullets were flying over their heads as they delivered the food to the front lines. The windshield of the delivery van was hit, but the driver was spared. Despite the danger, Alexander's people continued shuttling to the front lines, delivering four tons of sandwiches during the course of the three-day showdown, enabling the civilian defense line to stay in place.

Alexander and his people also made up a news bulletin summarizing the events, which they duplicated and took to the railway station in Moscow. They pressed copies into the hands of people leaving the city. This was one way of getting the word out.

6. Ibid.

"Better to Die Than Do Nothing": Dimad Diomushken

The morning of August 19, Dimad Diomushken had slept in.[7] When he met friends later, he couldn't believe the news of the coup. "It can't be true," he protested. "Didn't you see any signs of troops in the city?" his friends responded. When the reality had sunk in, Dimad says, "I was really afraid we wouldn't have another opportunity to change our country. [I knew] I would be ashamed if I did not do something now."

Dimad, who was twenty-five years old, worked as an interpreter. He had just become a Christian, and had been baptized only three weeks earlier. One thought that pierced him was that he had done so little to spread the faith he held dear. If the coup succeeded, what chance to witness would he have then? He headed to the parliament building not knowing what to expect there but certain that he must go. On the way he passed many foreigners in buses near the embassies, and he noticed that they were crying. "When I saw how many foreigners felt the same as we did," he recalls, "I felt the world would help us in this situation."

When Dimad arrived at the building, he saw old and young together, some carrying flags, a diverse group of people melding together in a most unusual body of support. He also saw a group of Christians distributing copies of the Gospels near the building. Their presence confirmed what he had been thinking — that now was the time to take a stand and accept the consequences. "I thought, 'Our folk is not lost at all. We have a chance to change our lives. We can do it with the help of Jesus.' In this difficult situation, I knew I had to act."

He remembers that he was thinking very lucidly. *"The rest of my life depends on how I respond right now,* I decided. [I made the decision] with a clear mind, not with emotions. Of course I was afraid, but I knew I had eternal life. I knew when I received Jesus Christ that I had nothing to be afraid of. I [also] knew if I didn't change something now, I would never be able to."

7. Based on the author's interview with Dimad Diomushken in Moscow on March 18, 1992.

Getting information on what had occurred was extremely difficult. But as the news filtered back into the country through foreign radio broadcasts, the city began to heave and swell. While many people stayed home out of fear, others decided that "they would rather die together than do nothing," as Dimad put it. He looked with wonder at the crowd gathered around the parliament building, all different kinds of people united by a single idea: "If we want to live here, we must do something ourselves. It depends on us."

Dimad recalls that the situation was very dangerous, but that the people gathered there remained unswayed. "I have never seen before such strong faces. There was a decision in their eyes. They knew some of them might not leave the [grounds]. They might not live." By the time night fell, several thousand people had gathered around the parliament building. When the sun went down, it was a deep red. When Dimad looked at it, he remembers thinking that "it looked dangerous, even frightening." But the people stayed. They hunkered down in improvised camps around the barricades and settled in for the night.

Bibles against Tanks: Shirinai Dossova

August 20, 1991
Reuters News Agency

At least 50,000 demonstrate in front of the Russian Parliament in Moscow. Thousands more protest in Leningrad. A night curfew is imposed in Moscow. Estonian Parliament declares immediate independence and calls elections for 1992. Three people are killed outside the Russian Parliament Building, shot by soldiers or crushed by tanks.

On the second day of the coup, Iven Kharlanov called Anatoly Rudenko at the Bible Society again, this time with the grim news that the storming of the parliament building was most probably imminent. He asked Anatoly to alert the Western media, and Anatoly agreed. Putting his chain of contacts into motion again, Anatoly manned the international phone line to get this news out of the country. Meanwhile, Father Alexander Borisov went to a printing plant that the Bible Society often worked with and had thousands more copies of Yeltsin's appeal printed for distribution throughout Moscow.

Father Alexander and Anatoly also teamed up with other Christians from *Licht im Osten*. First they helped load up a van with thirty crates of New Testaments that the organization had just received in a shipment from the West. Then Father Alexander donned his long robes of the Russian Orthodox priesthood and put on the badge that identified him as an elected member of the Moscow City Council. Dressed this way, he sat on the front seat of the van next to the driver. He hoped that the symbols of authority he was wearing would get them through the traffic blockades. These were everywhere now, guarded by tanks and troops. The ploy worked: each time the van was stopped, Father Alexander emerged, his long clerical robes swishing and his city council badge gleaming, and the van was waved through.

The driver managed to work his way to the very center of the city, where a hundred tanks now surrounded the parliament building. The crowds had swelled to the point that a solid mass of people now spilled into Manege Square, where people traditionally assembled for political rallies. Father Alexander and the teams from the Bible Society and *Licht im Osten* piled out of the van, taking copies of the appeal and New Testaments to hand out to the soldiers. They worked their way through the packed throng. To the delight of some and the bemusement of others, Father Alexander, dressed in his long priestly robes, made the sign of the cross for each of the tanks and the soldiers as he came to them. But all the soldiers clearly understood the gravity of the situation, and they accepted both the Bibles and the blessing with solemnity.

One woman in the group, Shirinai Dossova, strode over to one of the tanks and knocked loudly on its side with her knuckles.[8] She continued knocking insistently until a baffled driver thrust the hatch

8. Based on the author's interview with Shirinai Dossova in Moscow on March 10-11, 1992.

cover open to see what was causing the unexpected ruckus. When he looked at her, Shirinai thrust a Bible into the air toward him. The young soldier was so flabbergasted that he didn't know what else to do but take it.

"It says in this book that you shouldn't kill," Shirinai said in a firm voice. "Are you going to kill us?" She looked him right in the eye.

"We're not intending to kill anybody," the rather startled young soldier replied. It was obvious that he was in a position he didn't want to be in. When Shirinai looked at his fresh young face, she wondered if he really would kill if he were given orders to do so. How many others might there be like him?

Shirinai had joined the protesting crowd because she feared that the coup would mean going back to the awful times when it was impossible to preach. A convert from a Moslem family who had become a Christian four years earlier, Shirinai was a street evangelist. She preached with charisma and fire to crowds on the Arbat, the popular street in the heart of Moscow full of artists, tourists, trade of every sort — a place brimming with life. She too was brimming with life. Thirty-three years old, trim and attractively dressed, with glossy dark hair in a stylish chin-length cut, she exuded energy, and she commanded attention when she spoke. Her dark eyes were as penetrating as her words. Since she had begun preaching on the Arbat, the KGB had threatened that if she did not stop, the consequences could be lethal. "We have an order to kill you," she was told. She knew her phone was tapped, and threatening letters arrived at her home in waves.

Viktor Pavlovich, the man who had brought Shirinai to faith, had been imprisoned for twelve years for his belief. He had warned her that she might be arrested because she was a Christian, and that drugs might be used to extract a "confession" from her. But he had told her that with God, he had been free even in prison, and that without God, regardless of where he was, he could never be truly free. When the coup began, her mentor's words echoed in Shirinai's mind. She did not fear for her physical life, but says now that she "felt ashamed that she had done so little for Christ" since she had entrusted her life to him. The moment had come to act. That is why she now joined forces with Father Alexander Borisov and Anatoly Rudenko to counteract the coup with Bibles and prayer.

People in the crowd begged for New Testaments, but Father Alexander replied, "We must give them to the soldiers. We hope it will make their hearts softer." The team members systematically worked their way down the columns of tanks. They would hand out the little books until one box was empty, and then a team member would dash back to the van to get another. Invariably the tank drivers were stunned, but they accepted the books. Other team members approached the paratroopers who were stationed in the center of Moscow. To their surprise, the members of the special attack forces, the *Spetznatz,* also responded positively. Only one officer turned them away, but others in his unit offered to take a box of the Bibles and distribute the books themselves.

Some of the soldiers took the small volumes and tucked them into the inside pockets of their uniforms near their hearts, like talismans. Others paged through them, stopping here and there to read words that were basically unfamiliar to them. Some sat and read earnestly. Although — or perhaps because — Bibles had been so difficult to obtain for nearly seventy years, the sheer presence of the New Testaments had a power evidenced in the reverent way they were handled.

Anatoly distributed Bibles near the Bolshoi Theater and the central post office as well. Wherever he went in the city, he was besieged by people eager to receive one, but they accepted his explanation that the team wished to give the books to the soldiers first. Some began an impromptu effort to follow up on the team's initial contact with the soldiers, staying on to talk with them once they had received a Bible, asking plaintively, "You're not really going to kill us, are you?" Throughout the city, discussions were lit like small bonfires on the borders of confrontation.

Meanwhile, Shirinai decided that the time had come to go to Red Square, where the crowd had become a solid mass extending into nearby Manege Square. People in the crowd were too tense to talk; they stood and waited. Shirinai took a copy of Yeltsin's declaration and positioned herself on a nearby hill. First she raised the Bible in her hand and asked for the crowd's attention; then she began reading Yeltsin's declaration loudly and deliberately. The meaning of Yeltsin's plea for resistance to the coup was unequivocally clear, and Shirinai felt that she might be killed at any minute by the forces opposing him. But she was determined to finish what she had started. The crowd was silent as it concentrated on the plea.

The declaration concluded with the words "Thou shalt not kill." After she read them, Shirinai raised the Bible again and said, "Christ called for love and peace, and only he can stop hate and fighting. There is no peace in the lives of people who are not at peace with God, and without him we cannot live in peace with one another. Jesus rose from the dead," she continued; "he is alive here and now, and knocks at the door of our hearts. This kingdom will end in ruins, but God's kingdom is coming." By this time the crowd was somewhat stunned.

When Shirinai had finished speaking, a cluster of people pressed forward to thank her; some asked her questions. When a man hostilely pushed his way forward, demanding to know what denomination she was from, a nucleus of people around her spontaneously positioned themselves to protect her. After the man had gone, one of the men who protected her asked, "Is it necessary to preach? Reading Yeltsin's statement is dangerous enough."

"I disagree," Shirinai countered firmly. She knew full well that she might be risking her life, but she was prepared to do that. "I want to give my life for Christ. I didn't come only for a political statement. If I am going to be killed, then I want to be killed for Christ. The only real freedom is in Christ, not in *perestroika.*"

When Shirinai went to the parliament building, what she saw there made her weep. The improvised barricades were a pitiful sight; people were bringing bags filled with small pieces of wood, scraps of building materials, whatever they could hastily assemble. It was all so improvised, so absurdly fragile. An old woman she had passed had asked Shirinai if she were going to the soldiers. When Shirinai said yes, the *babushka* gave her bread to take to them.

Outside the building, the human wall of protection that had

been spontaneously formed was holding strong. The defenders, many of them young people, had joined hands, forming a human chain, a living barricade against the coming storm. Shirinai and a man named Viktor Boudien went to these people and gave them Bibles, then stood next to them to pray for them, for the city, and for the country. Next Shirinai made her way to the Tamanskaya tank division, whose soldiers had refused orders and changed over to Yeltsin's side during the first day of the coup. When Shirinai gave the tank drivers Bibles, they staunchly told her that they would obey only Yeltsin. Shirinai encouraged them not to change their minds.

All told, in a few short hours, 4,000 copies of the New Testament were distributed, along with the appeals urging the soldiers not to attack. Those who had distributed them went home to spend the coming night on their knees with others, deep in prayer.

"Dying Is Not Difficult": Nikolai Arzhannikov

Inside the parliament building, Boris Yeltsin and his government waited for the impending storm of troopers. Throughout the day there had been warnings that an attack on the building was planned for five p.m. Yeltsin had called all the members of the Supreme Soviet together to indicate the gravity of the situation. The women members of parliament were told that it would be in their best interest to leave, since their security could not be guaranteed. But Vera Boiko refused to go, as did all the women deputies. Meanwhile, tanks and troops continued to amass outside. Random shooting was audible.

Nikolai Arzhannikov had the unpleasant task of defending the building from the inside.[9] A member of parliament himself, he was a former police officer and detective who had been fired for trying to block corruption in the police forces of Leningrad. In 1989 he had been elected to parliament, where he was now vice-chairman of the Human Rights Committee. Nikolai had years of experience with

---

9. Based on the author's interview with Nikolai Arzhannikov in Moscow on March 18, 1992.

weapons, and he did not take lightly the responsibility that had been placed on him. He was waiting just inside the main door to the parliament building, his body taut with tension.

"I had a pistol in my hand," he recalls. "I knew that the attackers had automatic weapons. And I waited for the moment when the doors would burst open and someone would come rushing in. I would have to be the first to shoot. I would have to shoot either the head or the stomach of the person to kill him. . . . Perhaps I would have met this man in the streets of Moscow. Perhaps a sister of this young man I was to kill now was out there in the barricades. . . . It is not difficult to die yourself. The most horrifying thing is to send another person to death."

Nikolai was doing his best to prevent confrontation and injury and avoid using the weapons he knew so well. "When we heard that the attack was a real possibility, we announced through the loud-speakers that the crowds should move farther away from the building, so civilians would not be injured. The people were told what to do in case of a gas attack. We pleaded with them not to stop army vehicles by force."

Nikolai's vacation in the Urals had been brought to an abrupt halt the day before, when he had heard the news of the coup. It was clear that things were critical and he had to get back. Before leaving, he reached his aide in Moscow, who sketched out the situation for him. In March they had concluded that certain dangerous elements might try to stage a coup, so they had already made preparations for that possibility.

When Nikolai stepped off the plane, his aide had already mobilized eighty private detectives, many of whom had served with the army, the KGB, or the police and had quit on political grounds, disgusted with the old Communist regime. These were seasoned men who knew how to handle weapons. Some of them had battle experience from Afghanistan. They were given the responsibility of defending the parliament building. In an agreement with Yeltsin's government, they were given thirteen automatic weapons and were allowed to set up a communications network.

When Nikolai reached the parliament building, it was surrounded by barricades. Military vehicles were everywhere in the streets, and fear and alarm were thick in the air. The detectives and police from the defense group assembled and asked Nikolai what their legal position was. Nikolai answered them honestly. "If we win, we will thank you. If they win, you will be described as a group of bandits. Those who survive will go to prison, probably for a very long time." It took a moment for these hard, true words to sink in. But when they had, no one left.

These men knew from experience what close fighting meant. In military terms, there would be no more than thirty to forty minutes of active firing before the clash was decided. They could only defend their position — nothing more. They also knew that many of their friends would be lost if there was shooting.

When word reached Nikolai that three people had been killed by the tanks, the grim realities of the circumstances became clear. "It was only then that some people grasped the seriousness of the situation," Nikolai recalls. "As we came into the internal courtyard, preparing for the defense, deciding who would do what, one of the men was on the fire escape. If the attackers would break into the yard, he would be to their rear. When everybody was ready, he shouted, 'Should we retreat to the cellars?'"

" 'Yes, Sasha, we will retreat to the cellars,' came the answer. But everyone understood that he surely would not retreat, because he would be at the backs of the attackers, and after the first shots, they would turn back and were certain to shoot him. It was a serious psychological moment. Up to then, everything was like child's play. That was the moment when I personally realized that there is nothing more catastrophic for one's people than civil war."

Teams were assigned to defend specific areas. While it was thought that the sewage system or the underground passages used to send official communications and move supplies might be potential routes of attack, Nikolai and the other defenders concluded that an air attack with parachute troops was more likely. "Because there were thousands of people nearby, there could be little possibility of forces marching through the lines of defense made of human bodies. Only the most outrageous criminals would dare to do such a thing.

Those people didn't want to be compromised in the face of the international community. They wouldn't be forgiven for killing thousands of civilians."

The parliament building was full of international journalists, and the offices of Nikolai's committee became a kind of headquarters for them. They were up all night on the phone, sitting on the floor, passing along information on what they had heard to their home offices. When the warnings came that an attack was imminent, Nikolai and others tried to persuade the journalists to leave the building for their own safety. But they refused. The spirit of resistance had galvanized them too.

The earnestness of the resisters is vivid in Nikolai's mind. "Those were the days of some kind of revelation, when people were very honest, and those standing at the barricades were very sincere. Each one came here although he understood that he was running a risk. But they considered it their duty to be here. Of course life went on as usual on the outskirts of the city. But here, the atmosphere was quite special. I remember a touching pair, an old man and his wife. He had a string bag in his hand. There was some food in it and a gas mask. Everybody kept asking him, 'Old man, why did you come here?' He answered, 'Can't you understand that we have come here to defend democracy?'

"There were many young people here. Many were despised, distrusted. . . . There were great contrasts between the old man and these young people with green hair. But they found a common language. They understood each other. The people on the barricades shared a firm belief in the good of changes for the country."

Nikolai's own personal resistance was based on a moral conviction but not necessarily a religious conviction. The motivations of the other defenders varied as well, but all of them were united in the conviction that the moment of truth had come and that they must act. As Vera Boiko put it, "The people had changed. With the first freedoms, it was as if people had been given oxygen to breathe, and suddenly it was cut off. They had to have it back."

At ten o'clock that night, all members of the Supreme Soviet were asked to assemble in the Hall of Nations. General Konstantin Kobech, who was visibly perturbed, told them that the building was to be attacked by *Spetznatz* and the army's Alpha units at one a.m. "I don't know what your decision will be," he said, "but everyone must decide for himself [whether to remain]. The main thing is to avoid a conflict between the army and civilians."

At midnight, the electricity in the parliament building was cut off. The attack now appeared to be imminent. The parliament members, the journalists, Yeltsin — all huddled in the darkness of the blackened building, waiting. Outside, the people on the barricades waited tensely in the drizzle that continued throughout that dark night. But by the time the sky lightened on the morning of August 21, the attack still had not come.

At this writing, it is still not definitively known why. Did the weather prevent the planned aerial attack? According to one scenario, the attack was "scrubbed" by the troops themselves after they had done some independent reconnaissance. The *Spetznatz* and Alpha troops reportedly sent ahead some from their own ranks, dressed in civilian garb, to appraise the situation at the parliament building. They had not been accurately informed about the nature of the conflict or the massive civilian resistance. When they discovered the true state of affairs, they reportedly refused to obey the orders of their officers. Had the world's most fearsome military apparatus simply collapsed in chaos? Or had it all been staged? Was there another explanation?

"The People Were No Longer the Same"

August 21
Reuters News Agency

Yeltsin says members of the coup committee are trying to leave Moscow by air. Troops and armored cars begin withdrawing from the center of Moscow. Defense Ministry orders all troops to leave Moscow. The chairman of the Soviet Parliamentary Defense Committee says the coup committee has disbanded and two members are flying to the Crimea to meet Gorbachev. Latvia's Parliament declares independence. Soviet Parliament formally reinstates Gorbachev as presi-

dent. Main Soviet television news program quotes Gorbachev as saying he is in full control of the country and will resume normal duties in the next few days. Gorbachev returns to Moscow.

*　　*　　*

Father Alexander Borisov had spent the night praying for his country. When he learned from a foreign radio broadcast that three people had been crushed by tanks, he decided to hold a service to commemorate the dead. On the morning of August 21, he made a large wooden cross and, accompanied by the choir from his church, went to the place where the victims had died. The blood was still on the asphalt. For some reason, the rain could not wash it away. People had put logs and flowers there in a spontaneous memorial. In the eulogy he gave, Father Alexander said, "Though we do not know their names, they are righteous in the face of God. We must pray for them."

Just as he and the choir were about to leave, they received the news that the putschists had been arrested. "It was one of the greatest joys of my life," says Father Alexander. "A huge stone fell from my heart." Along with the choir, he made his way to the parliament building, and since he was once again wearing his clerical robes and his political badge, he was able to convince the troops and guards to let him pass — in fact, he was allowed into the building. Moments later he emerged on a balcony, where he took a microphone and preached to the tens of thousands assembled there. The choir he had brought with him then sang a joyous and grateful hymn of praise to God. The strains of their song wafted over a city, and a country, stunned but liberated.

*　　*　　*

The coup had been plotted over a long period of time by a group of military and government officials, according to Yevgeny Lisov, the head of the Russian prosecutors' group that subsequently investigated the coup. This conclusion was based on abundant evidence gathered during a four-and-a-half-month-long investigation, evidence that included hundreds of documents, interviews with officials, and the questioning of fifteen individuals charged with plotting the coup. As many had guessed, the incident that had proved pivotal was Gorbachev's decision to sign a new union treaty on August 19.

According to the *Wall Street Journal*, "Mr. Lisov credited Russian President Boris Yeltsin and the Russian people who stood outside the Russian White House, as the parliament is called, with defeating the coup."[10]

If the conclusion of the man heading the investigation is true, then the individual decisions recounted here take on greater significance. These people exemplify thousands of others who at the critical moment were willing to resist and if need be risk their lives in so doing. Together, they may have been the decisive factor that broke the back of the coup. What prompted them to resist? A revolution of the spirit. As one participant put it, "The people were no longer the same." Confronted with the truth, neither were the troops who refused to fire on them.

The parallels to the revolution of 1989 in Eastern Europe are striking. Like the demonstrators who walked up to the armed troops in the streets of Leipzig, the courageous protestors in Moscow asked the troops of the coup, "Are you really going to kill us?" It became clear that the issue of "us against them" affected the troops too. The truth was that only a small elite held the ruling power, and they could continue to rule only if their subjects acquiesced.

While the political showdown took place in Moscow in August 1991, the revolution of the spirit had already been taking place all over the Soviet Union and the Eastern bloc in the years preceding it. *Solidarność*, where the Revolution began, was first described as the "huge forest of awakened consciences." This time it was visible in the human wall that surrounded the Russian parliament building. When the moment of decision came, a united mass of resisters dared to throw off the shackles of fear to confront their oppressors.

In the moral, political, and spiritual earthquake that rumbled across the entire continent, the Communist empire crashed to the ground.

10. Laurie Hays, "Report Finds Detailed Plans for Soviet Coup," *Wall Street Journal (Europe)*, January 22, 1992.

Psychiatric hospitals like this one were often used as "behavior modification" camps. Among other things, Soviet authorities used mind-altering drugs to try to force dissenters to become "loyal" citizens. © *ARC; courtesy of Keston Research Photo Archive, Oxford, England*

Ute and Manfred Gohlke decided that their family wasn't going to have anything to do with Communism. As a consequence, their children — Christina, Annedore (left rear), Stefan (middle), Beate, and Matthias (front) — were discriminated against in school. © *idea-bild, Germany*

Polish students cheer the arrival of Pope John Paul II on his first pilgrimage to his homeland in June of 1979. The "spiritual earthquake" that began here would later give Poland, as well as Eastern Europe, political freedom through peaceful revolution.
© J. Zywicki; courtesy of Keston Research Photo Archive, Oxford, England

Pope John Paul II with Polish Solidarity leader Lech Wałęsa. They are looking at a model of the monument that was erected in Gdańsk to commemorate the workers' movement.
Courtesy of Keston Research Photo Archive, Oxford, England

Above Left: Czechoslovakian leader **Father Václav Malý** in 1987. A principal member of Charter 77, Father Maly had been stripped of his official responsibilities as a priest, but continued to hold clandestine communion services.
© *Keston College*

Above right: Václav Benda, one of the Czechoslovakian leaders of the Committee for the Defense of the Unjustly Persecuted. © *Palach Press*

Below left: Czechoslovakian intellectual and writer Václav Havel became a spokesman for the independent intellectuals in his country and a leader of the Velvet Revolution. Havel claimed that the biggest challenge to Communism's "culture of the lie" was living the truth. © *Palach Press*

Below right: Irina Ratushinskaya, a Russian poet and writer, felt called to speak the truth that she as a Christian knew — and was imprisoned for it. © *Keston College; all photos courtesy of Keston Research Photo Archive, Oxford, England*

This worship service, held at the restored Danilov Monastery in Moscow in June 1988, marked the close of the celebration of the Millennium of Christianity in Russia. © *NCCC-USA; courtesy of Keston Research Photo Archive, Oxford, England*

Alexander Zaichenko, an advisor to Gorbachev's chief economists, wrote the report which told Gorbachev that the USSR couldn't compete with SDI. Zaichenko surprised many by revealing his Christian faith during a television interview in 1990. *Courtesy of Licht im Osten, Germany*

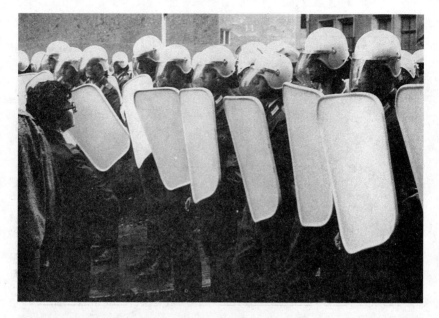

East German police braced for conflicts in Leipzig on October 7, 1989, as the nation stood poised on the brink of civil war. Two days later, live ammunition was distributed, and reservists were asked to sign statements saying that they would fire on members of their own families who were demonstrating.   *Photo by Tobias Rossa; © Gustav Kiepenheuer Verlag GmbH*

Christian Führer, pastor of the Nikolaikirche in Leipzig and leader of the *Friedensgebete*, the "Prayers for Peace." The Nikolaikirche, the site of the meetings that helped spark the "peaceful revolution" in East Germany, is in the background.
Photo by Martin Naumann, courtesy of Christian Führer

October 9, 1989: A crowd of nearly 70,000 moves through the streets encircling Leipzig after the *Friedensgebete*, carrying candles and demonstrating peacefully. Risking their lives, they faced down troops armed with live ammunition, water cannons, and attack dogs. The order to shoot never came.   *Photo by Heinz Loester;* © *Gustav Kiepenheuer Verlag GmbH*

After the protesters had circled Leipzig for the seventh time, the Berlin Wall fell in an echo of Jericho.   *Courtesy of Licht im Osten, Germany*

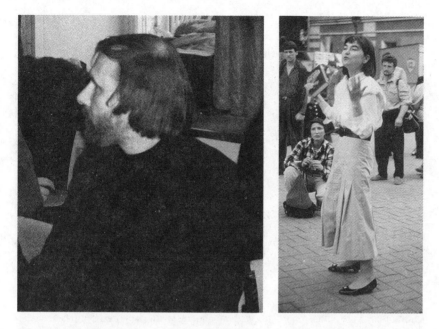

Left: Alexander Borisov, president of the Bible Society in Russia, passed out Bibles and copies of Yeltsin's appeal to soldiers during the attempted coup against the new Russian government.   *Courtesy of Licht im Osten, Germany*

Right: Evangelist Shirinai Dossova preaching on the Arbat in Moscow. During the attempted coup, she faced soldiers in tanks with her Bible and shouted, "It says here not to kill."   *Courtesy of Licht im Osten, Germany*

Hands reach for a Bible, evidence of the spiritual hunger that has been unleashed in the former Soviet Union since the fall of Communism.   *Courtesy of Licht im Osten, Germany*

Uwe Holmer and his wife, Sigrid, opened their home to deposed Communist leader Erich Honecker and his wife. Angry protesters threatened to bomb their home.
© *idea-bild, Germany*

As Russia rebuilds, it is bolstered by acts of Christian charity, which were previously prohibited. Here a mission doctor visits an elderly woman in need of care.   *Courtesy of Licht im Osten, Germany*

PART III

Candles of Hope

© Harald Kirschner

CHAPTER 10

The KGB and the Stasi:
Repentance and Forgiveness

O nce the monolith of Communism had been overturned, in-
credibly ugly creatures scurried out from beneath its exposed
base. Those who had collaborated with the Communist apparatus
— whether KGB, Stasi, or darkness by any other name — were unexpectedly thrust into the public eye. There have been many sur-
prises, deeply disappointing ones.

One can only guess how many millions were involved in gathering information on their neighbors, colleagues, and friends. But as
the myriad files have been declassified and put into the hands of their
victims, numerous explosions have rocked the emotional landscape
of the entire Communist empire. Trust has been irreparably damaged. Friendships and marriages have been blown apart, politicians
have been ejected from office, pastors have been catapulted from the
pulpit. Many are devastated by shame; others want revenge; some
have committed suicide.

The motives of the collaborators were as individual as they were.
A few were were moved by idealism — but many more were prodded
by fear of reprisals, blackmail of the crudest sort, rewards of money
and favors, or cold-hearted ambition. Personal weaknesses provided
levers of persuasion. Alcohol abuse, marital infidelity, financial in-
solvency, stealing on the job — all were useful grounds for recruiting.
Many agreed to cooperate with the KGB or the Stasi to keep the truth
from being exposed. The only thing that really worked well in Com-

munism was its secret police. One can say without exaggeration that they were virtually everywhere.

How all-encompassing this apparatus was, and how ruthless, goes beyond what most of us can imagine. The truth is stranger than the most bizarre fiction. In the relentless pursuit of information, Stasi and KGB victims were kidnapped, beaten, blinded, cut, burned with cigarettes, injected with drugs, stripped, frozen, and sometimes left to die. Informants' eyes and ears gleaned information from virtually every apartment, factory, school, letter, and phone conversation. No one and no place was immune. Powerful microphones in vehicles posted along the street could pick up conversations in living rooms. Neighbors filed meticulously detailed reports on everything they saw. What informants couldn't unearth would be wrung out of victims by interrogators using drugs, weapons, verbal abuse, and sheer brutality. The groans from untold numbers of victims have risen to the heavens in unfathomable misery.

Virtually everyone was confronted by the security apparatus at some point. The higher the level of responsibility an individual had, the more likely it was that the encounters were frequent. Scores of collaborators have been unmasked since Communism fell. But uncertainty still clouds the question "What is an agent?" If it is anyone who ever talked to the Stasi or the KGB, then virtually everyone was one. If it is anyone on whom the Stasi or the KGB had a file, then a big chunk of the population comes into question. Does it mean anyone given a code name in the files? Then Solzhenitsyn, called "Spider" by the KGB, and Sakharov, dubbed "Hermit," were "agents" too. If it means a person who regularly met with the secret police, then we get into a clearer target zone. But some of these people were sources without knowing or wanting to be. Others knew full well that they were talking to the secret police, but deliberately told untruths or withheld information that could be damaging to others.

Every institution had informants, and the church was no exception. Revelations in the wake of Communism's collapse have documented compromise in church circles in such detail as to make virtually anyone a cynic who wasn't one before. According to some estimates, nearly a third of those in the church under Communism collaborated as informants. In every country, stories are surfacing that document hypocrisy and corruption from the highest to the lowest levels. The church was not a shining city on a hill.

On the other hand, some Christians had unavoidable contacts with the Communists through their work. Lawyers and clergy who regularly handled cases of political prisoners and emigrés negotiated with the Communists out of necessity, oftentimes succeeding in obtaining freedom for those they represented. Did their contact indicate collaboration? If the Stasi or the KGB kept a file on their meetings, did that mean these people were informants? What appears to be a black-and-white issue at first glance has a disturbing number of gray shades.

Precisely when cooperation becomes collaboration is a thorny question. Manfred Stolpe in Germany and Metropolitan Pitirim in Russia are two such troubling cases for the church. Evidence from Stasi and KGB files indicates that these representatives of the church may have done more than simply represent the interests of believers. Both have been accused of being active agents, but both have staunchly denied it. The resulting debacle has cast a shadow not only over them but over the face of the church.

There are others who have admitted their longtime collaboration as informants and who entered into this activity willingly. Consider the cases of these two very different Stasi informants.

Two Different Informants, Two Different Stories

Jutta was anything but your ordinary nurse — her profession was deceptive packaging. She was the daughter of two doctors, her divorced mother being a prominent heart surgeon in Karl-Marx-Stadt in East Germany. Jutta was the product of a relatively well-to-do upbringing, a sophisticated woman whose growing-up years had schooled her in the social graces: her parents had given frequent parties, and the house had often been full of visitors. And then there were her looks. She was unusually striking, a dark-haired beauty with a riveting glance that arrested both men and women immediately.

She had a touch of the theatrical in the way she moved, and she was aware of its effect. She could pick up the nuances of situations and knew how to read people, so she was adept at ingratiating herself wherever she went. She took on the colors of her changing environment with grace and charm, an object of fascination for others. She was a perfect chameleon.

Her code name was Dissa Juko.[1] She was an informant for the Stasi. The fact that her mother was her boss in the hospital where she worked and was also a Stasi informant was convenient: it allowed her to leave for her little missions on short notice without cumbersome explanations. The liberal social life that she had grown up with at home had taught Jutta early on about the pleasures and uses of her abundant sexual charms. They helped her gather information, initially on the doctors in her mother's hospital, then later on foreign students and international business contacts. The little gifts of cosmetics, jewelry, and art that she received from her sources were welcome prizes. And there was the occasional trip to Bulgaria, Czechoslovakia, or Romania to do "fact finding."

Dissa Juko proved so thorough that the Stasi used her often to get information. The techniques she used to establish contact varied, but one became a favorite. She would appear at the door of a prominent man's home to deliver a money order for a hundred marks. When the surprised recipient would say that he didn't have any idea what it was for, she would propose that at least they could have a pleasant evening with it. The element of the unexpected, the striking looks of the bearer, the dinner that followed, and the consumption of sufficient alcohol before being invited to her apartment — these proved irresistible to ordinary mortals. Once Dissa Juko mastered that technique, her bold charm proved enough to snag even the larger fish in the pond. Her clientele included cultural celebrities and increasingly prominent figures in politics and the economic world.

---

1. The story of Dissa Juko is based on the author's interview with Rüdiger Knechtel, and on the writing of Dissa Juko's third husband in *Stalin's DDR: Berichte politisch Verfolgter*, ed. Rüdiger Knechtel and Jürgen Fiedler (Leipzig: Forum Verlag, 1991), pp. 239-52.

From time to time there were little "mishaps" — unwanted pregnancies or inconvenient diseases — but since her mother was a doctor, she was quickly fixed up and put back into action. Jutta had given birth to a son, but with her mother's help she sent him to a state-run institution during the week. Later she was to lose her right to raise him at all, the authorities citing her lifestyle as grounds for removing him from her care. And it was true that her life was not exactly conventional. Her information-gathering activities took her into bizarre places at unusual times. But there were other destabilizing elements in her life as well. While the parties she had grown up with at home had introduced her to alcohol and sex as recreation, she had also discovered the recreational use of drugs — particularly morphine.

By her third marriage, however, Dissa Juko had changed, or at least appeared to be different. Having married a member of the church, an honest man, she led a conventional life, shunning her earlier extravagances. Her clothes were unremarkable, she wore no makeup, and she moved in church circles unobtrusively. Her husband knew nothing of her past. When the grass-roots groups of the gathering revolution were meeting under the roof of the church in 1989, Dissa Juko was there with them. She marched with the demonstrators when they took to the streets. What she thought and believed can only be guessed at. Either she had experienced a genuine change of heart, or she was the perfect plant. She could have been merely a secret drug addict who sold any information she got to support her habit, or an informer who didn't know how to get out.

Whatever her motivation, she apparently couldn't live with it. When the Communists were toppled in East Germany and it was clear which way the country was headed, Dissa Juko decided that she couldn't go on. She wrote a note to the Stasi in January 1990, informing them that she was quitting. The next day she committed suicide.

*   *   *

There were some people who saw no contradiction between Christianity and socialism, and in an attempt to reform the latter made a Faustian deal with their Christian conscience. Peter Zimmermann is such a man. A respected theologian at the university in Leipzig, he was a Stasi informant for fifteen years.[2]

When Russian tanks crushed Czechoslovakia in August 1968, rolling through woods he knew well as a boy, Peter Zimmermann was seized by a desire to influence the world of politics. He decided he must qualify himself to play such a role. He began by joining the Communist youth organization, the FDJ, the first in a series of choices he hoped would permit him to change the existing order. He saw no contradiction between his faith and his political pursuits; instead, he saw himself as undertaking a mission "to prevent misunderstandings between Christians and Marxists." This was something he wanted to do from the inside.

Zimmermann became a noted theologian at the university in Leipzig. While some thought that a counterrevolution had to be waged through the church, Zimmermann disagreed. His mission was to reform socialism, not destroy it. As he explains it, "equality and solidarity" are the two characteristics most necessary in a society, and he believed that a strong state was necessary to guarantee them.

In 1973 Peter Zimmermann became a Stasi informant. He had become involved in the Christian Peace Conference, an international pacifist group that had international contacts which the regime wanted to monitor, and he reported on what took place there and elsewhere in the church. For the next fifteen years, in fact, he talked with Stasi officers every three to four weeks about church affairs. He was sometimes summoned by an irate phone call from a Stasi officer and ordered to appear in an apartment deemed "safe" for a debriefing. He says that sometimes the officers would demand to know the background of a synod decision, or the text of a speech by a churchman, or the meaning of a text the church had published. He was also asked to predict the outcome of upcoming synod votes. What he disliked most was the secretive slinking around and the orders not to discuss these matters with anyone else.

Peter wasn't handsomely paid as an informant. Over fifteen

2. This narrative is based on the author's interview with Peter Zimmermann in Leipzig on March 1, 1991.

years, he claims that he was paid a total of two to three thousand deutsche marks from the Stasi directly, and the same amount from local officials. He admits he was given quicker approval for trips to the West than most, but protests, "I have a clear conscience. . . . I got no car for what I did. I got no house. . . . I worked of my own free will; I wasn't blackmailed for material reasons. I didn't have a girl-friend or sexually transmitted diseases, I wasn't a homosexual, I hadn't stolen any silver spoons. I was not tempted by material advantages. . . . It was really my intention to influence politics."

Did he? "In the best cases, maybe something worse was prevented. But that's not what I intended. I didn't want to just prevent a worse alternative, I wanted to change things fundamentally." When he saw the state use violence against its own citizens, did he ever question his commitment to socialism? He says no. "Violence was a result of the imperfection." One had to accept the evil that came, he says, whether it was from "political wrong decisions, stupidity, or whatever, [and] view it as a part of the process leading to a goal."

But his commitment to socialism was to vanish. "Now my trust that a strong state is necessary to make political and social progress has been not just shaken — it is gone. The biggest political mistake which was morally wrong was the illusion that it was necessary to work with a socialist secret police to accomplish progressive changes. . . . It will do whatever is necessary . . . up to killing, torturing, and all the other things. I must admit that."

"These were very bitter lessons," he says now. "Never again."

Peter remained an informant for the Stasi until the beginning of September 1989. Shortly thereafter, he was to play a critical role in the showdown in Leipzig. When events hurtled toward a crisis in October, he joined the conductor Kurt Masur, cabaret artist Bernd-Lutz Lange, and three Communist party secretaries — dubbed the "Leipzig Six" — in facilitating the dialogue between the church and the Communists on October 9 as Leipzig stood poised on the brink of bloodshed. Their effort probably helped prevent a civil war. In a sense, Peter had a foot on both sides; he was a hinge figure uniquely positioned at that crucial moment.

Once the regime had been toppled, Peter's past relationship

with the Stasi burdened him. He wanted to make a clean breast of it, but he didn't know how. In the spring of 1990, he asked one of the advisors to the new government of Lothar de Maiziere how a hypothetical "friend" of his who had collaborated with the Stasi could come clean. Both knew that Peter was talking about himself. But Peter didn't have a clue that the newly elected prime minister was soon to be derailed himself by accusations of Stasi collaboration. Under fire, de Maiziere stepped down. In the feeding frenzy created by his accusers, disproving allegations was impossible.

Peter had also discussed the case of his hypothetical "friend" with a man from one of the "basis groups," who had advised him that the sooner he made his Stasi collaboration public, the better. Just two days later, the German radio station Deutschland Funk broadcast the list of the Stasi collaborators from the church and theology department of the university in Leipzig. The "basis group" had given the list to the radio journalists. In a few hours, it became widespread public knowledge that Peter Zimmermann was an informant. He had a lot of explaining to do, first to his wife and family, then to his colleagues at the university, where he was later dismissed.

People's reactions to the news varied widely. Some were shocked; others said they should have guessed it sooner. He wishes that he had come clean earlier; in any case, he was relieved to have his guilt out in the open. "I couldn't have lived with it," he says now.

How Is Forgiveness Possible?

In the wake of Communism's collapse, the issue of guilt and forgiveness is a critical one, both for victims and for perpetrators. There is an enormous amount of accumulated hate, resentment, and anger that needs to be dealt with before healing can begin. Families who have lost members and people who have been denied justice, whose ruined lives can no longer be salvaged, are furious. Victims of betrayal are justifiably angry. Trust has been shattered, hope demolished, and many are psychologically, physically, and spiritually sick as a result.

Throughout the former Communist empire, victims are confronting their oppressors in their newfound freedom, and they want justice. Some have narrowly escaped lynching. Those who have been wronged seethe inwardly when they see the same old Communist faces in new positions of authority, while their situation is still woefully inadequate. There is nothing more consuming than justified anger. It can devour a tremendous amount of human capital.

The wounds are so deep and fester so persistently that they cannot be healed by any simple means. People who have suffered abuse cannot simply say it didn't matter and forget. On the other hand, those who wronged others may suffer tremendous remorse. In fact, many were so consumed by their guilt that they — like Dissa Juko — committed suicide. The only path from this festering hell is the one of repentance, forgiveness, and reconciliation. It is not an easy path to take, and no one can walk down it without help.

People who suffered under the Communists justifiably claim that anybody who grew up comfortably in the West is not entitled to give a moral lecture on forgiveness because Westerners cannot understand how difficult their situation is. So perhaps a story from Corrie ten Boom will illustrate how one can take the difficult path of reconciliation.

Corrie and her family, who harbored Jews in their home in Holland during World War II, were eventually found out and sent to concentration camps. They all died there except Corrie, who watched her sister Betsy suffer from beatings and ultimately perish in Ravensbrück in unspeakable misery. Despite the horrors she had suffered at the hands of Germans, Corrie came to Germany after the war to deliver a Christian message of reconciliation. Little did she know that she would literally come face to face with her enemy there. At a church service in Munich, she spotted a man who had been a guard at Ravensbrück. When he came up to her, suddenly all the horrors were real again: the screams, the stench, her sister's pain-blanched face. What would she do? What could she say?

> "How grateful I am for your message, *Fräulein,*" he said. "To think that, as you say, He has washed my sins away!" His hand was thrust out to shake mine. And I, who had preached so often . . . on the need to forgive, kept my hand at my side.

Even as the angry, vengeful thoughts boiled through me, I saw the sin of them. Jesus Christ had died for this man; was I going to ask for more? Lord Jesus, I prayed, forgive me and help me forgive him.

I tried to smile, I struggled to raise my hand. I could not. I felt nothing, not the slightest spark of warmth or charity. And so again I breathed a silent prayer. Jesus, I cannot forgive him. Give me Your forgiveness.

As I took his hand the most incredible thing happened. From my shoulder along my arm and through my hand a current seemed to pass from me to him, while into my heart sprang a love for this stranger that almost overwhelmed me.

And so I discovered that it is not on our forgiveness any more than on our goodness that the world's healing hinges, but on His. When He tells us to love our enemies, He gives, along with the command, the love itself.[3]

Some years later, that same scene was to be replayed between a Communist and a Christian in the Soviet Union. In 1988, in the city of Rostov, a man approached the evangelist Joseph Bondarenko and begged him for forgiveness. Bondarenko had no idea who the man was or what he was talking about, but then he reached into his pocket and pulled out his KGB identification. "I am the one who put you behind bars. Please forgive me!" he pleaded. Bondarenko must have known what Corrie ten Boom had felt. Like her, he was powerless to forgive on his own, but able to forgive with Christ's help. He learned that Christ makes reconciliation and forgiveness possible.

Only months after the failed coup attempt in the Soviet Union, the Supreme Soviet issued an invitation to leading evangelicals in the United States to come to Moscow to serve as government advisors. Those who responded called themselves Project Christian Bridge; the group was made up of radio and television broadcasters, educators, publishers, Russian scholars, pastors, businessmen, and mission executives. What they discovered in the highest echelons of Russian

---

3. Corrie ten Boom with John and Elizabeth Sherrill, *The Hiding Place* (Washington Depot, Conn.: Chosen Books, 1971), p. 215.

government surprised them. Philip Yancey chronicled the group's experiences.[4]

He vividly remembers General Nikolai Stolyarov, who introduced himself to the group as vice-chairman of the KGB. A handsome man with strong features, Stolyarov had emerged from the attempted coup as a popular figure, having flown to Gorbachev's *dacha* to rescue him. Gorbachev had given the former air force general his new post at the KGB. "Meeting with you here tonight is a plot twist that could not have been conceived by the wildest fiction writer," he began. "How to bring peace and quiet to the hearts of people is a great problem for us. We are united with you in working together against the powers of evil."[5] At this point eyebrows were raised.

"We realize that too often we've been negligent in accepting those of the Christian faith. August 1991 shows what can happen," he went on. "But political questions cannot be decided until there is sincere *repentance*, a return to faith by the people. That is the cross I must bear. In the study of scientific atheism, there was the idea that religion divides people. Now we see the opposite: love for God can only unite. Somehow we must learn to put together the missionary role — absolutely critical for us now — and also learn from Marx that man can't appreciate life if he is hungry."

At that point, according to Yancey, the group was astounded. *What did he say? Is the translation accurate? — "Repentance"? "The cross I must bear"? Is this really the KGB talking?*

Joel Nederhood, a broadcaster from the Christian Reformed Church, rose to question him. "General, many of us have read Solzhenitsyn's report of the gulag. A few of us have even lost family members there. . . . Your agency, of course, is responsible for overseeing the prisons. How do you respond to that past?"

"I have spoken of repentance," Stolyarov answered. "This is an

---

4. Philip Yancey's article entitled "Praying with the KGB" (*Christianity Today,* January 13, 1992) provides the basis for this account. Yancey has since brought out a book with the same title: *Praying with the KGB: A Startling Report from a Shattered Empire,* ed. Liz Heaney (Portland, Ore.: Multnomah Press, 1992).

5. This and subsequent quotations in the description of this encounter are taken from "Praying with the KGB," p. 18.

essential step. . . . There can be no *perestroika* apart from repentance. The time has come to repent of that past. We have broken the Ten Commandments, and for this we pay today."

Next John Aker stood and said, "General Stolyarov, I am a pastor from Rockford, Illinois. I began a career as an army officer and was trained as an army intelligence agent. I taught courses in Soviet-bloc propaganda and participated in two high-level counterespionage activities involving KGB officers.

"I grew up as a young boy in America very much afraid of the Soviet Union. That fear turned into distrust and finally, in the army, it turned into hate.

"General, you said something tonight that touched a chord deep within me. I have one thing to add, though. You used the phrase, 'That is the cross I must bear.' I went through a time when guilt over things I had done as an army intelligence agent was destroying me. I couldn't bear that guilt, and I seriously considered ending my life. That's when I realized I did not have to bear that cross forever. Jesus bore it for me.

"Jesus' love for me has given me a very real love for the people of the Soviet Union . . . and I have found them to be loving, kind, and searching people. General, I mean it sincerely: As I think of you, I will pray for you."

It was clear that General Stolyarov was moved.

Alex Lenovich, the man who had been translating for him, spoke next. Decades ago he had escaped Stalin's terror and emigrated to the United States. For forty-six years he had been broadcasting Christian programming — which was often jammed — back to his homeland. People he knew who were Christians had been tortured and persecuted.

"General," he said, "many members of my family suffered because of this organization. I myself had to leave the land that I loved. My uncle, who was very dear to me, went to a labor camp in Siberia and never returned. General, you say that you repent. Christ taught us how to respond. On behalf of my family, on behalf of my uncle who died in the gulag, I forgive you." Then he reached over to Stolyarov and gave him a bear hug.

Stolyarov whispered to him, "Only two times in my life have I cried. Once was when my mother died. The other is tonight."

Driven to the Brink of Suicide:
Irmgard Kneifel

In many other situations, the oppressor never asked for reconciliation. Despite that, forgiveness was still possible, but in a different way, as Irmgard Kneifel discovered.[6] Like many political prisoners, she had been put into a prison cell in East Germany with a criminal who collaborated with the prison officials. A slight, gentle woman, Irmgard found herself confronting a large, muscular opponent who had been given license to abuse her physically, verbally, and psychologically. This woman beat her, harangued her, and spread rumors that Irmgard was insane in an attempt to isolate her from the other prisoners.

Irmgard's husband, Josef, was in prison for blowing up a monument as a political protest against the Soviet invasion of Afghanistan, and Irmgard had been imprisoned for not reporting him. Now she didn't know the whereabouts of her husband, who had also been jailed, or what had happened to their eighteen-year-old son. Prison officials, including the chaplain, told her that if she would divorce her husband, she could go free. But her Christian conscience didn't allow her to make that decision. Increasingly she felt consumed by the hell of incarceration. "There was no way to run away, turn around, stop your ears or strike back," she explains. "Screaming or crying didn't help, and there was no one to ask for help." Finally, she felt that she couldn't take it any longer. She decided to hang herself.

She looked around her prison cell. She knew that she had an hour and a half before her cellmate would return. She had a Bible on her bookshelf, and she pulled it out to seek one last thought before she died. She opened to a psalm.

The psalm spoke directly to her situation, she recalls. "I read how [the psalmist] was in such great need, what he had to suffer, and how he overcame. . . . There have always been people who torture one another and others who have been forced to suffer through

6. This portrait draws on the story of Irmgard Kneifel in *Stalin's DDR: Berichte politisch Verfolgter*, p. 127, and on the author's interview with her on May 10, 1991.

it. It became so clear to me that the psalmist had also experienced terrible things. That was a great consolation to me."

And then something inexplicable happened. "I could suddenly see the innermost soul of my cell-mate, the woman who worked for the Stasi [whom] I had been locked up with. She had tortured me in the most demonic ways, terribly, day after day, always with cruelty and mean-spiritedness. . . . Suddenly it was clear to me that if she did such mean things continually, what it must look like inside this woman — how terrible and dark! I could see how deeply unhappy she must be. She had nothing inside her other than evil thoughts. And then there came to me a kind of pity, not looking down on her in any sense, but a genuine feeling of compassion for her and for her inner misery. . . . I could suddenly see things totally differently."

And with that, Irmgard's intention to commit suicide was gone. Her circumstances hadn't changed, but with a new insight, her reaction to them had. "It saved my life," she says simply.

But her struggle wasn't over. For two years after her release from prison in 1982, Irmgard waged an inward battle against the former cellmate who had tormented her. She was still outraged, and she wanted revenge for being driven to the brink of suicide. She nurtured the plan that when her husband got out of prison, he would give her tormentor a beating. *He'll settle the score once and for all with her,* she thought to herself, nursing her bitterness. *Josef will do it for me.*

One night she attended a church retreat, where she was reminded of the need for spiritual cleansing of the dark corners of one's soul. She balked. No one was going to get near the secret place where she kept her plans for revenge. Still, she wrestled with the thought for the entire evening. But she kept coming back to the fact that her anger was justified — and in that case, why should she let go of it? Wasn't the desire for justice something good?

But, despite this reasoning that repeated itself in her head, Irmgard knew intuitively that while the object of her hatred never felt her loathing, she could feel the traces of hate in herself, and she knew they were poisonous. In prison she had been the victim of physical abuse; now she was the victim of her desire to get even. Both were damaging. Irmgard hesitantly asked others at the retreat to pray about this with her.

Irmgard can explain what happened next, but she cannot explain *how* it happened. In the space of a prayer, the entire burden of her accumulated hate, frustration, pain, and desire to get even was lifted from her. It was as if a cancerous growth had been expertly removed by a skilled surgeon. "I would never have thought it possible," she says frankly. "It was really gone. And the feeling has stayed away since. People who don't believe in God can't imagine such a thing. But there are really experiences when you know that something happens that you cannot do yourself."

"Love Your Enemies": The Holmers Take in the Honeckers

> If your enemy is hungry, give him food to eat; if he is thirsty, give him water to drink. In doing this, you will heap burning coals on his head, and the Lord will reward you.
>
> Proverbs 25:21-22

When Erich Honecker was deposed on October 18, 1989, he left office as probably the most hated man in East Germany. At seventy-seven years old, he was also ill. He had malfunctioning kidneys and was also suffering from cancer, and he needed medical attention. Having been unceremoniously relieved of his premier position, he had to evacuate the quarters at Wandlitz where he and his wife, Margot, had lived comfortably while they both held the scepters of power. Now no one was willing to give him a place to live — not the Communist party, in which Honecker had spent his entire life as a loyalist, not his daughter, not a friend anywhere in the country. And the lynching mood of the public had made him a moving target for potential violence. He and his wife had good reason to fear for their lives.

In one of the least likely twists in the turn of events in East Germany, Erich Honecker and his wife were taken in by a pastor, Uwe Holmer, and his wife.[7] The couple did this despite the fact that

---

7. This account is based on the author's interview with Pastor Uwe Holmer and

they had suffered under the Honecker regime: because of their Christian faith, eight of their ten children had been denied higher education by the policies Margot Honecker had established as Minister of Education during her husband's regime. Pastor Holmer led a Christian community for the mentally handicapped, the aged, and epileptics in Lobetal, outside East Berlin.

His wife stood behind the decision to take in the Honeckers, but their children were skeptical initially. "At first their chins just dropped to the floor," his wife reports.

"That's totally crazy! The very people who couldn't stand the church . . ." one of them erupted. But when they thought it over, they realized that their parents were right. "It's clear that if you've been asked to do it, then you should."

This was by no means an easy decision. Pastor Holmer was certainly no friend of the Communist regime. Not only had his children been blocked from higher education, but his telephone had been routinely tapped for years, and his mail had been monitored. The Stasi had kept noticeable tabs on him. But as a matter of faith, he took the directive to love your enemies literally, and so he opened his door to Erich and Margot Honecker. They moved in on January 31, 1990.

Word got out immediately, and the public was outraged. Crowds of angry people swarmed in front of the Holmers' house from the day the Honeckers moved in. The telephone rang incessantly. Letters poured in — 3,000 in all over the next months. All the pent-up resentment and hatred for the abuses and inadequacies of the entire Communist regime was focused on this one man. And as far as the average person on the street was concerned, anyone who would take him in was either collaborating with the Communists or insane.

"They should have taken Honecker out and put him up against the wall and shot him, just like in Romania," exploded a man from the neighboring village. "I would have gladly shot him myself. I don't understand why they did that for such a pig. He's the worst kind of scum there is."

---

his wife in Lobetal in January 1991, and on the reports of *Idea* magazine and correspondence by Pastor Holmer.

He was not alone in his opinion — the crowds that gathered in front of the Holmers' house every day shared it. The family received bomb threats on five separate occasions, but the police said they couldn't guarantee the safety of the Holmers or their guests. Despite all this, the Holmers were unflinching. "When we are convinced by God that what we do is right in His eyes, then there is nothing that can shake us," Mrs. Holmer explained when asked how she and her husband responded to the bomb threats.

The Honeckers were stunned by what they observed from the relative safety of the house. All those years of his regime, Erich Honecker had believed that the cheering masses assembled for military parades had marched by in adoring jubilation. The hatred that he could now clearly see directed at him in such ugly forms left him speechless. (He was also suffering physically. He had been operated on for a dysfunctional kidney nine days before he arrived at the Holmers, and he was suffering from extremely high blood pressure as well, so he was physically quite weak.) All that had happened politically was still so fresh and undigested that he appeared to be shell-shocked by the impact that had knocked his regime flat.

Margot Honecker was as dumbfounded as her husband. She was reputedly an even more passionately committed Communist than her husband, and the radical changes and the vengeful reactions to them now didn't fit anywhere in the picture of the world that she and her husband had acquired from their ideology. In a classic denial, she claimed, "We have certainly made mistakes, but that everything was wrong — that just can't be true." Her husband remained similarly staunch in his views. According to Pastor Holmer, "Erich Honecker was convinced to the end that it would have been good to hold onto communism."

The deluge of public protest against what the Holmers had done was so great that eventually Pastor Holmer wrote a letter to explain their motives:

It has become clear to us in a new way that to forgive is not an easy thing. Injustice is a reality. And the remembrance of it grows easily in our hearts, turning to bitterness and dividing us from one another. In light of that, God's forgiveness becomes even greater for me. It was not easy for HIM to forgive either. His holiness demanded fair justice and punishment for our sins. . . . To make forgiveness possible, he laid our sins and our punishment on Jesus, his son. Only then was the path to forgiveness cleared. Forgiveness is granted to everyone who asks for it — every single person! In recent days it has become apparent to me in a new way how much it cost God to forgive my sins. The joy of this gives me the strength to forgive other people. . . . The Lord has charged us to follow him and to take in all those who are troubled or burdened . . . to follow his commandment to love our enemies; and to live by the prayer he taught us in these words, "forgive us our trespasses as we forgive those who trespass against us." . . . [W]e want to live by Christ's example.

Pastor Holmer has done a great deal of thinking about forgiveness and reconciliation, which he sees as two different things. "Reconciliation can only take place when it is desired from both sides," he explains, "but forgiveness can be one-sided." Holmer's forgiveness of Honecker was in fact one-sided, since the deposed Communist leader remained unrepentant.

One evening as Pastor Holmer concluded a television interview, a man from the audience approached him, a dark scowl on his face. "You speak so quickly about forgiveness," he said. "You cannot imagine how hard that is for me. I spent fifteen years in Bautzen" (reputedly the most brutal prison in the GDR).

Holmer fixed him with his clear gaze and replied, "I have forgiven Honecker only for the wrong that he did to me. I cannot forgive him for his wrong to you. But you must forgive him for that. Otherwise the bitterness that you harbor will consume you."

The man stared at him for a full minute without blinking.

"You're right," he admitted grudgingly. "I have to. And I will. There is no alternative."

"There Is Hope in Forgiveness"

The spirit of forgiveness can infuse an entire crowd, as it did during the so-called Velvet Revolution.[8] On November 26, 1989, more than half a million people assembled on Czechoslovakia's Letná parade grounds in a spontaneous demonstration. Only nine days earlier, riot forces had viciously clubbed demonstrators as they marched to Wenceslas Square, wounding hundreds in a bloody confrontation, although many had offered the riot squads flowers, candles, and their opened hands in gestures of nonviolence. One demonstrator was rumored to have died. The incident proved to be the spark that ignited Czechoslovakia's resistance.

After that, events had unfolded with head-spinning rapidity, and now Václav Havel and Václav Malý were addressing the huge crowd that had gathered despite the freezing temperatures. Their commitment and enthusiasm for change were inspiring. When the Communist prime minister appeared and reviewed his proposals, the crowd shouted him down at first, but eventually cheered his promise to support demands for democratic change. And their enthusiasm mounted steadily. When Alexander Dubček appeared, they greeted him with tumultuous applause. When Václav Benda read the names of the political prisoners who had been released, they cheered for each. After the last name was read, they took out their keychains and jangled them, half a million people making "music" to express their desire for freedom. When folksinger Jaroslav Hudka, whose music had been banned, appeared before the crowd, they became ecstatic, singing with their arms raised in the victory sign, laughing, then crying for joy.

In this volatile atmosphere of emotional pyrotechnics, two men appeared next to Václav Havel, who led them forward. Then Father Malý introduced them as high-ranking members of the security police responsible for the bloody beatings in the demonstration nine days earlier. At this news the crowd turned ugly, booing and hissing

---

8. This rendering of events is based on Bud Bultman's description in *Revolution by Candlelight: The Real Story Behind the Changes in Eastern Europe*, ed. Harold Fickett (Portland, Ore.: Multnomah Press, 1991), pp. 208-13.

at the two men. "They have come to apologize," Malý shouted into the microphone. The crowd subsided into icy silence.

What happened next is powerfully recounted by Bud Bultman in *Revolution by Candlelight*:

A tall, good-looking man wearing a fatigue-colored parka stepped forward and looked at the stony faces.

"My name is Ludwig Pinc," he told the crowd. "I'm a lieutenant in the Prague police department. We see that it's a tragedy that we were enlisted to stop the democratic changes now taking place. Most of us joined the public security [force] with the understanding that we would use our power to fight against the criminal element, not to oppress regular working citizens."

The statement elicited cheers from the crowd.

"We share some of the blame for what happened during the last days," he said. "After the unpleasant events on November 17, there's a growing animosity of citizens toward the police. We want to tell you that none of our members had the legal right to use force to suppress the people. But this order didn't come from the police. This was a decision made by the higher-ups in the government."

He was interrupted by jeers. "What lies!" the crowd shouted together.

Malý put up his hands to hush the crowd. The young officer continued facing them, standing stiff and formal. He raised his voice to be heard over the angry chants. "We want to give you our support for the new democratic changes in our country. I want to express our profound apology that our leaders set us against the people of our own country. Last week, the striking students offered their hands to us in friendship. We want to reach out and accept their outstretched hands now."

It was an emotional moment. A few in the audience wiped away tears with their sleeves. One of the other junior officers standing to the side joined his colleague at the podium. He was wearing the red-banded green cap of the security police.

"I just want to add that I hope I never see the day when the people of this country stand against one another," he said.

When the two finished speaking, Malý took the microphone. His face was solemn. The crowd was still.

"We have to be proud of these members of the security police who came forward to apologize," he said. "They could be risking jail for their actions, and we have to protect them. Thank you for your understanding. Whenever there's political change, there's always the danger of the powerless seeking retribution against the powerful. Now, I'm not asking you to forget what those in power have done. But I am asking you to show forgiveness. Forgiveness is more than a word. There's power in forgiveness. There's hope in forgiveness. Now, will you accept their apology?"

There was an ominous silence. Then, a chant commenced, faint at first, but growing louder and louder, until the voice of half a million became one voice.

"We forgive you! We forgive you!"

Malý stood there, tears in his eyes. When the chanting subsided, he said, "I would like to end this special moment with a prayer. Those of you who know the words, I invite you to say them aloud with me. Those of you who don't know the words, pray with me in your hearts."

He began reciting the Lord's Prayer. Some in the audience prayed along, others fumbled for the words, until Letná field rang with the sound of a prayer that no one had dared to utter in public in more than forty years.[9]

In that moment, healing descended on a nation.

9. Bultman, *Revolution by Candlelight*, pp. 211-13.

CHAPTER 11

Epilogue:
Candles of Hope

What gave people the courage to cast off their fear and confront Communism? For many, it was their faith in transcendent truth. It was not a coincidence that Communism crumbled when many Christians stood up for what they believed and became crystallization points of resistance. The leaders of the revolution had various political opinions and came from different denominations, but they shared a vision of human beings as moral agents with individual identities and dignity and rights independent of the state. These leaders proclaimed that truth by living it and willingly accepted the consequences.

This is not to suggest that the church was simply an agent of politics, which is what the Communists suspected all along. The situation was more complex than that. It was not "the church" which sounded the death knell of Communism. It was the personal decisions of scores of individuals who for moral reasons cast off Marxist-Leninist ideology. The moral revolution preceded the political one, and it had been years in the making. There were, of course, many people who resisted Communism for moral reasons that were not based on Christianity. But Christian believers were among those who rejected Communism, and they did so because of a fundamentally different vision of humankind, of morality, and of God. They were convinced that there are eternal truths worth suffering and even dying for.

Solzhenitsyn claimed that the worst aspect of Communism was not its violence but its untruthfulness. Like many others, Václav Havel concluded that the only way to challenge the assumptions of the "culture of the lie" was to live the truth. The moral realm has tremendous power, as does the witness of deeds. Havel put it this way: "It is . . . becoming evident that a single seemingly powerless person who dares to cry out the word of truth and to stand behind it with all his person and all his life, has surprisingly greater power, though formally disfranchised, than do thousands of anonymous voters."[1] Thousands of individuals who made such decisions contributed to the moral, political, and spiritual earthquake that ultimately toppled Communism. Theirs was, in Havel's phrase, "the power of the powerless."

Working amid the Rubble: Leaders of Moral Renewal

While this earthquake has toppled the edifice of Communism, a reliable new order has not yet emerged from the chaos. In *Rebuilding Russia*, Alexander Solzhenitsyn warns that his country must be careful not to be crushed beneath its rubble. Russians have acknowledged with surprising candor the moral failure of their country and their present need to build a moral foundation. Many insist that the crisis is not economic or political, but rather moral and spiritual. The editor-in-chief of *Pravda* has said, "Morality is the worst crisis, worse than the economic and political problems. Christian values may be the only thing to keep our country from falling apart."[2]

There are signs of health. It is striking to see what kind of spiritual hunger has been unleashed since the old deity of Marxism has been toppled. The people who gave up the promises of Com-

1. Havel, quoted by Timothy Garton Ash in "Does Central Europe Exist?" *The Uses of Adversity: Essays on the Fate of Central Europe* (Cambridge: Granta Books, 1989), p. 179. This is an illuminating collection of essays on the changes in Eastern Europe preceding the peaceful revolution.

2. Quoted by Philip Yancey in "Praying with the KGB," *Christianity Today*, January 13, 1992, p. 19.

munist ideology are looking to the spiritual realm to satisfy the hunger for permanent things. In the former Soviet Union, the result is a religious revival of major magnitude. Its breadth and intensity are genuinely inspiring.

But there is a shadow falling across this bright development. Unfortunately, starving people will eat virtually anything set before them, and the result is that many have eaten at the spiritual smorgasbord now offered and have tasted the exotic fruits to be found there. Only later do they find out these fruits may make them sick. Every manner of sect is on the streets seeking new members: the Moonies, Hare Krishna followers, sorcerers, occultists, Satan worshipers, New Age believers, scientologists, bizarre faith healers, hypnotists — everything imaginable on the spiritual spectrum. They have descended full force on people who are unprepared to separate the spiritual wheat from the chaff. False spirituality is proving harder to combat than atheism was.

Since Communism collapsed because of moral failure, the key to rebuilding the former Communist nations lies in moral renewal. In virtually all these nations, there is emerging a nucleus of leaders — in the institutions of government, the military, the economy, the media, and among educators — who are committed to a moral and spiritual renewal. If they are successful, they have the potential to reach significant segments of their society. If the moral fabric of these countries can be knit anew, these individuals may be among the critical agents of restoration. The three Russians subsequently profiled are representative of the scores of others, here and throughout the Eastern bloc, who are working to make a difference.

Mikhail Kazachkov

Former dissident Mikhail Kazachkov, who spent fifteen years in the Gulag, became known in the West as "The Man in the Window." When A. M. Rosenthal of the *New York Times* visited the Soviet Union in 1988 to write about the abuse of human rights there, he was told that some of the prisoners he wished to visit were too ill to see him.

Although Kazachkov had been hidden from view in the notorious Perm 35 camp, when Rosenthal visited there he flung open a hospital window to shout, "We want to see you." Moments later the window was slammed shut. The two men eventually met in 1991.[3]

In 1975, when he was thirty years old, Kazachkov, then a physicist, was arrested in Leningrad and accused of "high treason" for contacting an American consular officer in his attempt to emigrate. He received a fifteen-year sentence. Six of those years he spent in solitary confinement; he also spent two years waging hunger strikes. In 1992, Kazachkov authored a survival manual to teach prisoners how to exploit the rules of the internally corrupt system in the Gulag. It was distributed without charge to thousands of Gulag inmates.

A symbol of resistance to the oppression of the Soviet system, Kazachkov, who is Jewish, has since become active in helping build a moral foundation for a more open and democratic Russia. Soon after his release from prison, he became a board member of the Open Christianity University, centered in St. Petersburg, which teaches Western values. After his arrival in the United States, he was named a fellow in the Human Rights Program at Harvard Law School. Currently he is a research associate in the Fletcher School of Diplomacy at Tufts University. James Billington, the librarian of Congress, has called Kazachkov one of the leading figures in Russia's Judeo-Christian renaissance.

In February 1992, in the home of Elena Bonner in Moscow, Kazachkov brought together other prominent Russian dissidents to launch an endeavor to help undergird political and economic reform. As he put it metaphorically, "It is absurd to expect a high-rise building to stand without a proper foundation." Kazachkov and his group are convinced that it is crucial to convey the moral values which make the practice of democracy and a market economy possible. To that end, they have established two firms, Freedom Channel in the United States and Persona in Russia, to produce television programming on these issues for Russian viewers. They have already put together a professional team that has produced well-received docu-

3. A. M. Rosenthal, "Man in the Window," *New York Times*, February 5, 1991.

mentaries, and they have successfully negotiated for regular broadcast time on the Russian airwaves, and now reach millions of viewers.[4]

Alexander Zaichenko

Another key individual attempting to repair the moral fabric of Russia is Alexander Zaichenko, a former economic advisor to Gorbachev.[5] Today he is the president of the Association of Christians in Business, as well as the director of the research program on business and entrepreneurship for the Academy of the National Economy. He believes that without a moral foundation, the economy cannot flourish in a democratic society. He asserts that the modern free market is not only an economic but also a moral phenomenon. "Soviet citizens were taught that religion was just a way of escaping to a world of illusions offering a kind of compensation for material hardship and social injustice. Most had no concept of the crucially important influence religion has had throughout history on the development of personality, public institutions, culture, and, in particular, the economy. When an individual finds liberation in Christ, this liberation gradually turns into a code of conduct."[6]

Before the collapse of Communism, people worked and toed the line out of fear. Being three minutes late for work could result in up to a year in prison; being caught stealing could mean execution. But now the incentive to provide for oneself and one's family can be harnessed for good, engendering productivity without coercion. Zaichenko contends that the desires to be responsible for one's actions and to work with discipline are moral products of

4. This portrait is based on the author's interview with Mikhail Kazachkov on February 3, 1993, in Washington, D.C., and on written materials provided by him subsequently.

5. For the personal story of Alexander Zaichenko, see Chapter 6.

6. Zaichenko, "Faith Can Prosper," *Frontier*, April-June 1993, p. 24, excerpted from "Christianity as a Means of Economic Renewal of the USSR," published by the Soviet Union Network, Winnipeg, Manitoba.

spiritual growth, which he believes will be accelerated by privatization.[7]

Anatoly Pchelintsev

While there are some in the Russian military who would like to return to the old order and would be prepared to use force to do so, there is a growing cadre of young, principled men who see things differently. Lieutenant Colonel Anatoly Pchelintsev is one of them. A thirty-eight-year-old military lawyer and instructor in the Military Institute, he founded an association of Christians in the military called Faith and Courage in December 1991.[8]

Soon after he joined the army, Pchelintsev jumped from a plane in a parachuting exercise. When his first parachute refused to open, he grasped for his emergency chute. But it, too, refused to open. Just seconds before impact, his emergency chute, which had gotten tangled up with his main chute, puffed open just slightly, braking his speed as he smashed into deep snow. Pchelintsev was injured but, against all odds, not seriously hurt. Experts who analyzed the incident said that it was technically impossible for the tangled parachute to open the way it did. The incident caused him to think hard about the existence of God, and what possibly could account for his own life being spared.

Pchelintsev later studied law at an elite military institute usually reserved for the budding protégés of privileged families — which his was not. He was to join the ranks of those handpicked to be future leaders of the country and be groomed for further responsibility.

Eventually Pchelintsev became a military lawyer. When he was confronted with the fact of religious persecution in the army, he concluded that it must be stopped. Because he defended victims of

7. Drawn from the author's interview with Alexander Zaichenko in Moscow on March 11, 1992.

8. Drawn from the author's interviews with Anatoly Pchelintsev on March 12, 1992, and on November 13, 1992; and her interview with Vadim Solod on March 12, 1992, in Moscow.

persecution and discrimination, his work brought him into contact with Christians, and this contact made him think more deeply about his own belief. The watershed came in 1990 as he stood at his mother's grave: he was overwhelmed by a desire to repent and make a commitment of faith.

Pchelintsev had begun to write articles on the issue of the rights of believers and the need for new laws to protect them. When the first article appeared in 1989, it rankled both politicians and military men. In 1990, he wrote another article advocating alternative military service for religious believers, and it appeared in the most widely read paper in the Soviet Union. Some wanted Pchelintsev removed from the army because of it. But in the changed climate of *glasnost* and *perestroika,* he was not ousted. In May 1991, he presented a paper on alternative service to the Defense Committee of the Supreme Soviet, but his plea fell on the deaf ears of the old guard.

After the attempted coup in 1991, Pchelintsev joined with navy captain Vadim Solod, who was formerly with the Military Political Academy of Lenin, to found the group called Faith and Courage. This was their response to what they perceived as a spiritual crisis in the ranks of the army and navy. Like Pchelintsev, Solod, who was trained for the KGB attack forces, experienced a complete change of orientation. Although, as he admits, many of his colleagues don't understand the goal of Faith and Courage, others have joined him and Pchelintsev. They are convinced that the more officers they reach with the message of Christian faith, the more likely it is that the military will be stable.

Today Anatoly Pchelintsev is an advisor to the Russian parliament. In that capacity he has drafted new legislation for Russia, including a bill on freedom of conscience. In the fall of 1992, Pchelintsev, along with other young Christian lawyers, founded a group that defends victims of human rights abuses. When they announced their intentions to take such cases, they were deluged with pleas for help.

What the East Can Give the West: Spiritual Riches

There are scores of other endeavors to rebuild the moral fabric of the former Communist nations: these are only a few examples meant to illustrate both the need and the potential. There are clusters of people in the upper echelons of government, in economic groups, in education, in publishing, and in newly founded political parties who have a clear vision of the moral needs of Russia and the other former Communist countries. Constructing a moral foundation for these countries is the prerequisite for any stable political democracy and productive economic order. Only if such efforts succeed is there hope for an exodus from the rubble.

Solzhenitsyn has observed that the former Communist empire is now beginning to embrace democracy at a time that it is not at its healthiest. The aspects of materialism that doomed Communism have produced another bloom in the West, prettier perhaps, but equally deadly. A twenty-year-old woman from East Germany has astutely observed, "We know now that the god of Marxism was a false god. But we don't want to worship at the golden calf of the West either."

To believe that the West holds the keys to the spiritual salvation of the East is to embrace an illusion. The spiritual heritage that shaped Western civilization as we know it has been consumed, spent, exhausted. Both American and European democracy were originally imbued with a sense of Judeo-Christian morality and responsibility. Both the culture and its institutions rested on a foundation of belief in God. But that is no longer the case. The twentieth century has taken the cultural and spiritual heritage of the West, lived off its capital, and handed it back depleted. The fruits have been consumed, the branches snipped, the roots long forgotten.

Precisely at the time when the West is preaching capitalism and democracy to the East, few in the West espouse the spiritual values that make their practice fruitful. The flowering of Western civilization to which we are indebted was based on the precept that the individual would be motivated by self-interest, while restrained by transcendent moral and spiritual values. That is no longer self-evident to many.

In the absence of these values, new democracies in the East are likely to be troubled, just as they are increasingly in the West.

Both the East and the West are confronted with the same need. No society can live harmoniously in responsible freedom without acknowledging and renewing its moral roots. People in the West have watched the dissolution of the Soviet empire and have been self-congratulatory about Communism's defeat. They have rushed to fill the gaps with a transfer of material wealth from West to East, believing that will solve the problems. But there have been bitter disappointments on both sides. Materially, most people in the East are worse off than they were before the fall of Communism. And the Western attempt to provide "spiritual aid" has been similarly flawed. So many Westerners have stormed the former Soviet Union with good intentions but inadequate preparation that some have suggested that they could do more good by staying home. According to John Aker, president of the Slavic Gospel Association, many church workers from the U.S. exhibit ignorance, indifference, and insolence, insisting that their own way is the only way.

Still, there may be another transfer in the making, one of another dimension, a transfer of wealth from the East to the West. The years of persecution endured by believers in the East have produced spiritual riches of strength and perseverance and wisdom. These riches are sorely needed in the West, although few are aware of their spiritual poverty.

During these years of oppression, Christians who attempted to live their faith were subjected to tremendous pressure. Either they were crushed by it, or they emerged with their convictions crystallized in resolve. They were forced to find answers to the most pressing questions in life: Why am I here, and what purpose does my life serve? They concluded that the purpose of life is to live in harmony with God, to love and serve him. The sacrifices they made in obedience to living this belief go beyond the realm of our experience. Their faith has been tested in ways that most of us in the West are not only unfamiliar with but can scarcely imagine. Only when we try to imagine how the consequences would affect us personally can we begin to get a sense of how dearly they have paid for upholding their beliefs. How many of us would willingly sacrifice the education of our children and both their job opportunities and ours for faith? Given the choice, how many of us would willingly go to jail for our beliefs — or die for them?

The persecution and suffering that Christians in the East endured had a purifying effect. The spiritual fruits they have borne differ from those from the shallower soil of less hostile climates. The formation of character under pressure is an uncomfortable subject for most Western believers. Yet the Bible links suffering to joy and hope and mature belief:

> Consider it pure joy, my brothers [and sisters], whenever you face trials of many kinds, because you know that the testing of your faith develops perseverance. Perseverance must finish its work so that you may be mature and complete, not lacking anything. . . . Blessed is the man who perseveres under trial, because when he has stood the test, he will receive the crown of life that God has promised to those who love him. (James 1:2-4, 12)
>
> We also rejoice in our sufferings, because we know that suffering produces perseverance; perseverance, character; and character, hope. (Rom. 5:3-4)

The kind of character produced in the crucible of conflict is striking. Crystallized conviction and courage enabled those who resisted Communism to burst free in spirit. Their feats are no less than those of the heroes of faith in biblical times.

Solzhenitsyn has written about the believers behind the walls of the Gulag. He describes their presence there as a "self-confident procession through the Archipelago — a sort of silent religious procession with invisible candles. . . . Some among them were mowed down by machine guns and those next in line continued their march."[9] According to Whittaker Chambers, a witness is someone "whose life and faith are so completely one that when the challenge comes to step out and testify for his faith, he does so,

9. Solzhenitsyn, *The Gulag Archipelago*, part IV, chapter 2.

disregarding all risks, accepting all consequences."[10] These people lived his words.

Those who survived exhibit a remarkable attitude shaped by hardship. Alexander Firisiuk's daughter recently scoured stores everywhere in Moscow trying to obtain milk for her child. For three days she could find none and returned home frustrated. "What kind of a country is this where a mother cannot get milk for her child?" she asked plaintively. But eventually she came home triumphantly carrying milk. "No mother[s] in any [other] country could be as happy as we are. No American can understand how we rejoice at finding something we have looked so long for. We have such great joy!" Whether one sees scarcity as a source of bitterness or a source of joy indicates a remarkable difference in perspective.

Alexander Firisiuk went to the hospitals to visit the children of Chernobyl. He looked into their eyes, and he came back from the experience changed. "Since then, I have a different attitude toward my own life. I feel the guilt of our system in this tragedy. While we still have time, we must speak about hope, eternity, the new heaven and earth. There is no hope for these children. . . . But when they take Christ into their lives, something appears in their eyes: joy. Pray for the joy to spread to us."

A profound difference in spirit is evident here. These Christians are not filled with bitterness toward their oppressors; they have forgiven them. They have responded to their circumstances not with despair, but with thankfulness to their Creator for the good things he has given them.

A time of great tribulation may lie ahead for our civilization. The crucial question in a crisis is not "Why?" but "How should I respond?" Just as those under Communism defined their faith by the way they lived it, so do we as we work out our response to our own trials, whatever they may be. We don't know how we would respond in circumstances like those that nearly crushed others in the rubble of Communism. But when we face crushing circumstances of our own, perhaps the stories of these people's lives will offer encourage-

10. Chambers, *Witness* (1952; rpt. Washington: Regnery Gateway, 1980), p. 5.

ment. The formation of the spirit is like the formation of coal in the earth. The enormous pressure that is exerted over time creates either dust or diamonds.

Irina Ratushinskaya, who was convicted of writing Christian poetry, was incarcerated in the part of a Russian prison called the "Small Zone." It was there that she wrote this poem, which speaks eloquently of God's presence in hardship:

> So tomorrow, our little ship, Small Zone,
> What will come true for us?
> According to what law —
> Like an eggshell over dead waves?
> Covered in patches and scars,
> On the word — the honest word — alone —
> By whose hand is our ship preserved,
> Our little home?
> Those of us who sail to the end, row, live to the end —
> Let them tell for the others:
> We knew
> The touch of this hand.[11]

---

11. Ratushinskaya, "So tomorrow, our little ship, Small Zone," in *No, I'm Not Afraid* (Newcastle upon Tyne: Bloodaxe Books, Ltd., 1986), p. 130.

Bibliography

"'Abbat' vykhodit no svyaz" ("'Abbat' Makes His Contact"), *Argumenty i fakty,* no. 1 (January 1992).

Andrew, Brother, with John and Elizabeth Sherrill. *God's Smuggler.* Old Tappan, N.J.: Fleming H. Revell, 1967.

Ash, Timothy Garton. *The Polish Revolution: Solidarność.* London: Granta Books, 1983.

———. *The Uses of Adversity: Essays on the Fate of Central Europe.* Cambridge: Granta Books, 1989.

———. *We the People: The Revolution of 1989.* Cambridge: Granta Books, 1990.

Bahr, Eckhard. *Sieben Tage im Oktober (Seven Days in October).* Leipzig: Forum Verlag, 1990.

Bauman, Michael. "Reality, Religion and the Marxist Retreat," in *Man and Marxism: Religion and the Communist Retreat,* ed. Michael Bauman. Hillsdale, Mich.: Hillsdale College Press, 1991.

Besier, Gerhard, and Stephan Wolf, eds. *Pfarrer, Christen und Katholiken: Das Ministerium für Staatssicherheit der ehemaligen DDR und die Kirchen (Pastors, Christians, and Catholics: The Ministry for State Security of the Former GDR and the Churches).* Neukirchen-Vluyn: Neukirchener Verlag, 1991.

Bourdeaux, Michael. *Gorbachev, Glasnost and the Gospel.* London: Hodder & Stoughton, 1990.

———, with Michael Rowe. *May One Believe in Russia? Violations of Religious Liberty in the Soviet Union.* London: Darton, Longman & Todd, Ltd., 1980.

———. "Look to the East," *The Tablet,* January 2, 1993.

258

Bibliography

————. *Risen Indeed.* Crestwood, N.Y.: St. Vladimir's Seminary Press, 1983.

Broun, Janice. *Conscience and Captivity: Religion in Eastern Europe.* Washington: University Press of America, 1988.

"Brühl aus Morokko: 'Ich musste mich anpassen' " ("Brühl from Morocco: 'I Had to Go Along'"), *Morgenpost,* March 21, 1992.

Bultman, Bud. *Revolution by Candlelight: The Real Story Behind the Changes in Eastern Europe,* ed. Harold Fickett. Portland, Ore.: Multnomah Press, 1991.

Bürgerkommittee Leipzig, ed. *Stasi intern: Macht und Banalität (Inside the Stasi: Power and Banality).* Leipzig: Forum Verlag, 1991.

Buss, Gerald. *The Bear's Hug: Christian Belief and the Soviet State, 1917-1986.* Grand Rapids: William B. Eerdmans, 1987.

Chambers, Whittaker. *Witness.* 1952; rpt. Washington: Regnery Gateway, 1980.

Chronicle of the Catholic Church in Lithuania, vol. 1, nos. 1-9, 1972-74; vol. 6, nos. 40-49, 1979-81. Trans. and ed. Nijolé Graęzulis. Chicago: Loyola University Press and the Society of the Chronicle of Lithuania, Inc., 1981, 1989.

Cohn, Norman. *The Pursuit of the Millennium.* London: Granada Publishing Ltd., 1970.

"Deckname Conrad: Gespräch mit einem Informaten der ehemaligen Staatssicherheit" ("Code Name Conrad: Conversation with an Informant for the Former State Security"), *Die Union,* January 30, 1990.

Desel, Jochen. *Oskar Brüsewitz: Ein Pfarrerschicksal in der DDR (Oskar Brüsewitz: One Pastor's Fate in the GDR).* Lahr-Dinglingen: Telos, 1991.

Deyneka, Anita and Peter. *A Song in Siberia.* Elgin, Ill.: David C. Cook, 1977.

Dobb, Michael. "In Hard Times, No Time to Hunt Down KGB Agents," *International Herald Tribune,* February 12, 1992.

"Dr. Hartmut Greim alias IMB Boysen, trotz Stasi in den Wüstenrot-Chefsessel; Buchautor Rüdiger Knechtel war sein Opfer" ("Dr. Hartmut Greim, alias Informant Boysen, in Boss's Chair at Wüstenrot despite Stasi; Book Author Rüdiger Knechtel Was His Victim"), *Bild,* March 25, 1992, p. 5.

Ellis, Jane. *The Russian Orthodox Church: A Contemporary History.* Bloomington: Indiana University Press, 1986.

Ericson, Edward E., Jr. "Solzhenitsyn and the Rebuilding of Russia," *Intercollegiate Review,* Spring 1992.

Funderburk, David. "More Ceauşescus? Continuing Threats to Religious Freedom," in *Man and Marxism: Religion and the Communist Retreat,* ed. Michael Bauman. Hillsdale, Mich.: Hillsdale College Press, 1991.

CANDLES BEHIND THE WALL

Glenny, Misha. *The Rebirth of History: Eastern Europe in the Age of Democracy.* London: Penguin Books, 1990.

Gorbachev, Mikhail. *Perestroika.* New York: Harper & Row, 1987.

———. *Perestroika,* rev ed. New York: Harper & Row, 1988.

Gorischeva, Tatiana. *Die Rettung der Verlorenen (Saving the Lost).* Wuppertal: Brockhaus, 1982.

———. *Von Gott zu reden ist gefährlich (Talking about God Is Dangerous).* Freiburg im Dreisgau: Herder Verlag, 1985.

Gueffroy, Karin. "Es hat keinen Befehlsnotstand gegeben" ("There Was No Compulsion to Obey Orders"), *Freie Press,* December 14-15, 1991.

Hadon, Sven. "Terror gegen Stasi-Aufklärer" ("Terror against Stasi Exposer"), *Bild,* January 19, 1991.

Havel, Václav, et al. *The Power of the Powerless: Citizens against the State in Central-Eastern Europe,* ed. John Keane. London: Hutchinson, 1985.

Hays, Laurie. "Report Finds Detailed Plans for Soviet Coup," *Wall Street Journal (Europe),* January 22, 1992.

Hill, Kent. *The Soviet Union on the Brink: An Inside Look at Christianity and Glasnost.* Portland, Ore.: Multnomah Press, 1991.

———. *Turbulent Times for the Soviet Church.* Portland, Ore.: Multnomah Press, 1991.

Horn, Gyula. *Freiheit, die ich meine (Freedom That I Mean).* Hamburg: Hoffman & Campe, 1991.

Ich liebe euch doch alle!: Befehle und Lageberichte des MfS (But I Love All of You! Orders and Reports of the Ministry for State Security). Berlin: Basis Druck, 1990.

"Jaruzelski Rethinks," *International Herald Tribune,* March 6-7, 1993.

Jones, E. Michael. "The Untold Story: Religion's Role in Liberating Eastern Europe," in *Man and Marxism: Religion and the Communist Retreat,* ed. Michael Bauman. Hillsdale, Mich.: Hillsdale College Press, 1991.

Khorev, Mikhail. *Ich schreibe euch, Kinder (I Write to You, Children).* Gummersbach, Germany: Verlag Friedensstimme, 1986.

"Killing of Rebel Soviet Priest," *New York Times,* September 15, 1990.

Kirkpatrick, Jeane J. "Exit Communism, Cold War, and the Status Quo," in *Man and Marxism: Religion and the Communist Retreat,* ed. Michael Bauman. Hillsdale, Mich.: Hillsdale College Press, 1991.

Klose, Kevin. *Russia and the Russians: Inside the Closed Society.* New York: W. W. Norton, 1984.

Knechtel, Rüdiger, and Jürgen Fiedler, eds. *Stalin's DDR: Berichte politisch Verfolgter (Stalin's GDR: Reports of Politically Persecuted).* Leipzig: Forum Verlag, 1991.

Bibliography

Krakhmalnikova, Zoya. "Hat Russland eine Hoffnung?" ("Does Russia Have a Hope?") *HMK Kurrier, Stimme der Märtyrer,* 1/93.

———. "Once Again about the Bitter Fruits of a Sweet Captivity." Thomastown, Vic., Australia: Orthodox Action, 1989.

Kunze, Reiner. *Deckname "Lyrik" (Codename "Lyrik").* Frankfurt: Fischer Verlag, 1990.

Lewek, Antonin. "New Sanctuary of Poles: The Grave of Martyr-Father Jerzy Popieluszko." Warsaw, 1986.

Maaz, Hans-Joachim. *Der Gefühlsstau: Ein Psychogramm der DDR (Blocked Feelings: A Psychogram of the GDR).* Berlin: Argon Verlag, 1990.

Magirius, Friedrich. "Wiege der Wende," in *Leipziger Demontagebuch.* Leipzig: Gustav Kiepenhauer Verlag, 1990.

Marx, Karl, and Friedrich Engels. *Gesamtausgabe.* Berlin: Dietz Verlag, 1974.

———. *Werke.* Berlin: Dietz Verlag, 1974.

Meyerson, Adam. "The Ash Heap of History: Why Communism Failed," *Policy Review,* Fall 1991.

"A Murder Most Unholy," *Chicago Tribune,* September 16, 1990.

Neues Forum Leipzig. *Jetzt oder nie — Demokratie: Leipziger Herbst '89.* Leipzig: Forum Verlag, 1989.

Nisbet, Robert. *History of the Idea of Progress.* New York: Basic Books, 1980.

Plowman, Edward. "From China to El Salvador to Romania: How Religion Is Faring around the World," in *Man and Marxism: Religion and the Communist Retreat,* ed. Michael Bauman. Hillsdale, Mich.: Hillsdale College Press, 1991.

Polosin, Vyacheslav. "The Eternal Slave of the Cheka," *Izvestiia,* January 22, 1992.

Porter, David. *Laszlo Tökes: Im Sturm der rumänischen Revolution (Laszlo Tökes: In the Storm of the Romanian Revolution).* Wuppertal: Oncken Verlag, 1991.

Ratushinskaya, Irina. *Grey Is the Colour of Hope.* London: Hodder & Stoughton, 1988.

———. *In the Beginning.* London: Hodder & Stoughton, 1990.

———. *No, I'm Not Afraid.* Newcastle upon Tyne: Bloodaxe Books, Ltd., 1986.

Riecker, Ariane, Annett Schwarz, and Dirk Schneider. *Stasi intim (Stasi Insider).* Leipzig: Forum Verlag, 1990.

"Russia Meets the Market," *The Economist,* September 15, 1990.

Sawatsky, Walter. *Soviet Evangelicals since World War II.* Scottdale, Pa.: Herald Press, 1981.

Schlossberg, Herbert. *Called to Suffer, Called to Triumph*, ed. Al Janssen and Steve Halliday. Portland, Ore.: Multnomah Press, 1990.

Schneider, Wolfgang. "Oktoberrevolution 1989," in *Leipziger Demontagebuch (Leipzig Demonstration Journal)*. Leipzig: Gustav Kiepenhauer Verlag, 1990.

Shirley, Eugene, Jr., and Michael Rowe, eds. *Candle in the Wind: Religion in the Soviet Union*. Washington: University Press of America, 1989.

Smith, V. Dale. "The Underground Breaks Free," in *Man and Marxism: Religion and the Communist Retreat*, ed. Michael Bauman. Hillsdale, Mich.: Hillsdale College Press, 1991.

Solzhenitsyn, Alexander. *The Gulag Archipelago*. New York: Harper & Row, 1973.

———. *"One Word of Truth . . ."* London: Bodley Head, 1972.

Staatsbürgerkunde 7. (East) Berlin: Volk und Wissen Volkseigener Verlag, 1983.

Staatsbürgerkunde 8. (East) Berlin: Volk und Wissen Volkseigener Verlag, 1984.

Swoboda, Jörg, ed. *Die Revolution der Kerzen: Christen in den Umwälzungen der DDR (The Revolution of Candles: Christians in the Upheaval of the GDR)*. Wuppertal: Oncken Verlag, 1990.

Ten Boom, Corrie, with John and Elizabeth Sherrill. *The Hiding Place*. Washington Depot, Conn.: Chosen Books, 1971.

Thorkelson, Willmar. "East Germans Said to Have Had Plans to Arrest Activist Clergy," *Religious News Service (RNS)*, October 2, 1990.

Uzzell, Lawrence A. "The KGB's Agents in Cassocks," *The Christian Science Monitor*, April 28, 1992.

———. "Word and Deed: Russia's Religious Reform," in *Man and Marxism: Religion and the Communist Retreat*, ed. Michael Bauman. Hillsdale, Mich.: Hillsdale College Press, 1991.

Vins, Georgi. *Wie Schafe unter Wölfen (Like Sheep among Wolves)*. Neuhausen-Stuttgart: Hänssler Verlag, 1989.

Weigel, George. *The Final Revolution: The Resistance Church and the Collapse of Communism*. New York: Oxford University Press, 1992.

Yancey, Philip. "Praying with the KGB," *Christianity Today*, January 13, 1992.

———. *Praying with the KGB: A Startling Report from a Shattered Empire*, ed. Liz Heaney. Portland, Ore.: Multnomah Press, 1992.

Zaichenko, Alexander. "Faith Can Prosper," *Frontier*, April-June 1993.

Index of Names

Index of Names